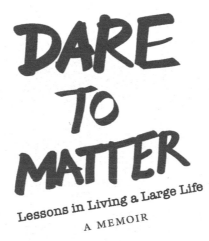

DARE TO MATTER

Lessons in Living a Large Life

A MEMOIR

SHIFRA MALKA

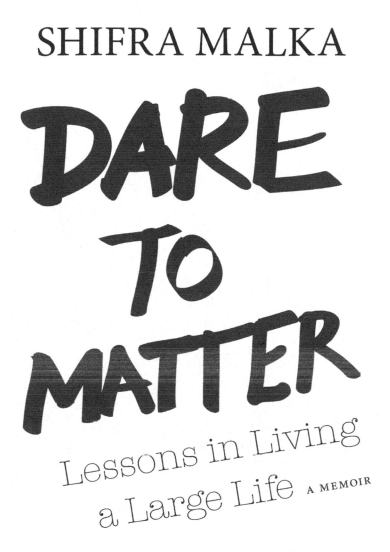

DARE TO MATTER

Lessons in Living a Large Life A MEMOIR

GREEN PLACE BOOKS | Brattleboro, Vermont

To G-d, (Ribono Shel Olam / Master of the Universe)
who breathed a piece of His Divinity, a soul, into us humans,
so that our lives would matter.

To my Parents, who brought me into this world,
and then bravely let me bring them
into my world of mattering.

To my Children, who trusted me to bring them
into this world, and to their spouses and children
for joyfully joining our world.

To Zack,
who is my whole world.

Printed in the United States

10 9 8 7 6 5 4 3 2 1

Green Writers Press is a Vermont-based publisher whose mission
is to spread a message of hope and renewal through the words and
images we publish. Throughout we will adhere to our commitment to
preserving and protecting the natural resources of the earth. To that end,
a percentage of our proceeds will be donated to environmental activist
groups and The Southern Poverty Law Foundation. Green Writers Press
gratefully acknowledges support from individual donors, friends, and
readers to help support the environment and our publishing initiative.
Green Place Books curates books that tell literary and compelling
stories with a focus on writing about place—these books are more
personal stories/memoir and biographies.

Giving Voice to Writers & Artists Who Will Make the World a Better Place
Green Writers Press | Brattleboro, Vermont
www.greenwriterspress.com

ISBN: 978-1-950584-42-0

Cover design by Asha Hossain Design LLC

THE PAPER USED IN THIS PUBLICATION IS PRODUCED BY MILLS COMMITTED
TO RESPONSIBLE AND SUSTAINABLE FORESTRY PRACTICES.

CONTENTS

PREFACE

A Purposeful Word

I did not choose this story; only to tell it. A hard decision, and a demanding one, that many times had me rethinking why I'd put myself through the rigors of writing it. Since it does little to serve my image, it must have something to do with serving my purpose.

While we humans are busy being alive, and even great, we make mistakes. We are supremely well-intentioned, and *we are often astonishingly misguided*. And there are consequences.

And though thoroughly convenient to do so, it is nearly impossible to judge the people in our lives with absolute accuracy. Because the confluence of factors that bear down on a human being at any given moment can never be fully known or replicated by oneself, certainly not by another.

Best we can do is to tell the story of *our* experience, and share the lessons learned as we found ourselves in the nexus of others' lives, and they in ours. It is valuable to acknowledge and appreciate the ways we have profited, while minding the collateral damage *as we experienced it,* and to heal it as necessary.

A Word About Purpose

Funny thing about our lives is that we can seriously miss out on them, and never even realize it. We can walk past our highest purpose for being here and completely devalue it because we don't recognize it.

Many people, if not all, find themselves wondering about their purpose in life and what makes their lives meaningful and worth living. Surely you, as I, have been given ideas early on from others who help us to understand that "success" makes this whole living thing worthwhile. Sounds great until we stop and ask, *what is success*? What makes our lives large and powerful? Here again, others try to have us understand that success means *having . . .* possessions, positions, prestige, an array of unending iterations of advantageous circumstances that place us in power, pomp and privilege.

And here's the main point of it all: *This success is supposed to release us from the deepest fear that we are not special.* It validates that we are indeed set apart from the mass of humanity which seems destined to travel its journey unobserved and uncelebrated, unadorned and unprivileged by society's admiring eye. It confers on us largeness and importance. It whispers that now we can justify our existence. *That we matter.*

And then we watch those icons of success crumble. In recent years, a staggering number of our fellow humans who had inhabited the highest, coveted places of success in media, fashion, business, politics, and medicine have been undone by their inner challenges. After working so hard to finally make it, to "become," they have *un-become.* We were shocked and saddened, for example, that famous designer Kate Spade and celebrity chef Anthony Bourdain opted out of their lives, within one week of each other. We are increasingly bereft of our illusions about success, leaving us to redraw the lines of our thinking of what *really* makes our lives matter.

I cannot know how deeply this question agitates inside of others, but seems to me that most people ask it, then move on about their daily lives without having to fully answer it. Maybe they are too busy being successful. Or maybe they renegotiate their definition, by choice or necessity. Not me. I found myself standing in the pain of this question over and over again, intensely and consistently, without letup. And then, when given the opportunity, to write a whole book about it.

Perhaps I should have seen this coming...that I'd write on this topic. I was born to two people who are an exquisite study in opposites—in background, in personality, in temperament, and in outlook. Though challenging, I quite loved learning from them two completely different languages of how to be human, and great, though not perfect. Nobody is.

You will hear more about Father and Mother; that they are extraordinary examples of people with uncommon grit, a self-less capacity and yearning to build their community, and the deep desire to help their children strive for excellence in mind and character. They'd say that the happiness of their children was paramount to their own. They built a family on ideals of faith and duty, always trying to do the right thing, even when it got very, very hard. Indeed, they earned their true image of earnest, G-d fearing people who put others' interests ahead of their own, over and over again, until it became their pattern of being, their identity.

And into this partnership entered a child named Shifra. I know her well; she's the third of six children born to this couple. She is the really stubborn kid who unravels the nerves of those who try to reason with her, but so un-gritty and vulnerable that she cries over nothing and wants to quit at everything. Her mind is always asking *what* and *how*, while her fearful imagination bears down with *what ifs* and *whys*. Her heart is tethered to the unseen, deeper side of things, not at all grounded in observable order and behavior. Her parents are people who are strategic and pragmatic; there is simply no time to speak to or soothe childish imaginations. There is life to be lived, reality to nurture; a business to build and a family to feed, clothe and educate.

.

I give them all the credit in the world, and many Hallmark cards too. How easy could it have been to put up with a child like me?

Clearly, this dynamic duo of creative chaos married to impeccable order yielded, well, a problem: a child who could not conform, or perform, to their personal understandings of success. *Nobody's fault; everybody's challenge.* Above all . . . *mine.* Because all I really understood growing up was that I couldn't seem to ever be of any particular value, to make any meaningful contribution that would make me matter. And that I was all on my own, utterly alone, in trying to fill that deepest of questions.

You and I both know that this question of mattering does not ever totally go away; but, if left unconsidered, it compromises the power of our voice. And just to be clear, our voice is who we are at our core.

And if five decades of this life have taught me anything, it is this: There is only one real choice we will make in our life— to opt in or to opt out. Simply put, to build or to destroy— ourselves and others. *Dare to Matter* is the choice to build.

PART ONE

Discovering Self

Diets were built on the belief that if I trusted myself, I would destroy myself . . . We live the way we eat and eat the way we live. Our relationship to food is a perfect, one-hundred percent, exact reflection of what we believe about being alive. About what we deserve. About what's possible and what's not possible. What we feel hopeless about. What we feel despairing about.

—GENEEN ROTH, author, *When Food is Love*

Discovering Self is about choosing to live life on your terms. It is an invitation to discern what is personally healthy, what is deeply nourishing.

Eating was the first portal through which I consumed my ideas about mattering. It would take me many years to connect that unless you are fully present to your inner emptiness and fullness, food cannot satisfy you. And even then, it can only satisfy a piece of you. Other hungers cannot be stilled with food. While that may be quite uncomfortable and inconvenient to know, it is also the beginning of growing a sense of mattering that will fuel your life in meaningful and miraculous ways.

CHAPTER ONE

The Heart of
Non-Mattering

One ship drives east and the other drives west by the same
winds that blow.
It's the set of the sails and not the gales that determines the
way they go.
                    —ELLA WHEELER WILCOX, author-poet

I GOT THE CALL WHILE VISITING ISRAEL.
She, Israel, was clearly a land calling her children home.
Her Judean hills were unfolding one into the next—stretching
outwards, always upwards—holding visible signs of incredible
welcome.

"She died."

We weren't expecting Aunt Rosalie to die *yet*. Though
admittedly, I sometimes wondered why she'd want to hang
around in a life that didn't seem to matter.

To be clear, she mattered to me. I cherished the cards she
mailed me for my birthday and the money she sometimes
included in them. I also adored the way she nonchalantly dismissed simple protocol with the twist of her left hand, bent on
undermining authority, as she drove her little black car through
the red light. And, how else would I have learned to mindlessly

nibble a biscuit while patting my growing midriff, oblivious to the trail of chaotic crumbs on my mother's perfectly clean floors? Still, I had good reason to wonder if and how she mattered to anyone else in my family, or to the world at large.

Aunt Rosalie was my father's older sister, his only sibling. I watched her and my father, ten years her junior, share their mother, my Grandma Lolly. Their lives could not have landed them more different roles. Hers was to dutifully serve her mother, while his was to be doted upon. As they each played their roles superbly, I noticed early on that Aunt Rosalie's voice was often dismissed by family and friends as unimportant, silly, hostile, even crazy. I caught the roll of their eyes or the small smirk of their mouth when she'd state her opinion on anything, even something as mundane as "nice weather we're having, ain't it?" And this increasingly reverberated with me, that my emerging voice was beginning to be similarly silenced; that what I had to say did not matter and was not worth listening to.

The main echo, clear if not always loud, was that I was a lot like Aunt Rosalie. And that I should stop being like her immediately, if I knew what was good for me, which apparently I often did not. I wasn't at all sure what that meant, because I didn't look like her in the slightest. She was a slim, black-haired female, with an olive complexion, and her face sported full, well-shaped lips with lively almond-shaped eyes the color of lima beans. At 5´4˝, a respectable height for a woman of her time, Aunt Rosalie stood on two light legs that wore high heels with a model's grace. The pictures I had seen of her younger years surprised me. She was smiling, and possessed the type of pretty that said, "I care enough about myself to wear attractive clothes and tasteful make-up." Her beach photos captured an enviable comfort with herself, obviously accustomed to drawing favorable attention from others.

By the time she was in my life, Aunt Rosalie was a lonely, fear-filled, and unfulfilled woman. Dull-colored pant outfits draped her sagging spirit. Argumentative words in her charming Southern drawl fell out of her mouth in a half-baked, cynical way. She had become increasingly known throughout the family for her manipulative maneuvers, for her imaginative and irrational ideas, and for her provocative personality. Recounting conversations she had overheard was a specialty of hers, replete with subjective commentary toward the negative side of things. I'd seen her, on occasion, fingering a piece of mail in our house that obviously wasn't addressed to her. And standing behind a doorway listening in on a conversation belonging to someone else was a definite pastime. She'd often take the opposite side of a widely-held opinion just for the fun of it. I don't think she did any of this purposely to get attention. I am not even sure she was aware of it at all. It was just the way she existed here.

I knew that earlier in her life, she had done more than just exist. She had served as the volunteer president of her city's local women's organization, arranging day activities and overnight trips for her female friends. She had also worked in a department store, even once buying a coveted baseball mitt for my father with money she saved from a week's worth of work. Still, these noble acts could not garner her any enduring honor or respect. Rather, she somehow suffered the harsh and distant whims of others, managing to invite rejection from friends and strangers. Maybe she didn't expect people to see the good in her, which made her resort to defensive plays of character that naturally offended most people who didn't know how to understand her.

Unwilling Child Witness

Throughout the years, Grandma Lolly and Aunt Rosalie were dutifully invited to our home, if not exactly joyfully welcomed. They'd come take up residence on the kidney-shaped, red velvet couch with my father wedged between them—one ear open to each. The glass-topped oval desk, adorned by two identical red and gold paisley velvet chairs at each edge, sat off to the side just for show. Its job was to hold my father's hats, car keys and a book or two. A single chair sat importantly behind the desk, though it was not available to us children who might have wanted to lazily sit there. And in an opposite corner stood a gold-edged, six-foot fountain which, when turned on, sent beads of oil sliding down delicate harp-like strings. It always felt to me like it was crying.

While my mother was often working hard at her home desk or in the kitchen, we children would be summoned by name to entertain our grandmother/aunt duo. They would take turns restlessly pacing between the living room and kitchen, in search of someone or something with whom to engage. This aimless chit-chat walk must have irritated those in my house who were doing the important daily business of living life. But that did not include me because my life, I had often been advised, was not as important.

Just like Aunt Rosalie.

These seemingly too-frequent visits from Richmond to our home in Baltimore featured on-edge and over-the-edge power struggles. Angry words were easily exchanged over Aunt Rosalie's habit of leaving, on my mother's kitchen table, her used Styrofoam cups of coffee that my mother was expected to serve her. Quietly taking her garbage, food and otherwise, was a recurring challenge indeed. Aunt Rosalie's quirky, predictably unpredictable behaviors drew out the powerlessness in others, particularly my mother. Sometimes this made my aunt seem powerful to me—that she could provoke such chaos in my usually generous, kind, unflappable mother. But then again, it looked to me like Aunt Rosalie herself always came up looking powerless, too. Always coming in second, if at all.

Understand that on our home turf, hard work marked by quantifiable accomplishment and acclaim was prized above all. For us children, that meant academic success, a pleasing appearance, and a happy disposition; while for my parents, increasing business success and community involvement took first prize. As my mother stood her superior ground by virtue of, well, her virtuous character marked by admirable achievements, Aunt Rosalie would trail behind. It seemed that these two women couldn't be equal; if one was ahead, the other had to be behind. As a baseball fan, I can tell you that even though the home team has the advantage, the visiting team is not doomed to automatic failure. But they do have to fight hard to win. In this comparative game, it seemed to me that to score, one had to have more to show for oneself. One had to be more, do more, have more, than the other to claim victory, and definitely had to prove they had the popular vote of an unquestioning majority, known as us children.

To my young eyes, it seemed that Aunt Rosalie could never win in any category, least of all in her parenting of her one daughter, an adored cousin of mine named Sylvia for whom I felt a sisterly cherish. I am not sure how one can accurately assess winners and losers in the tough sport of parenting, but I do know that Sylvia often had to put her mother in her place, even if that meant kicking her—which once left my aunt with a broken arm and a badly damaged self-worth, if she even had any. And on our home front, I well remember the time when, because we did not have enough beds to host them overnight, they'd opt for the local hotel—but not before setting the stage for a lingering struggle. Their hotel had a pool and, of course, they asked us children to join them for a swim, but neglected first to secure my mother's approval of their plan. Excited, we asked my mother for permission to have fun, and when denied, I knew we had been pawns in this round of *let's prove who's boss around here*. Of course, our anger was provoked against our mother, for pre-adolescents cannot yet sense any context beyond immediate, beckoning water to cool off a hot summer's day. How uncool to all.

Grandma Lolly and Aunt Rosalie did not speak this language of superiority well. If I intuited correctly, they were instead well-versed in the democratic model of everyone being equal. Status was an entitlement, not something that had to be earned or deserved. I remember that in this ongoing game, when my aunt would pitch the smallest word or smirk, striking down a food or fashion choice, my mother's glances would punish Aunt Rosalie for daring to say something designed to put her on more equal footing with my mother. But that would not stop

Aunt Rosalie from trying to make my mother lose her superior standing, provoking her until the breaking point.

Breaking points were painful to watch. They sounded harsh and seemed unfair to those who didn't see how and why they had formed. As a first-hand, unqualified child witness silently recording the unsavory goings-on in these inner chambers of power, I found it impossible to judge who mattered and who didn't. I desperately wanted both to matter. My loyalties, divided between my mother and my aunt, begged my compassion for each of them. The agony of trying to judge who was right and who was wrong, who was good and who was bad, overwhelmed me. In rendering judgment on each, while struggling to vindicate both for their human vulnerabilities, I exhausted my natural reserves of childhood joy and innocence.

I cannot totally explain why I positioned myself as judge in a case between two women I considered powerful. Maybe in handing down the verdict, I could rearrange my own identity for the better, at least in my own mind. Put myself on a bit of higher ground. One thing was certain: this long-lingering drama wounded me for much of my life. It was traumatic to see in the raw how people can wound each other, destroying a sense of worthiness in both the actors and the spectators—possibly the most vulnerable of whom was me. I say *traumatic* because traumas, I'd come to learn, can be *slow, steady, seemingly unremarkable assaults on something intrinsic to the healthy functioning of a breathing organism.* Consistent, enduring messages of non-mattering fit this ill.

Crumbs of Mattering

Interesting that it was on this ground of non-mattering that I actually tasted some mattering. I was the one who'd go over to Grandma Lolly and Aunt Rosalie to make them feel welcome. To throw a crumb of mattering, of worthiness, and of belonging. And that crumb fed me, too. Not out of spite for my mother, not of duty to my father, but because my nature was to accept others. And besides they were funny and fun, informal and laid back—qualities that were a nice contrast to the more reverent, straight contours of our home. They also seemed fair to me, which somehow nobody else knew how to be. Because they asked me to be something that no one else needed or wanted from me—to be myself. Being my unintimidating self was the only condition for their friendship. They did not make fun of me. They did not insist on comparing me with my sisters, or point out how I came up short or wide or inferior. And I understood that in this colder climate of mattering, I, as they, had none of the accomplishments that mattered, and therefore, together we could not matter much—if at all. To me, that felt quite important.

Pre-scripted: My First Role

The language of not mattering is held together by notes of disdain and discounting. Its main sound is guttural and harsh: *Do not be who you are.* Worse, *who do you think you are?* Curiously, not mattering was most effectively spoken when my mouth was closed, while listening to others speaking to or about me.

"What will ever become of you? Nothing, that's what."

"You make everything so complicated."

"You are in your own world; snap out of it."

"You have no common sense."

"Don't listen to her; she doesn't know what she is talking about."

"She is so stubborn and difficult."

It was vowelized with ridiculing looks and sighs of desperation or embarrassment. And I began to speak it to myself: *Why must you be different from your sisters and your friends? Why can't you just be normal, just do it like everyone else?*

I had been given my script early on. As mentioned, my main role was cast like Aunt Rosalie, with my big line: *Do not be like Aunt Rosalie, to whom you are so similar.* And I'd overtax my brain wondering what it was about her and me that made our roles so parallel. Was it our shared green-eyed perspective on life that left us feeling small in our own eyes, prompting us to then act in accord with that unflattering assessment? Maybe it was the inability to restrain our impulsive emotions, eating whatever and whenever we wanted, saying what we pleased, and showing great frustration easily and intensely when things did not go our way. Was it the way we could spin people's heads with our imaginative account of something that didn't quite happen in the way they experienced it that left them checking to see if their heads were on straight? Or could it have been the special powers we both seemed to have when it came to drawing out my mother's long, forgiving limits, leaving her undermined and powerless, yet somehow eliciting my father's pity for us rather than for her?

Lessons in Loyalty

All loyalties were put to a great test in this ongoing drama spanning nearly four decades of my life. It was much more than just my own loyalties to my parents and aunt that begged for some objective relief. My father's allegiance to my mother came under much scrutiny, as did hers to him, in these murky matters between spouses. I call them *fault lines*, as in shaky ground beneath all who tread, a consuming place for all to be amply faulted and hurt. And somehow, I was caught smack in the middle, which couldn't have been too helpful to my already vulnerable (dis)position.

It was a confusing test for all, and here is what I began to understand. While Grandma Lolly busily exercised her well-intentioned but naïve efforts to maneuver everyone into one big smile, all sides indulged in an array of provocative actions, no doubt each in justifiable self-defense. But this would only serve to fire up their complaints with charges of *she said/she did,* which were maddening to all. My young senses strained to take it all in, to make meaning of it, to rewrite the script of who provoked whom, and who deserved what. How could they all be right and all be wrong? In truth, I ached for my mother, my aunt, my grandmother—and for my father who was caught in between. I watched as they all agitated for dominance with him, and he, the peace-loving negotiator who knew how to make money by buying and selling homes, could not buy the peace in his own. He could not make it clear who deserved his loyalty, *and that was because he himself did not always really know.*

Parenthetically, as the mother of one son, twenty-four years young, I am terrified to tell you what I'm about to say. Let the secret to a loving, peaceful, respectful marriage be known right here: Your wife or your life. In other words, your wife comes first, your mother—second. Of course, it is usually a very happy perk that once that score is settled, everyone is given their due in honorable, respectful, and even loving ways. A man cannot negotiate his wife's well-being and status as his prized priority. *Non-negotiable.* My husband Zack knew this, and it is the rare occasion that I've had to review this with him.

How could my noble, peace-loving father not have his loyalties clear? For one thing, he possessed a fierce foundation of respect for his parents. The divinely ordained mandate to honor one's parents motivated his exemplary show of grateful submission to his parents' desires. Close attention to these, no matter the cost, was paramount. Overlaying that, my father grew up in the South, observing the rigid family structure wherein a man was served by his wife with due respect and reverence. All womanly actions were poised at showing unquestioning loyalty to their husbands, thus ensuring their domestic peace. His mother, my Grandma Lolly, dutifully worked alongside her husband, Grandpa Barry, in their small convenience store. She had to suffer long days manning the store, and even worse, had to keep a loaded .32-calibre handgun right beneath the cash register. While it badly scared her to be in its proximity, my father made some good use of it. Barely able to see above the counter, one day he picked up the gun and instructed the unfortunate customer who had just entered, "Mista Andason, put ya hands up and move against the wall." Frozen in fear, Grandma Lolly cajoled him into setting it down, while Grandpa Barry entered just at that moment and laughed.

Toting around authority in a playful but dangerous way did not stop there in Richmond. A man expected his wife to be strong and submissive at the same time, to be available for him and his children—but always him first—and for his children to practically raise themselves without much fussing. And while the submissive wife piece was somehow lost on me, the hierarchy of values regarding work and children was pretty clear in my little mind. Yes, when I'd grow up, I'd be hiring a nanny to care for my children, if I had any, so that I could go make money. Nothing other than that seemed necessary, worthwhile, or respectable. (Real-life scripts do look different, but that's a story for later on.) So with this thinking, my father could easily have expected my mother to understand that short-term accommodations to his mom and sister were part of her loyal service to him. It would be many years of resentful bouts by my long-suffering, afflicted mother before he had even an iota of understanding that some things just don't work the way he thought they ought.

So yes, while I knew why my father's loyalties were often unclear, here is what I had yet to clarify: my sensitive spirit was inhaling the unhealthy air of this ongoing drama of difficult, painful relationships between ever-evolving personalities. Frightfully unaware of this dysfunction, they were all helpless in how to heal it. There was more than enough self-righteousness casting its angry fumes, burning holes in my soul caught in this all-consuming and growing powerlessness.

All were just playing out their part, and it made sense—poor though it might have been—for them to be doing their thing. But following scripts with misguided characters is asking for a lopsided performance, which everyone predictably gave.

Taking It Personally

I pondered deeply throughout the years if Aunt Rosalie could have blossomed, if only given the chance. I believed the words of Margaret J. Wheatley: "A weed is but an unloved flower." Had anyone ever tried to water her? Why was she so easily discarded?

I felt wounded for her. And for me. Would I be given the chance to blossom? Or would I be discarded too?

I would come to understand that her poorly tolerated, crazy-making, disordered personality with its subsequent anxiety and panic disorder—maybe a touch of other clinical stuff like schizophrenia—would have likely been well-served by today's scientific knowledge of mental health and its cadre of capable, compassionate practitioners. How sad that she would not have that benefit.

As for me, all these thoughts traveled deep into the recesses of my heart, becoming stored as feelings of profound unworthiness. That I would never matter. Not being invited to be who you are creates an unwelcome divide in the spirit, obstructing a healthy path towards wholeness. And I was left, in the dark of many nights—days, too—to wonder what work or accomplishment I'd ever do that would change that.

This fallout registered on me personally, birthing a great loneliness. Not-mattering and loneliness are twins (emptiness a triplet) sharing the same faint heartbeat of a life yet to be lived. They coexist in a colorless and dark place, desperately agitating for the relief of a redemptive light.

This underbelly of the human psyche is an intensely cold and despairingly empty place. And I'd come to learn that very little can satisfy the growing hunger these twins endure. One can never be enough, have enough, or do enough. *Enoughness* is the word I use when I talk about this concept. And for now, I just want to say that this *enoughness* is not within the rational and reasonable reach of this twin pair.

It was in the deep cracks of this shaky ground shifting dangerously beneath me that my spirit could get caught and fall. Which I did, many times.

Complicated Matters

One more thing you should know: Mixing this language of not-mattering with the natural tongue of a complicated child yields the kind of kid that gives parenthood a really bad name.

Turns out, complicated children can be difficult to raise. While their siblings manage to keep frenetic pace with their mother in a store, the difficult child often becomes lost and must be led by the hand of a caring adult to the store office to sit with a lollipop until her frustrated mother claims her, muttering something like, "You know, some kids are just so . . . ," with the last word trailing behind like the lost child. Or even older, at the amusement park, somehow the uneasy child becomes separated from the rest of the family, who then hears the lost child's name announced over the loudspeaker, with directions to the little red caboose where the child can be retrieved—this thirteen-year-old who is waiting with the three- and four-year-olds, obviously themselves difficult children in training . . . or this is the child who sits at the table with her eyes closed and declares that she cannot listen to you because she is thinking. When she is told to stop thinking so much, she replies, "I'll think about that." This is the child who says she sees extra light in the room; why can't anyone else see it? She is the one crying hysterically that she has hepatitis, not considering that the carrot she ate lent her a temporary yellowish tint, and that she will indeed survive. And, for the life of her, she cannot understand that one and one is two, and not eleven.

A difficult child is one who must be carried because she screams and swears that her slightly sprained foot is broken, only to hobble off to participate in a game of bowling later that day . . . or the one who excitedly waits to get her ears pierced and somehow manages to lose the brand new diamond earring the evening before, while showing them off to her brother . . . or the one who, clad in her older sister's undersized coat that does not button on her (more important to look good than to be warm), falls one morning while running down the hill to school and loudly refuses to go to class until a pair of clean socks is brought straight from home. Surely you have seen this willful child on the amusement park children's ride, and as it is ready to spin in the air, she screams at the top of her ten-year-old lungs, "I am dying. Stop the ride NOW and let me off." Or you are waiting by the escalator, rushing to go on with your day, and this kid is standing and shrieking, "I am scared, I am scared." All of her mortified family has already gone up and down twice while she dissolves into a puddle of sobs. Maybe you saw the child who bolts up from her raised child seat in the middle of having her hair professionally cut. She furiously protests, "This is the worst haircut I ever had. It is so short. You are a terrible hair chopper. I'm calling the police!" What about the child who, on a family boating trip, lowers herself carefully into the pedal boat where her sister is patiently waiting in the othel, and somehow she, a fourteen-year-old, is suddenly drowning and needs to be rescued by the amused lifeguard?

Unconditional Love

Some people are born with simple natures, while others have a more complicated orientation. That, in my experience, does not ever change. It would be many tears later that I'd manage to learn this important distinction: I may be complicated, but I can learn how to not be difficult.

For all humans, simple or complicated, receiving unconditional love is a gift. For the complicated amongst us, though, it is critical; nothing less than spirit-saving. Unconditional love, loosely known as acceptance, allows everything in life its individuality, its purpose, and its power. To matter. To be less difficult, and less dangerous, we humans learn to function healthfully within some limits—moral, legal, social, financial, corporal, time, and space—though it is paramount that we try them on for size and grow into them when ready. But, overly limit-loving people—controlling, really—can be toxic for those more complex natures whose breath thrives on pushing limits of individuality and non-conformity. With unconditional love, we can extend a potent belief in the worthiness of the complicated person, activating natural wellsprings of hope and drive and discipline. *And ultimately, of mattering.*

But many humans, it seems to me, have a hard time loving unconditionally; especially Americans in an image-driven and overconsuming society. With this, we deprive the human soul of its main nutrient: Hope. As I've heard it said, "They tell you what you can't do, never what you can." Yes, indeed.

Healthy Boundaries, Happier People

Allowing the rightful position of each individual allows healthy boundaries for all, forming the basis for well-functioning relationships.

Aunt Rosalie would not, maybe could not, abide by simple, reasonable limits, which made it seem like she was always selfishly manipulating everyone around her. She was in her seventies, and I half her age, when on a weekend visit to my home, I decided to educate her not to walk into my bedroom without first knocking on the door. I gently retrained her by asking, "Aunt Rosalie, please go out and knock before you enter." With my hand in hers, I lovingly guided her to the other side of the door to practice this simple etiquette of respecting someone's boundaries.

Perhaps it was too late for her, but it was perfect timing for me. Because by that point, I had become conscious that the life I was redeeming with my own was hers. Perhaps there was truth to the idea that I was like her. But maybe I could find a way to matter anyway. *And if I could, then I could make her matter, too.* Making her matter seemed extraordinarily important to me, because often just thinking about her unseated a deep, ready tear for life's potential untapped. Using the similar raw materials of her emotional timbre, I could choose to fashion all that oppositional, limit-breaking and manipulative movement into a reasonable coherence of care and courage. Learning which limitations to honor and which to override, where to take "no" for an answer and when to insist on a "yes," to whom and for what. When to impose my will on others, and when to depose myself . . . *knowing full well not to ever take credit for being given the opportunity that she didn't have.*

Safe, but Not Sane

As for Aunt Rosalie, her spirit had deteriorated on the inside decades before her seventy-five-year-old body gave way, too. Her worsening dementia, which had urged us to place her in an assisted living facility in her final year, exaggerated everything about her that made her difficult to have around. She was argumentative; nothing was pleasing to her. No friend could be found, no food could fill, and no activity could interest her. And now, as she was dressing herself in a pair of stockings, with one stocking on while leaving the other hanging off to the side, we could all agree that her cognition was objectively impaired.

Her stay in the facility which my parents generously funded kept her safe, though not sane, and provided for her basic food, shelter, and medical monitoring. I'd often chat with her on the phone, until she'd announce that she had some "strange" people in her room. And though it was often tricky to sort out what her baseline pattern of creative thinking was, seeing these non-existent people surely passed it. By the end of her life, I had watched an anxious woman grow into a full-blown panic case, always in great emotional pain. In her constant refrain, it was like "being up a river without a paddle." I had glimpsed up close how perhaps Aunt Rosalie was her own greatest victim, for she could not speak the truth about herself and her life.

Responding to the Call of Her Death

The call of her death came to me on an Israeli Friday morning, seven hours ahead of the American clock. As my ears heard my parents delivering this sadness, the hurt settled inside, leaving me to ask but one question of them: Should I cut my trip short and fly home to deliver the eulogy in person at her Sunday funeral? No, I'd stay and deliver the eulogy remotely from a phone in Israel, and it would be broadcast there in Richmond's funeral parlor.

As it happened, the eulogy coincided with a meeting that I had already scheduled, which could not be changed for another time. Left with no choice, I turned to the office manager in whose office I was meeting, "Strange, but true... I have a eulogy to deliver in a few minutes. Can I use your phone, and how about your chair?" After securing his slightly amused permission for his space, I dialed in my formal, but not final, respects to my Aunt Rosalie for having been my aunt—and a woman from whom I learned lifelong lessons about mattering. A person whose circumstances can still evoke in me a trilogy of feelings: sadness about our being, fear of our not being, and courage to become.

If life is our teacher, then handling rejection was Aunt Rosalie's lesson that she learned and endured throughout her entire life.

I don't know much about her early life, but it appears that from early on, her unique pattern of thinking and relating with others made her somewhat complicated to comprehend. But she was a study in persistence.

She exemplified an uncommon loyalty, an extreme willingness to submit herself to Grandma Lolly's wishes and needs. In these later years, she tried mightily to care for Grandma in an effort to help her remain in her own home. Even within her limited abilities, she had an unlimited drive to protect her, and above all, to honor her.

Beyond her relationship with her mother, Aunt Rosalie tried to extend friendship to those who would accept it. She never wanted to be shamed, or to shame others. Her friends found her endearing, and her sense of persuasion compelling. She had a special ability to convince others of the truth of things according to the way she saw it, an important talent I wish her life circumstances would have been better able to support and nurture.

My family and I shall personally treasure the encouragement she gave us in our various endeavors, and we will always appreciate her for letting us know that she cared about us.

Finally, the lesson of her life shall not be lost on us: The lesson that one need not define oneself by another's standards, and that one must not measure oneself against any soul other than the one G-d breathed into one's body. That each soul has a reason for being, and that all souls are precious and beloved by G-d who created them.

Prepare to Matter

As a speculative soul, I mine the idea that perhaps I was most fortunate to have my shadows clearly reflected for me so early on. Without my family's input directing my attention to my inadequacies, I may have been at the mercy of my own complicated nature, for we cannot easily see these kinds of things on our own. And although at a high cost, I cannot really know where I'd be better spent. Which character would I ultimately be playing had I been left to my own script, totally undirected? Who would I really be if I wasn't living my life in conscious pushback mode to the messages I was given? Whether or not I would have been fueled faster and further is a question I cannot answer. But as I continued to work out that question through my own parenting, I was left with a more pressing one that desperately nibbled at the crumbling edges of my unfolding spirit: *What makes a person matter? And would I ever?*

This I have learned well: Reading your life script and practicing your lines is the beginning of mattering. Not the script of powerlessness that people might give you; that keeps you small. Take the lines you have, and say them as if your part is big and powerful. Telling the real story, no matter how few the lines, is big and powerful. It matters because you do.

And it opens the door to bigger opportunities for which you are waiting.

CHAPTER TWO

First Step:
Prepare to Fall

It is by going down into the abyss that we recover the treasures of life. Where you stumble, there lies your treasure.

—JOSEPH CAMPBELL, mythologist

I WAS THE MOTHER OF THREE DAUGHTERS when my older sister Brenna told me, "Watching you is like watching someone run with her hands tied behind her back."

"What does that mean, Brenna?" I asked.

"It means you need professional help," she answered.

"As in pay someone to talk with me?" I countered.

I had to admit that Brenna was right. Not only had she always been older than me, she was also always wiser. Guess that's what happens when you are an August-born Leo, the oldest girl in the family and gifted with a fiercely independent spirit that understands things others can't or won't, and has the language to confidently articulate it. And she was naturally svelte, which I was not. Possessed of a princess-like composure conferred upon her by her status as the oldest daughter and granddaughter to two sets of grandparents, I'd frequently call upon her to get me unstuck in my life. And now, without me even having to ask, she had called it right. As the singer-composer Julia Blum sang in her song "Dream Big," *In my mind, I run. In my life, I fall.* I was running, but not managing to get anywhere.

Dr. Norma was one of the prominent therapists in my city, known for her creative methods for teaching children to be responsible for their emotional well-being as well as their academic progress. At the turn of sixty, she still wore a short, wavy mass of black hair around a face marked by clear blue eyes, clean chin lines, and a warm, understanding smile that promised to help you in a direct, but respectful, manner—hard-pressing if necessary, but never abusive. Her Italian values favored solid mothering, good food, and a driven work ethic, making this a good fit, clinically speaking. For the sake of my highest good, I could overlook that she was very thin, an enthusiastic, daily treadmiller, and a passionate cook who made her own yogurt.

Meeting in her home office situated in the enclosed patio adjoining her living room, I took for myself the red-cushioned white rocking chair facing her swivel arm chair at the side of her small, unimposing walnut desk. She was dressed in her neatly-pressed khaki slacks with a red turtleneck tucked over them at the waist. With her dainty gold chain resting quietly on her heart, Dr. Norma turned her head to me. It was on this third visit with her that I shared the dream.

"I love the feel of water, Dr. Norma. Water is still and graceful. My bath waters hold me in their embrace, often kissing away the coldness of a winter day. And the boating waters of summer invite the untamed spirit to rip through them, pretending to briefly dominate the unseen expanse of life."

But this body of water was different. I was surprised how often and how deeply this particular body of water flowed through my subconscious in the dark night hours.

"Shifra, where is the water? Do you recognize it?" asked Dr. Norma.

"She sits on the edge of Highview and Shorepoint Road, near my growing-up home. She is called Shore Valley Creek.

Shore Valley Creek starts on one side of the road and travels underground through a tunnel to the other side of the road. I don't think most people are aware that she does that, because she does this in a most secretive and unobserved way."

"Is the water quiet in your dream? Is there any kind of conversation between you and the water?"

I hesitate. "At first, the water is quiet and peaceful. She can be trusted. But then she twists and turns in fits of fury. We don't exchange words, only images. I am holding a small child, sometimes two, in the water. The child—no, both children—whose safety is resting perfectly in my hands begin to fall."

"What do you do when this happens, when they begin to fall?" she asked, inviting the drama.

"They begin to fall, and I reach for them. I reach for them, but I cannot grasp them. I cannot grasp them, so I reach for them more. And they are falling, falling, falling."

Dr. Norma turned to her desk drawer and withdrew a piece of paper. "Shifra, can you read this?"

let me fall
(from Cirque du Soleil)

JAMES CORCORAN AND JUTRAS BENOIT

Let me fall
Let me climb
There's a moment when fear
And dreams must collide

Someone I am
Is waiting for courage
The one I want
The one I will become
Will catch me

So let me fall
If I must fall
I won't heed your warnings
I won't hear them

Let me fall
If I fall
Though the phoenix may
Or may not rise

I will dance so freely
Holding on to no one
You can hold me only
If you too will fall
Away from all these
Useless fears and chains

Someone I am
Is waiting for my courage
The one I want
The one I will become
Will catch me

So let me fall
If I must fall
I won't heed your warning
I won't hear

Let me fall
If I fall
There's no reason
To miss this one chance

Lifting my eyes from the page, I asked, "Dr. Norma, what does this mean?"

"Shifra, it means you are about to do some important, life-altering work. Are you ready?"

> If not now, when? If I am not for me, then who will be?
> (Ethics of the Fathers *1:14*)

Do you want to live large, to matter?

Prepare to fall.

I knew that no one is too big to fall. Even if you are a bank. Remember that notion in the economic chaos of 2008—that some financial institutions were too big to fail? Lehman Brothers wasn't. It did. In September 2008, this venerated, 158-year-old titan totally collapsed. Bear Stearns and Merrill Lynch—among the most stable, exalted names on Wall Street—toppled like sandcastles (even though they were ultimately saved).

Falling. It is a huge piece of living. Have you noticed?

My life has been generous in that way, giving me ample opportunity to practice stumbling. I started young, and it began with overeating.

How, *while dieting*, had my 5′ 4″ body expanded to 200 pounds before I graduated high school? Geneen Roth, author of multiple books on disordered eating, posits the "Fourth Law of the Universe: For every diet, there is an equal and opposite binge. Every action has a reaction, and like gravity, every over-controlling diet that does not have your loving, realistic cooperation leads to a let-loose eating binge, to the eventual backlash on our healthiest intentions." I began to realize that my life was minimized to just two compartments: my dieting days and my bingeing days.

Like a venomous snake, these coiled issues of eating, body size, and mattering slithered around my life for decades. Lying low at times, it would spring up at others, keeping my joy in a chokehold. I had come to agree with Geneen, that "diets were built on the belief that if I trusted myself, I would destroy myself. . . that my hunger was bottomless, that I was crazy and self-destructive." Trying to figure out this growing, illogical insanity that had sucked my life dry, I got heavier by the day, further eroding any sense of trust that I could get myself out of this desperate pit. The scale would steadily climb, reaching 240 pounds.

Being fat was a public affair. Some years ago at a family wedding, an older male relative approached me. It was in between the ceremony known as the *Chuppah* (literally, a canopy to which the groom and bride are escorted, usually by their parents, and under which they stand while seven blessings are said) and the seated formal dinner hosting more than three hundred guests in a large hall, decorated in purple and gold tones beneath two massive chandeliers giving off equal amounts of light and warmth. Soft music accompanied the guests to their tables, men on one side of the room and women on the other, in accord with the religious practice of modesty separating the genders at an Orthodox Jewish wedding. The male attire featured mostly dark suits buttoned over white shirts that were held closed at the top by paisley, striped, or floral ties. The women walked delicately on heels no lower than two inches, often much higher, beneath colorful dresses or two-piece outfits with careful lines and lengths protecting their feminine dignity.

This relative of mine was one of those really nice guys in his mid-60's whose exchanges with my siblings and me sometimes bordered on minding our business. His banter was consistently joking and jolly, always asking for a hug which he knew I would not give to the opposite gender because he was not my grand/father, brother, son, grandson, or husband. In his typical fashion, he found his way over to the women's tables so that he could catch up with his younger female relatives, which didn't happen often. After exchanging the pleasantries, he could not let the conversation end without surprising me: "When you get around to it, I would like you to lose some weight."

With a poise shaped from decades of experience with well-intentioned but misguided people, I replied, "Okay, so you want me to lose weight when I get around to it."

"Yeah, you know, you are attractive, and I want you to be the absolute best-looking you can be," he innocently stated.

Resisting the temptation to feel complimented, and looking at his own considerably overgrown belly, I countered, "Well, I'll keep this in mind. But you know what? I don't know if it's in the cards for me."

"It's in the cards. It's in the cards," he reassured himself.

I must be holding the wrong deck of cards.

Nike, You Got It Wrong

If I *could* "just do it," I would. Yes, Nike, I've been wanting to tell you that for a long time.

Being a young girl in a big body had its advantages. True, my body was too heavy to comfortably carry around, but I was noticed. *I mattered*—in the sense that my science teacher defined matter: taking up space. Wedged between my sixth- and seventh-grade years, I was eleven when my mother took me to Diet Workshop. Hoping to drop her extra fifty pounds hanging around after the February birth of her sixth child—a robust 8½ pound mixture of ruddy skin, an unruly black mop of hair, and a brilliant rattler of nerves who was now my fourth and final sister named Hadassah—my mother and I spent this summer before my Bat Mitzva focused on getting a thinner body. I dropped thirty-two pounds of myself. *How many pounds of shame is that?* I suddenly became beautiful. To say it another way, I now mattered because I *didn't* take up space. But the shame did not go away. Like fat cells, shame easily multiplies and gets in the way of a good fit.

Weight gains, weight losses, and weight regains were constant companions as I fell on and off dieting plans, none of which I could understand how to make work for me. Full friendships fed themselves on my dieting life, such as my relationship with my classmate Leah that centered on our weekly meetings, this time at Weight Watchers. Maybe their scales would be better balanced than the Diet Workshop scales. But when Leah lost weight and I did not (even after our joint session of eating excessively out of the same peanut butter jar), I thoughtfully advised her to continue on without me, and that I would figure out something else for myself, which I didn't.

In my senior year, I returned to Diet Workshop for my third time because they had upped their game, offering a new six-week session designed to accelerate our weight loss. So now, in addition to starving me, they had me paying to sit in circles of women twice and thrice my age and older, discussing why we ate so much. Well, if I knew *that*, I wouldn't be wasting my time going around in circles. After each session, I exercised my desperation by quickly splitting to the nearest ice cream store to figure out on my own *why* I could possibly eat so much. All I could think of was that it probably had something to do with how *good* the food tasted.

Full Body, Empty Self

My body may have been abundantly fed, but I was on empty.

My home was not always the best place to expect hunger to be consistently and deeply filled. Dinners that were meant for the whole family were barely enough to feed my double-portion hunger. Sitting alone at the kitchen table—my thin sisters had already contented themselves with a small plate of nutrition, followed by generous helpings of candy—I feasted over the daily *Baltimore Sun*, sports section first, while feeding every morsel of aloneness that I could. All the eating got done before my parents came home, so they could have the room they needed to unwind quietly after yet another grueling day at work.

In our home, one was encouraged to get A$^+$s, be thin and pretty, be quiet, be happy, and to limit expressions of fear. All of these were generally out of my comfortable, consistent reach. But the cookies in the breadbox, the cabinet closest to the floor, were well within my grasp. The breadbox, known in other homes as the candy drawer, held all the heaven you could possibly need on this earth. Creamy Kit Kats and exquisitely bitable Skor bars, Tootsie Roll candy that turned over and under your tongue as it blissfully melted away, and all other compelling combinations of chocolate and sugar, were there for the having. And when that could no longer satisfy . . . not to worry. With a half-body turn away, ice cream by the pint could be secured from the freezer and allowed to soften so it could slide down like a kid water sledding on a crazy-hot day.

And as I'd get scared or anxious about not being enough or having enough, I could reach for food because it would feed the emptiness and the fear. I would head to that drawer and, without even bending down, use my big toe to draw it open and restore myself to some balance. In those moments of unwrapping life's kindness—known to humans as candy or sweet calories—I held tightly to the imminent escape from life's gripping angst. As my lips tightened around the smooth edges of my richly-coated friends, an ocean of warmth flooded my belly with a delicious current of pleasure. So full, so satisfying . . . for thirty whole seconds, I was totally consumed by the absolute joy and comfort of being. But then, too soon after the swallow, the pit of angst began to fill again with fear, drowning me in familiar worry. I'd then help myself again to these household remedies for the loneliness of being too big in my body and too small in spirit. The only challenge was that I had to do it all in secret. If caught, I'd risk the food being denied me, or worse, be shamed for feeding my too-heavy body. If you were thin, you had permission to eat. If you were fat, you had the permission, the right, the duty to starve.

Skating: Lesson for Life

After I tripped into motherhood, I had a dream in which I was skating. I was carrying many, many extra pounds and as I twirled and swizzled with my pale-peach chiffon gown kicking up behind me, my concerned mother turned to Brenna, my older sister, and said, "She can't do that. She's too fat. Won't she get hurt?"

To which Brenna responded, "But, Ma, she's doing it."

Despite my notion that thin people could effortlessly skate and fat people would fall and maybe die, I knew it was time to stop dreaming and start skating. Skating would have me tread on my fears and begin to prove that others' presumptive limits for me don't get to define my path.

I phoned Courtney, the pony-tailed, thirty-something, skating teacher who taught nine-year old Basya—my second daughter, whose signature smile was as sweet as it was big—to skate, asking her when she could fit me in. Of course, I clued her in to several things: I'd probably be the hardest student she ever had, certainly the most scared, and probably the fattest. And also, we'd be skating to a piece of Yanni music. Would that be okay?

Bless her kindness for putting Yanni in the overhead speaker, powering my spirit. In our first lesson, I held her as tightly as an unsteady, newly walking baby holds on before knowing he or she can do this. Like the shiny shoes just placed on the novice young walker, my skates hugged ankles with just enough strength to stand on their own, held back by fear that can only be undone by actually taking the steps forward—with lots of encouragement from others. The air was predictably cold, hardly made warmer by my thick opaque leggings under a loose black skirt, hooded sweater, and still-dry gloves. My breathing was already labored with fright while I watched others rhythmically dance in this round space of life called the rink, circling it with ever-growing ease and passion. Legs burning already from standing on anorexic-thin blades stilting forward, I began to move across the ice with a slight uplift, carrying myself from one step to the next.

"Shifra, our first lesson in learning how to skate is preparing to fall. Today, I will teach you how to fall." *This should be easy,* I thought to myself. *I am a natural . . . at falling.*

Courtney showed me how to fall, which took a surprising amount of my courage—and finesse. Basic rule: Keep your composure, keep your hands close to you, get up quickly, continue with the move you fell on, and be prepared to fall again. It was that simple. I'd remember this long after leaving the ice rink. I could learn to stay composed after a fall which would allow for a quick rebound, and then to pick up precisely at the falling point. After three sessions of lovingly, securely holding my hands while skating around the rink, Courtney prompted me, "Shifra, it's time for you to skate around on your own. I will be right here in this corner, working with another student." And, pointing to the far right speaker, she smiled. "Yanni's here, too."

"Sure," I said, "I can do this." Knowing she had one eye on me from across the rink, I was ready. Forward I leaned, lifting one foot in the air and then the other in delectable slices of joy. It was on the second go-around, as I circled the far-end corner of the rink, that my skate got caught in a piece of music that sent me to the cold ground.

"Shifra, are you okay?" Courtney called out, her blonde pony-tail already swinging, as she started to skate towards me.

"Yes, I am fine; I really am. Don't come." And I really was. Because as I hit the ice, I broke my fear, and that, to me, was the dance I was really after.

Yes, I say *dance* because she is the mother of the arts. In the larger sense, dance represents the forward movement that has us flowing into our spirit, showcasing our release from its weighty bonds of human limitations. In this way, dance encourages the human spirit to articulate its intense and unspoken language as it seeks to convey the landscape of human dream and drama.

As I began to make my way back up, a guy whizzed by me on his skates to say, "We all start that way."

Do we? I wondered. Do we all start that way? Yes, that guy was right that we all fall, even if we are not all equally terrified to do so. I remember the day I put my then-nine-year-old Daniel on skates. No fear in his skates; the ice bowed to his bravado. No Yanni playing, the beat in his heart pulled him around in easy lines, with nary a falling moment on the ground. What a joy to watch that fearlessness in such a young child. I did not know that could exist, certainly not in one of my offspring. (But then again, Zack is his father—the man whose decision to marry me must have somehow bestowed on little Daniel a similar zest for taking on a challenge, indeed thriving on the edge of danger.)

To live large, you don't need a sizable body that takes up ample space. Nor a thin one that doesn't. You need your spirit, *yourself*.

"Success consists of going from failure to failure without loss of enthusiasm," said Winston Churchill. And for each of us, and for all of us, fat or thin, scared or stoic, we take the steps—and missteps—we need, to move us in the ways we wish.

Learning how to fall is one of life's greatest lessons. Prepare. It is often the first step in the journey. Small steps make large strides. Be willing to fall, for that is the pathway to rise.

CHAPTER THREE

Struggling to Matter

The privilege of a lifetime is being who you are.
—JOSEPH CAMPBELL, mythologist

FROM HIS FIRST CONTRACTING TUG on my inner conscience, my son Daniel waited forty-two hours to be born. If that sounds long, I'd say that it *felt* even longer. Forty-two hours is a few hours short of two full days and nights, which means I was going on a second night of no sleep. As I am not a particularly patient person, I suppose this was good training for motherhood. This waiting process definitely pushed my limits . . . as children do. I had only seen the inside of 3 and 4 a.m. when I pulled the rare all-nighter in high-school or college, after which I'd collapse into an undisturbed world of dreams for most of the day's remaining hours. But the thought of an epidural scared me more than being tired, so I wouldn't do anything to rush it along.

After thirty-seven hours of secretly hoping that this baby would birth itself suddenly at home, like those exciting stories I had heard and wanted as my own, Zack convinced me—with the wave of a bag of Skor bars—to check in at the hospital five minutes away. Dr. Hein was on call that Monday night in late

November. He was as close to a midwife as one could get in a doctor—which is why the majority of my friends engaged his services. It was his sparkling sky-blue eyes beneath a respectable head of light brown hair and his easy, warm smile that made his patients comfortable in his care. His gentle, respectful, hands-off, "let nature take its course" approach did much to keep me in good emotional form. He delighted me when he agreed that I, a multi-birther and 6 cm. ready, could "lobby labor:" to remain downstairs in the lobby, unadmitted, walking, talking, and eating. Actually, it was our "labor policy" that I did the walking and eating while Zack did the talking, until I told him I'd had enough and he should be quiet, *please.* Then I'd continue the monologue with this stubborn unborn, trying to get it to pick up some speed, while allowing Zack to close his eyes for a few minutes at a time. No sense in his going into a real sleep when I might need him any minute now. Laboring women aren't always at their most generous.

The lobby guard, stationed behind a small security desk, had me a little concerned, as he was casting us glances every so often—each time getting a bit more nervous-looking. "Don't you think it's time, Ma'am, to go on upstairs? Look at you, bent over and all, hardly able to breathe." I reassured him, in between those mounting waves of unreasonable pressure on my lower back, that I'd know when it was time to take the elevator up, that I was a reliable delivery person. Zack tried his best to do that special counter pressure on my laboring back, but in truth, even the strongest hands could not bring total relief. Using my own pillow from home to place over the back of my lobby couch chair, I'd lean forward on the pillow during the contraction, shifting the pressure off my back as I indulged in relaxing thoughts that I had been specially trained to think. The funny-sounding breaths I employed amused me more than relieved me, but I could see they unnerved my guardian behind the desk.

And then, finally, in the forty-second hour of this unearthly process, my little one made it clear that the time had come to admit us upstairs—and quickly—for his long-awaited show was about to begin. Barely into the brightly-lit birthing room, greeted by a refreshed-looking Dr. Hein and two nurses whose names I didn't care to ask, I knew talking time was over, because all I could do was breathe and bend, stand straight for a few seconds, and repeat. Still walking around—a laboring position that felt most safe and comfortable to me—I announced my intention to lie down for just a quick breather. But, before I could even turn my exhausted body towards the bed, I was awash in the joy of a miracle born. He had decided that now, this very moment, was the time for him to begin living. With my birth attendants standing along with me, little Dan emerged to a standing ovation. Defying conventional positions for being born, he signaled early on that he could thrive on the drama of quick, last minute-decisions about how to show up for life. If only I had known how spirited he'd be, I might have agreed to let him ripen a bit more inside of me.

To the point: No one is too small to live and to assert a presence.

Maybe there are better places to be, but if you are here in this world, you are here to matter. If you are among the living, find a way to do it, to live. If a seven-pound baby—in fact babies a lot smaller than that—can make it and thrive, so can we. *We have one life to matter.*

The Spirit to Survive

My own life started tenuously. I was four days old when my twenty-three-year-old mother hemorrhaged in the tub and was rushed to the hospital for four pints of blood. Left in the care of the nanny, a thirty-five-year old African American whose imposing six-foot frame and reputation as the local community's most competent baby nurse commanded the trusting obedience of newborns and their families she cared for, I suddenly turned blue. A baby gasping for life, I held tightly to Fanny, for my mother was not there. With quick-thinking breaths, she restored life to my little bones. Little bones apparently have big memories; I do not like to decorate myself or my home with the color blue, and the occasional bout of anxiety still typically begins with that feeling of needing more air. And something else . . . for years, I yearned to become a baby nurse when I grew up.

Clearly, this early trauma colored itself on my emerging psyche, inclining it towards a ready fear of death and hopelessness while simultaneously casting a glow of expectant anticipation for recovering the air of hope for myself. It seems that as a new-born baby, I wanted to give up on the life I had just begun. I was never able to understand the medical explanation of what happened, and therefore will speak to the metaphysical piece that holds some personal meaning. The breath of life had threatened to leave me, and then was compassionately restored in me. *But I'd come to learn that holding onto it isn't always as natural as it seems.* The capacity to opt into our lives and to inhale the life-sustaining air of a large life requires that we find, and act on, the hope that our lives matter. Over and over again. Like G.E.'s tagline, we have to bring good things to our lives, nothing less than our best selves. That is what we do when our lives matter, when we matter. *How large I hope . . . is how long I live.*

As for my postpartum mother, she came home healthy, but probably not ready to mother any child, much less a needy infant sucking her energy, time, and attention. It got harder for both of us. I was alive for nearly eight weeks before a new life took hold inside my mother; she was now expecting her fourth child in five years. Sima, whose large, cocoa-brown eyes innocently opened on a clear day nine months later in early October, would now imbibe my mother's sweet feedings, while I was relegated to bottled milk with an emotionless, man-made nipple to suckle.

Smack in the Middle

As a middle child now squeezed between a thin older and younger sister, I was a misfit from the get-go.

Our baby pictures hung on the walnut-paneled bedroom wall, happily enough. Dark-haired and bright-eyed Aaron, my brother and oldest sibling, was framed upright on the one side, while my older sister Brenna was propped regally on the left. And yes, I was nailed in the middle. My nine-month-old chubby face, surrounded by short, soft, lively dirty-blonde curls, is lit up with a smile, the kind of light you love to see in a baby. I am sitting in a loose light green dress with white sleeves grabbing my meaty wrists, but it barely covers the fullest, fleshiest, dimpled-at-the-knee doll legs, dressed in short white socks. Sima's baby picture is not there. I guess by the time she was born, the pleasure of parenting had worn thin, and everyone was too tired to snap a photo, even of an adorable, easy going new baby.

The photos may not be there, but the memories are. My mind flashes through those first few years and captures some disquieting images our family album might have preferred not to record. Every family has those, no? I am toddling around and opening drawers to see what's in them, and determine that they must be emptied. In an exceptionally tidy home, curiosity and its concurrent disorder is not an admired quality, and there is only one way to contain it. I am harnessed to my crib so I cannot climb out and roam free.

I cannot really say how it felt to be harnessed, for I do not remember. I can, however, imagine that I was frustrated by the limits this harness imposed on my curious movement to jump the crib, which of course was its job to prevent. This harness was the precursor to today's oft-debated leash-like contraption, used by some to protect their young, active children from running too far ahead on an outing. Padded knapsack-like bands hug the child's upper body, while an extended piece of the band is held around the hand of the caregiver, securely binding the two. In its earlier form, the harness consisted of two thin, tan nylon straps that fit over the arms and extended around the front and back of the baby's chest, with a zipper closing it down the back. In their peak time, harnesses were an important tool in good parenting, helping to shape the behavior of small children who otherwise could not be enticed to stay still in obedience of bigger wills. Perhaps it was the conceptual version of whipping the child into shape, which incidentally was another popularly recommended parenting technique that often failed to achieve any real lasting results . . . unless emotional scars count. Strapping me in between some thin but secure ropes fastened to the side of the crib bar, my parents intended to protect me from roaming and possibly tumbling down the nearby flight of steps, which was obviously dangerous for me, and most definitely scary for my tired parents.

But free spirits cannot be solved so easily. Free spirits may be tied down for a while, but they manage to find ways to manifest their strong presence, including making lots of funny noises designed to annoy, and perhaps even scare, others. They, the big folk in my life, my exhausted young parents, finally tried their hand at the popular hitting technique, only to later report that "our hands would ache" before I'd cry for them to stop. They'd tell me this story throughout the years with the most earnest of intentions, mostly as a way of sharing that they always had my best interests at heart, but my stubborn nature made their job quite challenging at times. Honestly, I cannot recall this, and I am not even sure I understand how a small child could provoke such powerlessness in adults, but who was I to argue with the story? And so I didn't.

But I do often wonder what that experience of being hit must have meant to such a small child. I had no way to know that a whole generation of parents was being taught that spanking children was an acceptable way of disciplining them, only to be redirected otherwise by Dr. Spock. Unfortunately, I was caught somewhere in the middle of that whole generational discourse on proper parenting and discipline. To be clear, it wasn't the physical scars I think about; it is the lingering messages that affected me. Were my parents giving up on me? And if so, maybe I should give up on myself? This recurring feeling would leave me breathless, cutting off the air of hope so that it could not circulate healthfully through my sensitive heart. I also questioned what would make a child so stubborn and unresponsive to her parents' sincere attempts to raise her? There had to have been something fundamentally wrong with me, I reasoned—further deepening my belief that I did not matter.

Cracks in the Foundation

My brother Aaron was busy being an oldest, while we three girls were always trying to figure out which two sisters would be best friends while excluding the third. Feminine cliques, apparently, start young. As the first grandson on both sides of the family, Aaron asked for nothing less than the moon, and while he may not have gotten that, he sure was the superstar. I never was a star, so I didn't quite understand how hard it could be, but apparently it was quite an imposition to be doted upon and to be entitled to the desires of one's heart. A fastidious, prince-worthy wardrobe of clothes and toys adorned his environment. As for Brenna, the oldest girl and first granddaughter on both sides, she was the adored one. She sat daintily and quietly, only asking for "happy days and happy nights." As far as I knew, that's what she had, so I wasn't clear why she needed to ask for that. I, no one's first or favorite, wasn't quite sure where I fit, or if indeed I did at all. Sima was quite content to just sit prettily, collecting everyone's admiration—until she wanted something that I had, which inspired her to use her long nails to intimidate me into giving it. Sometimes, we three girls found ways to have fun, even if it meant just waiting for the bus on our pillows which served as the pretend bus stop. Lots of pretending made my life bearable when the tensions of a busy and often strict home sometimes rose high, asking for an obedience and a conformity that I did not know how to give. Sometimes, it seemed that the relaxing, dream-driven bedtime could not come soon enough for me.

Mornings typically dawned happily, with the upbeat Jewish morning prayer that I remember my father using to wake us up—his first parenting task of the day. *Thank you G-d for returning my soul with compassion, Your faithfulness is great.* Faith in G-d was actually a refrain I heard often, as my parents considered G-d their partner in their unfolding business and communal ventures. I overheard—perhaps, technically, it'd be called eavesdropping—countless conversations from their bedroom next to mine where they discussed G-d's guiding, loving hand. Yet, somehow when it came to the family front, I wondered if they availed themselves of Him as much. Maybe they thought He'd opt out of this challenging partnership?

Soon enough, my own faith would turn to fear as my mother's Jamaican-born morning hire, Sandy, helped me dress for school. Brushing my hair was the first official fight of the day. A full-bodied, thick head of unruly hair that would not do what it was told attracted Sandy's frustration—full force. She tore into the task of straightening it and untangling it, which, as I recall, made me wonder why she couldn't just play with it the way I lovingly did my doll's silky hair. And as my mind wandered off to Karisa, my doll who I'd then hold with my imagination, Sandy found no choice but to jerk my face between her hands, and with a quick stab of the brush handle against it, she'd finally get me to stand straight so she could perform her paid duty to perfection.

There was more fear waiting for me at school. With a confused sense of excitement, I'd watch the hands of my pre-school teacher guide many a precariously loose tooth from the mouths of my friends and me. I wondered a lot about all that turning and twisting of the young, but stubborn tooth, which seemed almost ready to do what baby teeth do . . . naturally fall away, making room for the maturing one to grow in. If she did not help it, I ultimately reasoned, maybe it would never on its own figure out how to do what it is supposed to do. Yes, better to remain speechless and let her hurt us, for it was in our overall best interest. There was a lot of blood, I thought, for such a little tooth, but we were still alive—so all was good enough.

Perfect Mother, Thy Name Is Food

On the occasion that I would visit the home of a friend, I was surprised to see what kind of mothers lived with them and what kind of food they ate. I recall Mindy's mother standing in the kitchen, smiling and making popcorn at the same time. Mindy was the youngest in her family, and I remember when I was given a bag of fresh, hot, buttered popcorn to take home with me, I tried to figure out how I could become the youngest in my family or how maybe just to move into hers. And Lisa's mom actually sang gently while dressing the salad with glossy olive oil and balsamic vinegar. It sure was different in my house, where our notion of entertaining a friend was for the housekeeper to put us all in the bathtub and get us comfortable and clean. It wasn't too long before I had no playmates coming over. Actually, friendships were restored when the housekeeper's knees became too bad for her to lean over the ceramic tub, and bath-giving as a social activity promptly stopped.

While my mother didn't usually sing or laugh much, or even make popcorn, I generally liked having this woman as my mother. When she lovingly carved out time to accompany me on a class trip to the Coca Cola factory, where my friends and I were each given a free ruler and a bottle of Coke to drink, I fancied myself as my family's youngest, or maybe even as her only child. I delighted in her smiling attention, not to mention the honor of having this fashionably suited, high-heeled, bejeweled woman near me. Her rich looks, in particular, made me feel that I mattered, especially because my friends told me so.

Yet there were still times when that outer facade could not satisfy me enough. And while food did not sing or smile, either, it sure could feed the constant hum of fear and emptiness. It would catch each day's high and low notes, harmonizing them into one safe voice that said, "Everything is okay." Food would feed my uncertainty, my aloneness, my sense of being lost in this world. Yes, food would mother me. It could do all of the good things mothers do, but food would never abandon me. I could turn to it at whim, knowing it would accept my unhappiness with total equanimity, and certain that it was willing to be eaten up by me. How unselfish and comforting—and totally available. The food inside of me was all mine, belonging to no one else.

A Growing Problem

Toward the end of third grade, the year my teacher Mrs. Stewart made me hold my sharpened, yellow #2 pencil between my chubby second and third fingers—rather than with the third and fourth, the way I naturally did—my maternal uncle got married. I only had one of those, and it was a big enough deal that his three nieces, practically his little sisters, would be outfitted with new gowns. Three fluffy pink chiffon gowns with angelic floral crowns adorned the threesome who walked down the aisle, with me in the middle, of course.

By the turn of the summer, at the very beginning of my fourth-grade year, my brother was to have his Bar Mitzvah celebration. You know which gowns we, his three younger sisters, would be wearing? The ones from my uncle's wedding. Slight problem: In those passing three months, my gown no longer fit me. Completely taken by surprise, I began to cry. What would I wear? I'd have to have something different than my sisters who still could fit into their gowns. So began the first custom-made attempt to dress the growing problem known as Shifra. Miss Ann was promptly called to sew a gown for me. It looked nothing like the elegant gown that had fit me just a few months before, like the ones my sisters would be wearing. Miss Ann really tried, but I was confined to a boringly pale-pink cloth with raised, pimply rose-colored dots that deeply irritated me.

A Fabric Called Shame

By this age of nine, suitable clothing could no longer be found for me at the regular dress shops. Because the plus-size shops outfitted females much older than myself, my mother kindly engaged the services of her friend, a talented seamstress. On her table, I would begrudgingly fidget while she noted my heavy measurements for her challenging work.

The shame of being different, of being limited to unappealing jumpers draping a growing body and a sagging spirit that seemingly could never get enough of anything, would leave a scar so thick that it would—even decades later—superimpose itself on every fiber of my life. While my siblings and friends daintily clothed their happy, light spirits in frilly, stylish, cute clothes, I dressed my heaviness with amorphous, lifeless swatches of fabric whose threads could only be stretched so wide. This pattern of being different was being sewn further into my emotional wardrobe. This would become my familiar cloak, like the go-to piece of clothing every human surely has hanging on standby in their clothes closet for life's harder days.

And if you think clothing isn't a major part of who we are, try this on for size. Clothing is used to cover our bodies, it is true. Even truer, clothes have the power to hide or reveal our spirits. We demand that our clothing serve us for very specific purposes and in highly unique ways. Yes, we ask a lot of our clothing. We insist that our clothes tell others who we are. Surely, you have heard that clothes make the man. But do clothes really have the power to fashion a human being into something he is not?

"Crack" Addict

These threads of childhood get stitched into our emerging psyches. My childhood was full of them, some very tightly wound around me. The scars and cracks left behind as we grow do not just magically disappear. They demand, and deserve, our attention. When we use food, clothing, money, people, or anything to fill the empty spaces, we will likely implode. As with any resource that is abused, using it to plug up the holes eventually makes the crack bigger and much more dangerous.

Feelings of mattering and non-mattering run deep, very deep, core-deep. I saw that my body was becoming bigger and could not be "easily fashioned," and that my family and friends began to focus their attention on my size—not to mention my stubbornness—but I had no way yet to manage a healthy response. I could not make the connection between the reality of my urgent appetite and increasing poundage, and my deepening feelings of not mattering. This was way out of reach of my young understanding. All I really understood was that I was different, my body was getting heavier, and I had no clue what to do about it, nor did anybody else. Powerless and hopeless, once again.

Even if your mattering was given to you in the form of a worldly currency called "talent" or "fortune," you will still have to find a way to matter. Ever wonder how one can have all the food in the world, and still be starving? Or all the money or beauty or fame or any other advantage—and still manage to self-destruct? Mattering happens on the inside, and when it doesn't, the cracks open wider and destroy everything in its swallow.

I'll agree with singer-songwriter Leonard Cohen that "there is a crack in everything, that's how the light gets in," but only if we welcome it. There is great value in learning how not to block the light that wants so badly to come into our cracks, into our brokenness. For me, it would require many years of penetrating lessons to see the light.

CHAPTER FOUR

Tales From Inner Space

Every adversity, every failure, every heartache carries with it the seed of an equal or greater benefit.

—Napoleon Hill, author

T HERE IS A WELL-KNOWN PARABLE about an old Chinese woman who had two cans attached to a yoke. Every day, she would place the yoke over her shoulders and walk down to the river to draw water. She would then carry the water to her modest hut, where she would make good use of it. There was a difference between the two cans: One was whole without blemish, while the other had a crack on its side. Upon reaching her hut, it was obvious that the unblemished can could hold all its water, while the other was half-empty. The cracked can felt inferior to the whole one, and was ashamed that it caused the woman to lose half of her water. Feeling deficient and ashamed, it apologized to the woman for being defective. The wise woman smiled to the can and said, "Do you think I have been unaware of your crack and that half of the water leaks out? Take a look at the path from the river to my hut. Do you see all of those beautiful flowers on one side of the road? I planted those flowers there, and every day when I walk back from the river, you water those flowers for me. You are the reason that such beauty adorns the side of the road."

Whole or cracked, your contribution will take root in this world, if you—and those you trust to help you—wisely prepare the ground. As in this vignette, we are fortunate when we have the benefit of someone who can help us understand more about who we are and to hold a loving, hopeful version of who we can become and what we can accomplish—without condemning the brokenness, but instead using it well. And then as we unfold, we can see it for ourselves and ideally learn how to do it for ourselves... *To hold out hope for our mattering, in the face of the brokenness.*

If you want to live large, if you determine that your life is valuable, that you matter . . . have you taken the opportunity to reflect productively on past events? How have they shaped what you consider possible or probable? How might they be keeping you stuck in what may be a self-imposed block that disinvites you from moving further into your being?

It is hard to see past our struggles while we are submerged in them. Just trying to stay above the strong current of our being, we fight against being taken under by its overwhelming pull. It is only when we turn back to that *inner space* that, in a more collected moment ripe for reflection, we can name certain things in our lives and connect the dots to see how they affected us. And maybe even see the blessing in them. Making, and taking, the time to do this process with oneself or with a trusted other, will reveal the light between the cracks, the purpose alongside the path of pain. As pain subsides, we have the opportunity to glimpse the beauty that has been created in its stead.

One more thing about struggles: Our pain is highly subjective. How we experience anything depends overwhelmingly upon such variables as our personal innate sensitivities, our past experiences, and how we have been taught to think and feel about them. What shatters one person's barometer may barely register on another person's, if at all. Only you know where the pain is. *Keep your eye on your pain; that's where your prize is.*

An Inner Storm called Anxiety

The cracks in my young life deepened, as cracks are wont to do. And I, the free spirit, albeit troubled and troubling, had a knack for finding them. I surely would have fallen through them if I could have fit. But misfits don't, because they can't. Sometimes, it is defiance that gets in their way. Not being able to tolerate authority well, a strong internal opposition rises and rules. Other times, it is their intense curiosity that commands their interest and attention, rather than focusing on how to fit in. And even plainer, they may not fit because they just don't know how to sit quietly and unobtrusively like more sedate types.

As the intensely colorful autumn months of my fourth-grade year turned to winter's frost, the ground beneath my plump feet visibly shifted. Grandpa, father to my mother, became sick, and I became a very anxious child for all to see. I didn't think grandpas could just suddenly become sick, especially ones who were tall, strong, and very smart. My grandmother—whose life force had been poured into keeping her husband, two children, and home in a perfectly controlled, impeccably straight environment—would now be swept up in the details of nursing her husband back to life, which she did remarkably for the next twenty-one years. She would speak about his illness in grave details. Many times I'd hear her recount how she nursed him back to life. "I brought him home from the hospital with an open wound in his abdomen that I had to pour alcohol straight into." I understood little, just that he'd be wearing some kind of bag attached to his abdomen. Images of this bag, bulkily stored under a stylishly-dressed veneer, dripped into my mind, which was already overflowing with fear and pity. For a small child, hypersensitive to her own survival, this proved too much to bear. The anxiety started here, but didn't end here.

As with family members, storms have a way of developing together: "When it rains, it pours." I had finished my weekly

Sunday piano lesson with Mrs. Goodman, and was waiting to be picked up from her house. While looking out the window and waiting, I wondered why my fingers could not produce the music she was trying to coax out of me. Sitting on her fancy bench in front of the shiny, way too black and white keys of her baby grand piano, my hands would rummage around, trying to find their way into some happy sound. But I was totally lost. Mrs. Goodman then announced that she had to run some errands, leaving me with no choice but to wait outside for my ride, which was sure to come any moment. No one came for me, and the sky began to drop a peaceful, innocent snowfall, flake by flake. *I'd better go into Mrs. Goodman's neighbor, the Shermans, to keep dry, and call home again to remind them I am still waiting.*

An unusual and unpredicted thing began to happen. The snow suddenly took the Baltimore streets by force. This, my fourth-grade year, is the year of the December 1974 colossal Baltimore blizzard, a most unwelcome visitor that we are not prepared to host. Thirty inches of heavy wet snow and high winds break phone wires, topple trees, towers and antennas, and strand thousands of people along the highway. With a snowfall of several inches per hour, I was still hopeful that soon enough I would be gotten. Soon enough came and went, but it seemed that I was forgotten. The day turned dark, and I was still in the neighbor's home. A plan for me to spend the night at this home, which was actually the home of my classmate Mimi, was expediently, if not excitedly, arranged—and *that* should have been that. But anxious misfits don't just stop at *that.* The storm outside, I now knew, had left me stranded. Its chaotic nature began to seep inside and flood me with torrents of tears. Pulses of panic trampled my chest, breaking it into shallow, uneasy breaths. At first, I thought that I could make it. Just one night . . . how hard could that be? Too hard, it turned out. Phoning my parents at 10 p.m., I insisted that I would not be staying the night. "But, Shif, we cannot come get you. We tried, but even with our snow tires, the car cannot make it on the road." I tried to understand. But at 1:00 a.m., I imploded. "You must come get me now," I sobbed and pleaded and begged. And I knew that somehow they had managed to pick up Brenna from her friend's house.

I was picked up the next morning as the storm abated and the streets were being cleared. But for me, there was no clearing. My storm was just beginning, and was gathering frightening strength. And now, going to school became a monumental, scary task which left me crying every morning. At my locker, I'd beg Brenna, now in sixth grade, to "wait with me just one more minute, *please*, just one more." When Sima lay sick in the infirmary with a high fever, I begged her not to go home, for that would leave me in school alone. Completely wrapped in my terror, I could not consider that she, a child with 102-degree fever, belonged at home. Just looking out the class window every day, assessing my danger, became my primary lesson—with no teacher to help me understand the material. I became schooled in watching the sun walk behind the clouds, which was the cue to my hands to become sweaty, my throat to become tight, and for me to begin to think that this is what dying must feel like. I was in danger of something that felt very big to me, although I didn't have a name for it then. Now, I'd call it that primal fear of turning "baby blue," of being left without breath, and abandoned, but with no Fanny to breathe life into me again. Of being utterly powerless and alone. It was nothing less than the fight for my survival.

A Cloak of Fear

This anxious spirit began to dress itself around my life. It cloaked even the lightest of events with an opaque struggle.

For one thing, I began to beg my mother to have a baby. Lying as flat on the floor as I could with my oversized, nine-year-old belly, I swung my feet behind me in the air. "Please have a baby. I want a baby. I need a baby. You must have a baby," I wailed and willed and. . . .

One day, my mother announced that she'd be having a baby, whom she would soon enough name Rebecca, on April 23. How kind of my mother to deliver these beautiful six pounds of life, a huge gift to me, delicately wrapped with butter-smooth light skin and even-tempered lips turned upwards in a constant smile at me. But what could all that pining for another sibling have been about? Did I need a baby, a powerless entity, whom I could watch grow and see that she could be okay? And if she could be, then maybe I could too? If indeed my mattering was attached to another human being who'd need my strength to thrive, I certainly didn't have a conscious clue.

And then there were the smaller ongoing occurrences that consciously showcased my anxiety. "Um, I forgot to show the permission slip to my mommy to sign." With that lie to my teacher, I was sure I would not have to put myself on the unfamiliar bus and join the arduous class trip to Annapolis forty-five minutes away, for which all the other children were majorly excited. "No, thank you; I'd love to come to your house for the weekend, but we are having company at ours," was the way I turned down possible friendships if it meant I would have to leave my house for the night. When my classmates tried to surprise me with the cupcakes my mother secretly sent in to school on the occasion of my birthday, I ran out of the room, feeling cornered and powerless. I would not come back until the party was over.

Homework Wreaks Havoc at Home

At home I felt safer, but not totally secure. In my house where academic excellence reigned supreme, homework was king. Under my mother's overachieving eye for perfection, I felt enslaved to the nightly routine of hours of reviewing my school work and preparing for the next day. I deeply respect parents who consider it their high priority to dutifully sacrifice their time and energy to help their children with their homework. And while I am grateful for the benefits of having learned from such a loyal parent the discipline of following through on

gnments, I cannot dismiss the steep tension it created for
.e, day after day, year after year.

Of the four children who took their seat, one by one, at the
yellow square kitchen table to do homework near this queen
of discipline, none created more havoc in the home than me.
Night after dark night, I was relegated to the throes of despair
and defeat, since my mind didn't work the right way, like my
mother's clear and focused mind. I was often still wrung out
from the fear of the day, and my mind was in no shape to bend
itself around more information. And yet, what could I, a young
child, say or do? I tried to hang in there and fight to do what was
being asked of me, but many times it wasn't good enough, fast
enough, right enough. My mother tried her best, too, but how
do you influence a seemingly uncooperative child to do what
it takes to succeed academically? Although it was not often, I
feared catching the hopeless slap of my battle-fatigued mother
on my back. This left me on guard, having to prepare for the
next moment's lurking danger instead of focusing on memorizing the capital of Georgia or when Columbus set sail. No one's
routine was more grueling or dueling than mine. This well-intentioned drill lasted for hours. The longer the onslaught,
the more my mind became frazzled with raw fear that I'd be
wrong—and wronged.

Stung by the Blessing Bee

Take this for example: We had a schoolwide contest that awarded
prizes for memorizing the correct blessings to say before
eating food. In Judaism, there is a blessing for just about every
phenomenon and life cycle. As food figures very prominently in
the life of every living creation, it is simple gratitude to thank
G-d before and after eating anything, and there are specific
blessings for various food groups with which to do so. As it
turned out, I was chosen as the class winner to represent my
grade in this competition.

In preparation for the victory that my mother made clear
should be mine, we studied night after night, reviewing the

blessing for all sorts of stuff: kumquats, chicken soup, currants, and, of course, chocolate chip cookies. When we got to cooked carrots, it just made sense to me that it should not have the same blessing as the plain old regular carrot that grows from the ground. A carrot that was bathed and softened in water, it dawned on me, was special and should have an entirely different blessing, which I lovingly assigned to it. Night after night, as we reviewed the list, I would prepare to hear, "NO! Shif, what is wrong with you? It is not *that* blessing. It is the same blessing as a regular carrot—no difference." It got to the point that I honestly didn't know what the right answer was, and so in my nine-year-old mind, I just daydreamed about Mrs. Big Hard Carrot and the Little Soft Carrot who was always in hot water, and I couldn't understand why anyone would want to bless either of them.

The day of the blessing bee arrived, and up to the stage I soldiered in my custom-made bag—this one was the navy blue dress with red dots on the upper half intersected with a gold half zipper, and my black shoes with the wedge that gave me a winning lift. All things considered, this was my choicest outfit. Sitting on individual white metal chairs with some of our legs too short to reach the shiny wood floor, the row of eight competing elementary girls attired in varying colors and styles could be clearly seen by the excited audience of parents, siblings, and the rest of the elementary school children. Thickly-pleated gold curtains were held securely on each side of the stage by decorative tassels. The American flag stood proudly on the right side of the stage while the blue and white Israeli flag graced the other. A scalloped gold valance sat on top of the curtains, lending a formal decor to what essentially was our lunchroom, but called "the auditorium" on occasions such as this.

Round after round, the moderator served up all kinds of foods, and I was getting my blessings right. Then I heard an interesting food—it sounded very familiar—and I began to envision the hot water softening it and making it into something very different from the standard carrot. I blurted out the blessing I thought it should have. Somewhere from the middle of the audience-packed room, I was sure I heard, "NO, Shif!" I didn't know who to feel worse for—my mother, or me, or the poor carrot who couldn't receive its proper due. No, I just could *not* let that carrot be the same as all other carrots. By the way . . . my younger sister Sima won the contest.

Taking the Hit, Surviving the Hurt

Sometimes, I wonder why I continued to go to school, or more accurately, why I didn't just try to do what my brother had started to do. Aaron began to sleep in late, at first missing a carpool here and there. Challenging the status quo, he then clung more and more to his bed, leaving his seat in school empty for days at a time.

I loved sleeping just as much as he did. My bed was the safest place in my home. It also conveniently housed my food, which I secreted underneath. And even though Aaron wasn't beaten, past experiences taught me that I'd be mercilessly dealt with if I tried any overt opposition. I didn't want to be made lifeless; *something* in me yearned to survive. And I wasn't sure I trusted my parents or anyone else to protect that *something*. While I relied on them to safeguard certain things for me, like our home, our daily sustenance, and our honorable reputation, I wondered if they, or any adult, were capable of not harming that *something*. That *something* belonged to the world of my internal spirit. It was the small, flickering hope and the big, defiant longing that I could matter. But they, like most adults I knew, were much better-versed in the universe of the external senses. And this created a remarkable friction that branded my inner world with the lonely, sad streaks of non-mattering. I could not gain a foothold into mattering, because I could not carry myself into their world. I was in my own world, doing all I could do to survive its tumult. While its intensity, I realize, may seem dramatic, I cannot undo here its deep effect on who I was becoming.

It is a human's nature to be scared of that which we do not understand and I wondered if my parents were scared *for* me. I didn't blame them; I terrified myself, too. How would I ever make it? How could I ever matter? If I couldn't do the basics at the homework table, what would become of me? Those fits of fretting and frustration over the smallest things, like getting dressed in the morning, were not encouraging signs for a successful life. Like Aunt Rosalie, I was unable to summon the strength to defend myself from the onslaught of powerful judgments of others who didn't understand my difficulties. I didn't know how to.

Yet I have come to learn that it is a fact of living that we can unwittingly precipitate that which we fear. I have since learned how beneficial it is when we learn to express hope, and not fear, in working out the pieces of our lives, especially when it comes to our children. To acknowledge, even honor, limits while guiding them safely past. As an example, when our daughter Ayala routinely didn't get out of bed on time for middle school, we knew we had a choice to make: "To fret or to let." Remember, I was well acquainted with the unpleasant scenario of a teenager (my brother Aaron) sleeping late each school morning. In this case, we did our "deepest" to work with her, without incrimination, chiseling away at her resistance. We did not wish to make her scared for herself, rather to keep her hopeful that she'd be just fine. And to myself I repeated, "Build, don't destroy. And trust yourself to know the difference."

I might as well mention that when I found myself in the confusing role of parent, I'd work on finding that balance between my young homework table and that of Zack's childhood routine. My husband Zack came from a family focused on sledding in the winters, barbecuing in the summers, and singing all year round. Taking pictures of all that fun and then organizing it into albums occupied his growing up years. Homework was something to be done in between the fun. This huge contrast in our childhood home cultures was ripe for lots of discussion on our part. "Zack, we must help them with their writing assignments. I know their teachers said they are not allowed parental help, but I don't care. How else will they learn if we don't help them?" To which Zack would nonchalantly reply, "They can figure it out on their own. No great worries here." (Actually, this whole debate on whether or not they could receive parental help with writing assignments was more a political science lesson than an English one. The communist conversation contended that since all children could not obtain a similar advantage, no child should have it. The democratic discourse debunked that: Try to find a way to give that advantage to all, but don't deny it to those who can have it now.) Ultimately, the fun gene proved dominant, meaning that our children had to beg us to stop having fun so they could get some homework done, usually without my help. We'd just have to suffer the withdrawal of our children retreating to their rooms, leaving us with time to clean the house and have more conversations on how to be great parents.

Despite all this inner commotion as a child, I knew something really important. I knew I was here to matter. How could I know *that* when my experiences were speaking to me otherwise? It was that small but noisy voice inside that insisted I'd find a way to matter, *precisely* because others had told me I didn't, and that Aunt Rosalie didn't either. If we must name that voice, its first name is defiance . . . with courage as its middle name. All in the name of mattering.

Actually, I'm quite sure that we all somehow know we are here to matter. It's just that we may have to remove the blocks that have told us we do not. How do we remove the blocks? *By challenging them.* By staring them down and rearranging the power grid that denied you the power of your being. The people who have taken the liberty to assault our worthiness . . . who says they are correct? The circumstances that positioned us to appear particularly vulnerable . . . can't they improve? Our experiences that have highlighted our prescribed lines . . . what stops them from being rewritten?

And if we can identify one universal block, might it be

shame? Shame is one huge block that shuts down our matter-ing—quickly, quietly, and unequivocally. Shame messes around with our mattering in very powerful ways. I suppose there are good uses for the experience or emotion we call shame, but mostly, it is propped up by fear and violates our deepest selves. *Unless we confront the shame, our sense of passion and purpose will collapse into a heap of non-mattering.* For me, carrying the extra weight of a troubled childhood, in body and spirit, cre-ated the shame that had me crying over who I was and what I couldn't be or do—very similar to the cracked water can in the beginning of this chapter. The cracked can learns to take sight of the positive path of progress. Broken, maybe. Purposeless, hardly. Confronting shame is the willingness to stage an offen-sive against the lie that we do not matter and then finding ways to manifest our mattering.

Spirit—the non-physical part of a person that animates character, emotions and attitudes—cannot be seen, but is most definitely experienced. Similarly, shame cannot be seen, but is highly visible. This means that it needs our attention to heal; our mattering depends on it.

CHAPTER FIVE

Money: A Currency of Mattering

Legacy accounting: Will you have been an asset or a liability on the world's balance sheet?

—RYAN LILLY, entrepreneur

"BRENNA, what happens if we don't have enough money?" I would question my older sister when we were already in our beds for the night, before thrusting my nine-year old thumb into my mouth to ponder other such lovely, secure concerns. Brenna would usually stay quiet, maybe just uttering a quick thought: "Money's not everything, Shif. Just need enough of it to pay the bills." Only once did she elaborate: "If you're careful with how you spend your money, you won't have too many bills to pay." And I silently cried, terrified that I would have too many bills to pay and not enough money to do it.

This was a pattern that would persist—thinking about money, sans my thumb in my mouth—even once surprising Brenna and Sima years later when we visited Baltimore's Inner Harbor. I turned to them and said, "You smell fish, I smell money." I was acutely attuned to the profitability of the water-front properties being built nearby.

Father Tongue: The Art of Money-making

By age nine, I was skilled in the mother language of discipline, thanks to the rigors of my nightly homework routines. But it was my father's constant business phone conversations, conducted in the pretend privacy of our kitchen located right off our three bedrooms, that schooled me in this language of money and the art of negotiation. Puffing on his cigar, occasionally letting us in on the puff, he made his job seem easy and fun. My report cards with less than an A+ grade were mandatorily thrown his way for his quick glance and creative scribble—the flourish of a left-handed brain that convinced more than it controlled. Clearly, there were more important things in life—like money.

Even at that young age, I couldn't have agreed more.

I knew that money could buy some important things. My classmate Pearl had told me something I hadn't known: my father was the wealthiest dad in the school. She even suspected that the jewelry I wore was fake, that the real stones were in a safe. Pearl's facts weren't always reliable, so I checked in with Brenna about this. "Is it true that our father is the richest in the whole school?" But Brenna, even at her young age of eleven, could not be amused. She wouldn't answer, unimpressed as she was by the promise of fame or fortune. She's still like that—fiscally grounded and harboring little grandiosity, which leaves her with the energy to actually make money to pay her bills.

But I had a hunch about this currency. I saw that it could buy help in the house, which was convenient, because someone had to do the small, mundane things that mattered, especially when they were *not* done. That *someone* came in the form of many housekeepers through the years whose job included making us and our home look good. Far more pressing and rewarding tasks than tending to children and chores—like making money, running community organizations, holding endless committee meetings at our dining room table—had to be accomplished by my parents. It was obvious that my parents were fast becoming respected communal figures because of their talent, dedication, energy, and generosity. They were called upon from multiple directions, including needy individuals, schools, organizations, and a growing family of four children within five years (and later, two more to squeeze into this noble tension). In addition to their professional roles as co-owners of a growing real estate business, my father was the long-serving president of a local school, while my mother served as the youngest president of our school's Ladies Auxiliary. She shouldered the tedious burdens of coordinating everything, from the minute details of mailings to the lavish planning of luncheons. Without the compensation of even a dime, and sometimes less appreciation than that, she graciously grew the crucial funds for the school. Doing certain tasks that today's women wouldn't voluntarily do or even ask others to do for pay, she and her "ladies" cleaned chickens, cooked them, and served them to two hundred hat-clad, fancily gloved women at the school luncheons on the last Wednesday of every month.

Bilingual: Study in Opposites

If any kid ever worshipped its parents, it was me. For one thing, they were an exquisite study in opposites. The "opposites attract" phrase must have been coined by the person who suggested my parents as marriage partners. My father, having grown up in the South, had a casual, unvarnished, simple way about him. School was nothing more than a place to play ball and to learn the one lesson he ever needed to know: He who has the ball always gets to play in the game. Easy to understand that—no ball, no game. His clothes could hang about him with little finesse, but he sure knew how to skillfully dress his speech in a way that could easily negotiate conflicts and persuade people. He held money close to himself, not easily dispensing it unless the deal was right, i.e., brilliantly crafted in his favor.

Blessed with a plain but capable sense of other's true natures, especially the underdog, my father had an intuitive grasp of who wanted what, who was taking advantage of whom, and who to distrust . . . as it turned out, most people. He was the first one to know when he was being conned, even if he didn't quite catch it beforehand. I recall the time a Californian doctor and businessman wined and dined him over the prospect of a high-end commercial business deal with him. At the end of the meal, Dr. Gordon casually said, "Emanuel, you won't believe this. Someone stole my coat with my credit card in it. Can you loan me a couple hundred dollars for the hotel tonight? Of course, I'll have it wired to your bank tomorrow." Unsuspecting, my father invested his kindness in the doctor as a first deposit of trust that would surely earn him great dividends. It wasn't even twenty-four hours later that I saw my father begin to pace in his familiar nervous manner, finally looking up and declaring to my trustful mother, "Ruthie, I have been taken." He promptly made a round of calls to other business partners connected with the deal, who were similarly being duped but hadn't yet intuited their misfortune.

And years later, before the scandalous smells of the local Savings and Loan Bank diffused into public air, my father sniffed trouble. He rushed to stand at the head of the line to withdraw his money, hours before they closed down the bank, leaving a line of hundreds of angry people the poorer for the wait.

Even though introversion was his strong point—he often arrived late to a party and was the first to leave (shortening the time he had to interact with others)—my father could tell a great story and an even better joke, replete with the kind of humor that had all of us laughing; me the loudest. Apparently, humor is genetic, because he, his mother Grandma Lolly, and I would always laugh at similar things, like watching the unexpected deflation of big egos that come with a sudden trip or fall. I recall the time a school banquet dais seating dignitaries collapsed under their self-important weight, sending me into an unguarded, full-bellied laugh (after I knew they were not physically harmed) which I had to cut short when others squinted my way to quiet down.

Car gasoline bills were high in our family because my parents drove separate cars to events, accommodating my mother's extroverted need to be the first guest to arrive at a party and the last to leave. My mother stood tall for a woman, and was the local stores' dream customer because she could carry almost any style they had in stock. She'd pay for it, too, without ever asking for a bargain. In fact, the family joke was that the saleswoman would tell her something was on sale, but allow her to pay retail if that felt better to her. She was born to parents who invested their every dream and hope into her success, which she easily and obediently delivered. Valedictories and school presidencies, four-year college scholarships and editorships . . . the only thing she could not do was to catch that ball my father knew how to throw.

It was, I suppose, a dance of sorts: He had rhythm, she had rhyme. He could sing soulfully and do an easy, light-footed dance (especially the *kazatzka,* a popular Russian dance performed in a crouching position with the legs alternatingly flung forward and out to the sides), while she'd write mathematically-metered, purposeful poetry. He was full of feeling, ever reactive to the unseen, irrational pulse of life, while she wore the cool, poised, rational face of fact, accented with her signature Chanel ruby-red lipstick. He casually bent rules; she routinely made them. I knew who to approach when circumstances called for compassion and leeway, rather than logic and accountability. He worked in circles and notions, she in straight lines and numbers. Where he saw the compromise of a deal, she focused on the perfect promise of the ideal—and sometimes, the two were very far apart. He'd be inclined to purchase yet another business property, not necessarily considering the bank balance, which was her exclusive domain to record and mind. Yet, they were both extraordinarily generous in spirit, albeit in vastly different ways. He could easily cut people slack, and she could efficiently cut checks— which they both routinely did for me and countless others who needed these many, many times.

This tiptoeing around each other made for a complex, if not passionate, dance. For me who watched it up close, it was quite dramatic, and sometimes funny, confusing, or scary—always enlightening. Watching those two vastly different paragons of power taught me fundamentals for working with both types of personalities, and gifted me with one of my guiding principles: *Facts first, feelings second.* There is room, indeed a need, for both fact and feeling because both are hugely important to living life large. And one more thing was quite clear to me: that the right shade of lipstick is indispensable to a polished image, with warm orange being my version of her power red.

At Home With Business

For some unearthly reason, this illogical match made in Heaven forged itself into successful partnerships, both personal and professional. These two 'ships' rode high, with us kids along for the ride.

The seat of the action was our home. There were the upper quarters and the lower ones. The basement of our home housed the office. So far as I knew, most basements held the lighter side of life, such as the television and the board games. Not ours. Ours held "the business." Into the business walked secretaries who actually provided great entertainment for us, so I suppose that our basement did hold some fun, after all. Like the time short, round-bodied Ms. Cindy swiveled off her chair, unintentionally rearranging her little headpiece, which now sat backwards on her fuzzy, surprised head. There was the time when Sima and I realized that one of them had stolen some paper towels, so we casually took a walk down the block to stick my pudgy little hands through the open car window to retrieve the "quicker picker uppers."

Our toys were the now-old-fashioned calculators, adding machines, typewriters, and accounting ledgers. Above all, I was fascinated with the desks. After the close of the business day, I'd skip downstairs, plop onto one of the swivel chairs, and pretend to answer the phones in a big secretary voice. "How much money did you say you sent in the mail? I will be sure to let you know when we receive it." Then I'd shake my head and mutter under my breath, repeating what the secretaries always said in a funny kind of voice I couldn't quite comprehend. "Suuure, the check's in the mail."

My parents often recounted gratefully how they got their start in the real estate business. My father's parents, taking an umbrella's shelter on a rainy day, voluntarily traveled to inspect and purchase the first property for the business. With their own modest experience in purchasing houses in Richmond, Grandpa Barry and Grandma Lolly wanted to help their now twenty-six-year-old son, a father of two who was still studying in a *Yeshiva*, an academy for advanced Jewish studies.

To clarify: In the Orthodox world, many newly-married couples choose to allow the man to continue his Jewish studies in fulfillment of one of Orthodox Jewry's highest ideals—to amass the Divine knowledge contained in the Bible. A man endeavors to study, both for the sake of the special value of pure learning in fulfillment of a Divine commandment, and for the practical knowledge allowing for better adherence to the Biblical laws. The woman—who must be similarly knowledgeable in the practical application of daily Orthodox life, but is not obligated in the abstract learning—is often prepared to accept the responsibility to earn their livelihood until the couple decides, for any number of reasons, that the man will enter the work force. In this case, my mother loyally worked two jobs to support their spiritual ideal until she became pregnant with her third child, at which time my father began his entry into the business world. He naturally gravitated to the real estate business, following his own parents who managed a few small properties while primarily minding their grocery store.

Allowing my father to stay behind so that he could continue his daily study regimen, Grandpa and Grandma surveyed the property by themselves, determining to purchase it with eighteen hundred dollars. This depleted my parents' total life savings. Their exceptional parental devotion paid off handsomely, as this first transaction cleared the way for many others to follow, filling up our basement with files, folios, and funds. As the business grew, more desks populated the downstairs, while several employee cars lined up in front of our home during work hours. Their developing enterprise was sub-grouped into various companies named after some approximation of their children's names, which told me in my heart of hearts that all they did was truly in service of our family. That is not to say that they didn't enjoy their success, their accomplishments, and their honor. But I find it hard to believe that people would push themselves way, way beyond their limits, when their endurance begged to give way, if something pressing had not been fueling their furiously fast engine. For them, it was their growing family and their urgency to provide for us. *And there is no question, money meant love.*

So even though I could not understand their business ledgers downstairs, it was obvious that the numbers were adding up under their cold, calculated, unyielding discipline. Numbers do not have feelings; they do not get hungry or scared, and they can be counted upon any time. But since I was not a number, I belonged upstairs on the home front, where I couldn't be counted or put neatly on a page or summed up or calculated.

As with their business, my parents did invest in us, their children, and surely hoped for great returns. It's just that the process of ordering numbers around is hugely different than arranging human affairs. It is *so* not an exact science, with fewer objective ways to both measure and ensure success. Their personal stocks rose and fell many times, and like a stockbroker, I learned to watch it, predict it, and catch the fury of the fluctuation. I was ever alert to the slightest changes in their moods and circumstances, and knew when I could expect a day that made me feel safe and one throughout which I'd feel agitated. Unsurprisingly, my emotional stamina was directly tied to theirs which, I surmised, was tied to their financial success. They took seriously our financial well-being, making it clear to us that they wanted us to have things. "We are working to make it good for you," they'd say. And while Brenna would insist that Sundays become "family day," when we'd do something together as a family, I was content knowing that my father was "out on the street" as part of his responsibility to finance our lives. When I did get those things money could buy—the designer clothes, the high-heeled shoes, the sweet perfumes, the expensive cosmetics, and those "gorgeous" new earring hoops, all of which undoubtedly attracted my friends' admiration—I felt happy and loved. How else would I matter? Maybe if Aunt Rosalie would have had money to buy things, she could have mattered. *Yes, money meant love and mattering to me.*

But here was the growing question: *If my family's financial resources ensured that my basic physical needs were earnestly well-met—quite more than basic, really—why was I often very hungry, intensely cold, and despairingly empty?* Why was it never enough . . . being given the credit card to purchase a reasonable amount of clothing and jewelry each season, along with endless weight-loss programs to try to help me fit into these new clothes? Not to mention the make-up, manicure, and hair appointments. I continuously felt poorer and more scared that I'd never have enough money. As far as I understood, money was where it was at. Money absolutely meant happiness. Mattering. And I didn't have nearly enough of it.

When Money Means Mattering

"Shifra likes multiples," my father told Zack while we were dating. "I'm not talking about children, although she does love babies. It's about her clothing. You should know that she doesn't just buy one dress at a time . . . usually quite a few at a time. Very important to her." That was my concerned father's way of testing Zack's worthiness to marry me. As for Zack's response, let's just say that taking things lightly has always served Zack well. (Not to mention that he was grateful he wouldn't be forced to father lots of little children close in age.)

Shortly after Zack and I were married, he asked me if I preferred a loving husband or a wealthy one. *Thanks for asking.* If I couldn't have both, then *I'd opt for the wealthy one because money is a practical commodity and love is not.* Or, so I thought. Zack has spent decades showing me the value of a currency called love, and its ability to build and impact lives in ways similar to money.

I satisfyingly recall the many hair-brushing and braiding sessions that Zack has lavished upon me, as a doting mother might on her only child, and as in fact G-d Himself lovingly did for Eve in preparation for her wedding to Adam (Talmud, Volume 1: Chapter 9). While women spend money, lots of it, for a nicely-coiffed hairdo, I doubt money can ever buy the delight with which Zack smooths out my glory (hair is referred to in the Torah as the crowning glory of a woman), all the while wordlessly communicating enduring messages of mattering. The brush in his hand speaks, "I will always find your beauty. I will never let you be less than perfect for me, no matter what. Because you matter more than you can ever know." All with a few brush strokes. And for no money. An *interest-full* loan of love, to be repaid with my deepest appreciation for this Heavenly gift. I smile, and then sometimes I cry, contrasting his touch to that of my mother's morning helper whose tense hands tore into my mattering because she was frustrated by my stubborn head of hair.

Still, this "money or love" thing is a tangled mess of knots for me. It is a hugely tough one for me to answer because we live in the world of money. We can see it, hold it, and move it. It can take us places we desperately want, even need, to go physically, spiritually, emotionally. The questions keep coming: Can love do that, too? Can love be a potent energy that releases something big in us—and for us? Is love as powerful as money in helping us to achieve our deepest hopes and greatest selves? We can give it and get it. Maybe we can even describe what it looks like and feels like. But, for what can we exchange it, and with whom? Is love really a viable currency, a basis for trading one valuable thing in exchange for another?

Of Closeness and Connection

I am quickly reminded of the Torah lesson I learned regarding the punishment levied on the primordial snake who led Eve astray with his cunning arguments to undermine her reliance on G-d. G-d decreed that it shall forever eat the dust of the ground, essentially guaranteeing the snake its eternal and constant sustenance, without it ever having to worry. Therein, I was taught, is the curse: The snake would never be privy to a relationship with G-d. It would never experience the need, and therefore the opportunity, to connect to G-d. By being invulnerable and never lacking, it could never learn how to ask and then luxuriate in the relief of receiving—and in the subsequent bond of gratitude and closeness that would be created. *No love here. No connection here.* Ultimately, it'd be devoid of any possibility to expand its essence, its mattering.

It took me a long time to process this as a curse, because I wasn't sure if disconnection was such a high price to pay for always having one's needs met, the equivalent of having all the money one wanted. I could go for that . . . or could I?

I had to think about the meaning of disconnection. I needed to think about how disconnection *feels*. Cerebral doesn't cut it here. Here, the heart will have to assert its truth, no matter how taxing or frightening.

Without recrimination for my family who did the best they could for me with the resources that they had, undoubtedly spending more money on me than on my siblings, I sampled deep disconnection. Given my highly sensitive, complex nature and anxious childhood circumstances of belonging to confident, robust parents with whose pace I was way out of step, I was primed for this venomous pit of disconnection. Maybe we all are, at least at some stretch of our lives. There was a disconnect between money and mattering in my own life, and I, in the inner core of my being, begged to know if I would ever have enough of either. I, the child who had the most money but the least mattering, lived the cold experience of being alone, different, apart; the feeling that no one could give me anything bigger than money (because that was all I wanted), and that I could not give them anything valuable. *Disconnection.*

And while physical bodies are indeed separate entities, the

healthy spirit is not limited and confined. It feeds on human love, and expands most especially with Divine closeness. When we cannot connect with the Divinity in us and around us, we are constricted. And when that flow of love, of connection, is cut off, we cannot reach the inner places of wealth and enoughness. Just as a body and a soul that are no longer attached (*un*popularly known as death—or as an attached body and a soul whose connection on some level is disrupted and labeled "disease"), a spirit cut off from love is cut off from mattering, and ultimately from its highest self.

Love as an Asset

And so to the question posed and pondered—would disconnection get in the way of building the life I wanted?—the answer is: majorly yes. So, G-d, please don't ever make me a snake. But do tell me, is it possible that connecting to my life and mattering could happen with a different currency? Can we finance our dreams for large lives with more love than money?

In order to answer Zack's question about opting for wealth or love in a husband, I would need to know if I could define Zack's love as an asset that could grow this connection for my life. Could his investment of love yield dividends in the form of a life that I could grow, in accord with my deepest hopes for a large life? For a life that mattered?

These are big questions I think about—a lot. What I know for sure is that not only can love attract the seemingly smaller things in life like a baby's smile or a flower admiringly picked just for you, love can absolutely attract life's big things such as authentic and enduring beauty, trust, and honor. These acquisitions may look different from the ones money can buy, because these in fact cannot be bought. *Indeed, they must be wrought.* You know what I mean. Who do we instinctively hold up as heroes to our most innocent and trusting children: those who seek honor, or those who are pursued by it? Those who appear beautiful, or those whose actions are core-beautiful? The deep-pocketed, or the whole-hearted?

If we are to give Torah a few words here to define the currencies of might, wisdom, wealth, and beauty, we'd find (Ethics of the Fathers 4:1) their values being plotted along an inner, eternal graph rather than an external one. We'd be trained to readily admire strength in one who conquers evil impulses, discern wisdom in one who learns from others, appreciate wealth in one who has earned the capacity to be satisfied with his portion, and celebrate beauty in the face of one who reflects in it consideration of G-d's will.

I have watched all these questions begin to answer themselves in my children. I am amazed, if a bit clueless, how satisfied most of them are with fewer material things than I could ever be. How could that happen, when my own sense of well-being is often deeply shaped by external things? I have watched them respond to an inner definition of wealth, power, beauty, and wisdom. They must have discerned much of this from Zack who'd sooner give a hug and a heartfelt blessing than a cold, one-dimensional dollar bill. Then again, in between my often cold-tempered hands, I could warm a dollar bill rather quickly as I turn it into a life-giving entity. Doesn't that count for something?

As you can guess, this discussion does not neatly end here at the close of the chapter. As I continue to live the question of the value of various currencies, of reconciling the different set of assets available to me in my childhood home with those we can offer our children, I understand that there is a wise balance to be struck between the two currencies. This balance is highly individual for both parent and child, and fluid as our life choices and circumstances develop and unfold. Having everything easily in equal measure would bankrupt our spirit, while *having to make choices builds it*. It is only in the choice that our mattering grows.

Dollars and (Common) Sense
Since I am a vulnerable candidate for the illusion that money can answer the question of mattering, I recently turned in

curious conversation to my two youngest children whose teenage and early twenty-something years are being shaped by an unabashedly money-mattering world where money trumps all. Where having the most money will absolutely answer all of life's questions, and even secure world peace. Where deep pockets allow people the illusion that they are morally responsible, until they are exposed by those who know better. (2017-2019, thank you for making that happen.)

These two kids know that this is the world of money, that we consider money to be integral to ensuring our physical survival. The world has been arranged in this way; money translates into tangible things we need to live. And our psyches are innately wired to know what those things are. We learn, early on, what deserves our attention. We begin to form ideas of what we must have in order to survive. From youth, money grabs our respect, our desire. More precisely, the things money buys captivate our imaginations. Relentlessly. We learn who has what and who does not. We discuss others in terms of their "net worth," beginning the lifelong confusion of mixing the means with the end, *of what we have with who we are.*

Being different is often very cool; all kids know that. It's a curious thing about humans: we ache to be different, to stand out, to differentiate ourselves with certain things while we strive to be the same in other ways. We must have the latest spinner everyone else is circling on their ADD fingers, but we dare not drive the same car as someone else, for that could totally undermine our identity. Honestly, isn't that what fuels our economic system? By bankrupting people's mattering—through cleverly responding to people's hard wired, human needs, or even by creating them and prompting them to be uncomfortable with who they are and what they have (and mixing us up to think that what we have *is* who we are), we create an inner emptiness that can be capitalized. The message is clear, even if false: *You can buy your way into mattering.*

With all this in mind and mouth, I turned to our two youngest, green-eyed Daniel—the enterprising, cool, street-smart college graduate pining for his first breaks in the real estate business, and blue-eyed Ayala—our high-school senior whose user-friendly nature belies a sharp-witted, spot-on set of people-smarts which, with a charming twist of her mid-waist, brunette head of wavy hair, unwittingly draws out the truth in others with refreshing precision: If you had to choose, would you opt for a loving parent who can hug you with messages of mattering, making you feel confident, worthy, hopeful and secure, or a rich parent who can accommodate many of your material wishes? Which parent, in your opinion, is likely to help create a healthier, more whole child? I didn't know there were children in today's world who could value anything above money, or at least as much as money. But there are at least two: Daniel and Ayala.

They told me that there is no substitute for the love part. And that today's parents, including us, ought to continue to figure out how to do it, and not over-worry, because they will forgive our many mistakes (especially if given a little bribe of extra spending money). The chance that money will be used wisely by a child is greater if the child is more whole first, having then to depend less, rather than more, on money for their mattering. They reminded me of the cherished family vignette about Grandma Lolly, who was gifted by her furrier father with a luxurious fur coat, but would not wear it around her less advantaged friends. "How unwarm I'd feel in that coat." They agreed with me that filling children's empty holes with money is more than dumb; it is dangerous. It likely will create more problems than it solves, as it grants a false sense of self and security. Not to mention unnecessary jealousy in others.

How do they know that? Have they seen something growing up that I don't realize . . . like maybe a mother who has been agonizingly weighing this question in an ongoing struggle? And a father for whom this is not even a question, but a forgone conclusion? Wise children over here; I hope their mother is listening and learning from them.

Money Makes the World . . . Work

All that childish wisdom notwithstanding, in this world of money, seems that G-d needed a way to make people get out there and actually do something to build His world—and ours. Therefore, He created in our hearts a need, and for some an absolute love, for this tangible hope we call money. Incidentally, it is not a crime to have a lot of money. Nor is it a crime to have very little of it, though many people will have you believe that your life is less valuable, as intimated above. That *you* are less valuable because you could not or did not translate your life energy into a marketable currency. And that if there is little tangible in the way of worldly materials to show for your years on this Earth, then your life did not matter.

The Hebrew word for money is *kesef* (which literally translates as silver), which also means yearning—implying that humans always yearn for more, including (and particularly) money. Judaism is very sensitive to this steep tension, and constantly encourages us to navigate it carefully. Money has power, and confers power. It can make us feel large and alive. Money is employed in so many ways, some life-affirming and some life-destructing. But, it is not the money itself that matters. It is what we get to do with it. More, it is what it does *to us* when it travels through our hands. Manipulating human prejudice and pride, money can also inspire and translate the charitable impulse of the human heart into transformative action and reaction for ourselves and others.

When I hear people say that they could be so generous if they had money, I suggest the notion that we can start being generous with whatever currency we have now. Enrich the world with your particular wealth. You have extra time; give it. You've got abundant food; distribute it. A lot of good will; spread it. A list of impressive professional connections; share it. Surplus of courage; lend it. Wisdom; dispense it. Beauty; consecrate it. Honor; bestow it. Strength; galvanize it.

Generosity is found in the smallest things in life, as well as in the bigger arenas. Because generosity isn't about *having* money, it is about *being* wealthy. Generosity is about opening hearts, well before you open the pocket. An open heart is attuned to the needs of another, in addition to one's own needs that surely deserve due attention. Here's the smallest mundane generosity that just happened to me the other day. With no money down, no seconds lost, just the wish to be kind, someone offered to take my grocery cart that I had just finished unloading so that I didn't have to take the time to return it. (How did they know exercising isn't my favorite sport?)

As you prepare to receive the blessing for which you are asking so that you can "invest it, not spend it," exercise the currencies you already have. I have seen some people become the growing, expansive people they yearned to be when they were eventually blessed with their hoped-for opportunity, while others became even more tight-hearted, holding onto their newfound largesse and not dispensing it. Perhaps those who spent their time building themselves into the vessel that could hold the blessing are built by both the wait and the eventual receipt of their request, while those who did not were broken by it. Could that in part explain the documented phenomenon behind the surprising unhappiness and subsequent ruin of individuals who come upon sudden financial windfalls?

As for me, the moment that money stops being a major currency for transacting in this world, is the moment I stop needing it. Meanwhile, I'm fairly certain that my work is to keep my heart un-cynically open while waiting to receive more of the resources that make it possible to make an even greater difference for others. *To matter.* It is, I know, exceptionally painful not to have the opportunity to finance our dreams. *Yet it is large to choose to build with what we have, and not to destroy because we don't yet have what we feel is needed.* How many people do I know who cannot get out of bed in the morning to begin life because it feels so small to them? I well understand the great strength it demands from our inner being to show up in a life that seems so small. Yet doing just that—taking ourselves to the limit of our existing resources with the hope that it will open up to something bigger to show for our effort—is both large and noble.

To act large in the moment, despite the perceived smallness of the circumstance. An illustration: In the pre-Internet days, I drove to the bank and signed in for an appointment with the "lady in the back." The back of the bank is where you sit with a bank official whose job it is to take your money from you, all the while making you think she is doing you a favor. On that day, I sat myself down to speak with the good lady about how to invest some "disposable" funds that I had just earned. How I earned them, I really cannot remember. But I cherished the funds and wanted to kick off my investing dreams with them. When hearing the amount of the funds, she politely asked me to wait a moment. Upon her return, she explained that we'd be waiting just a brief moment for the chief financial advisor whom she just went to recruit. My face puzzled, "Why do we need that person?"

"Because $200K requires additional consideration," she calmly responded.

I had no choice but to ask her to cancel her reservation with Mr. Chief whose services were not needed for the $200 cash I had. Although I am not sure she could understand, I knew how big the $200 was for me and I treated it with respect.

Under His Loving Watch

At our wedding, Zack gifted me with something he knew I was deeply wishing for. After the *Chuppah* under which they become sanctified in a Jewish marriage, it is customary for the groom and bride to spend the first few moments of their married life in a private space, before rejoining the guests. Dining a little and touching up the bride's hair and makeup for "the pictures," it is a time for them to enjoy a new, tender closeness—and perhaps for the groom to give a gift. Although neither the gift-giving nor the choice of gift is mandatory, it is an appreciated display of generosity for the groom to delight his new bride with a piece of jewelry—often a pearl necklace or earrings.

Zack knew that I yearned for a particular gold watch. Despite my knowing that his presence was already an undeserved gift, I still wanted the watch. I cannot un-state the truth that it overwhelmed me with great joy to receive it from Zack, to hold it and wear it—at the wedding, and for many years after.

But then it happened. It was the day that I returned home from an outing with my children to see the house even messier than I could ever have made it. I knew my watch had been stolen. With no insurance to claim and with little funds to purchase a new one, Zack knew what this meant for me. And this is what he said:"I will not wear a watch on my hand until I find a way to buy you one for yours, similar to the one that you had."

And to this day, his hand remains watchless. And I remain under his special watch.

CHAPTER SIX

Finding Friends and Faith (and Funds) in the Fall

Always continue the climb. It is possible for you to do whatever you choose, if you first get to know who you are and are willing to work with a power that is greater than ourselves to do it.

—Margaret J. Wheatley, Management Consultant

R ABBI KAHANEMAN (1886-1969) was a world-renowned rabbinic figure, famed for building in Israel a *Yeshiva*—academy of Torah learning—known as the *Ponovezh Yeshiva* (named after the Lithuanian city of *Panevezys*). Originally founded in 1908 in Lithuania, the school and its then three-hundred students were annihilated by the Nazis in 1944, *along with his wife and nine children*. At the age of sixty-four and bereft of his entire world, the rabbi (who was miraculously saved) immigrated to Israel, whereupon he set his sights on a tall hill in the center of a particular area and made plans to purchase and build a school for no less than five hundred students. Did I mention that he had no money? Not even the small amount needed to send a telegram about this project to a prospective supporter in South America. Today, it stands as one of the largest *Yeshivot* in the world, with well over one thousand students.

When people saw him reaching for the hills, they knew he had suffered unspeakable losses and that he had no money. Some assumed that he even lost his mind. True, he had no money, but he most definitely had his mind—a quite focused one at that. What they couldn't see was his deep faith and far-reaching vision, those garments of the spirit indiscernible to the common eye. And while he surely articulated both of these—his faith and his vision—in his Heaven-bound prayers, he didn't neglect to invest unceasing effort in the millions of mundane details on the ground, no doubt attracting a supportive following who began to understand his conviction and character. Clearly, it was these non-material resources of faith and vision, not his pocket, which primarily influenced him to stake out the ground that money would later help materialize and build. Similar to the idea "You'll see it when you believe it," I'd say," *You'll see it when you can envision it.*" Because vision is a huge asset that requires the currency of faith, and the drive to live large.

This crypto-currency called faith is designed to work as a medium of exchange, just like money. But, it doesn't work in bills and coins. Rather, it requires trusting in the rightness of an idea and in G-d to make it happen. It affords one the ability to pay attention to dreams, to opportunities that are bigger than what's possible right now, but that can be pursued until they become "possible, then probable, and finally inevitable." Former Chief Rabbi of Great Britain, Rabbi Jonathan Sacks, said it this way: "Faith is the defeat of probability by possibility." While money might ultimately be exchanged, it is not the basis for the decision-making, as money is often not available until later on—a reality that chases away many a dream, in all but the most awake.

Friends in Unlikely Places
Putting our faith in money, one of our greatest worldly friends, is easy when you have it. *But what happens if someone doesn't*

readily have money on which to bank one's trust? Like Rabbi Kahaneman, he can place his trust in G-d . . . and in friends that G-d sends to us as His messengers. *Good friends matter.* And they help us matter. Finding friends whom we can trust with our profound sense of powerfulness, and powerlessness, is no simple task—no less for a child of nine.

Because at age nine, I had few friends and even less faith than that. And forget about vision. All I could see was a trail of despair and hopelessness behind me, and in front of me.

While I could count my trusted friends on less than one hand, I did have a very close friend whose presence was unquestionably paramount to my survival. This friend was always available, while keeping quiet and offering comfort whenever I needed. She never complained to me or about me and never even said a word when I cried to her, just offering me non-judgmental succor. From very early on in my life, this one friend stood by my side, cutely dimpled and short in stature but huge in significance. One of my elementary teachers even tried to separate us in school by insisting that I stop depending on her so much throughout the day. I admit that I wore her down over the years as I lovingly clung to her, my left thumb.

No wonder I thought to stick her in my mouth every night while talking with Brenna on our beds, and then again whenever we were taking a family photo—aptly called the 'shoot'—in which I was cajoled into conforming: sit straight, smile, and look happy. Having no intention of fitting in and getting lost in a picture, I collaborated with my thumb to suck more vigorously, even picking a piece of my upper lip for good measure. Drooping my head like a wilted flower, I kept my mouth as unhappy as I knew how, and spread my feet way apart, all in my best effort to communicate my truth: I was not happy, because I did not matter.

There was another friend with whom I had a connection. Actually, I cannot exactly call her a friend, although she filled in as one, in this fourth-grade year of weight gains, custom-made large clothing, snow storms, and exhausting homework sessions at the kitchen table.

My Hebrew teacher, Mrs. Ginberg, was celebrated for setting up her classroom in a way that accommodated individual styles of learning. She stood at the front of the classroom, but never in one place, always shifting and sharing her love from side to side. With the frequent, quick touch of her intertwined right index and middle fingers to her thick white glasses riding south of her wavy short black hair and large chocolate eyes, she'd easily offer us her continuously embracing smile. It seemed hard to overstay our welcome in her heart. Dressed in a compassionate glow on her thirty-year old, softly chiseled, light-complected face, Mrs. Ginberg injected joy and comfort into these early mornings of my long school days. In particular, it was her music station in the back of the classroom that gifted me with respite from the rigors of the regular classroom. Because she well knew that some children learn through diverse modalities and at varying paces, she arranged a short, rectangular table at the back of the room which held a tape recorder—the precursor to today's music-playing devices—that played her songs featuring the week's material she was teaching at the front of the room. One would go there if she was ahead or behind the class, or just needed to opt out of the group learning. With headphones on my ears, Mrs. Ginberg's musical voice would float along my mind, chasing away the anxious hum of my life.

Music was like that, I have noticed. A friend in its own right. It could, and still does, create a safe zone inside my mind where I take refuge from worldly reality. While words often get hung on fragments of human subjectivity, melody moves me past earthly defenses. It ushers me along the path of unguarded emotion, often creating a motion that may have been blocked before. While words push my thoughts concretely into a box, melody pulls them out—sneaking right past my resistances like the baseball batter whose home run sweeps the loaded bases, freeing the other players to run home. There is a dance in that run, a place to roam unfettered in the uncluttered expanse of spirit. Music moves us from the world of perceived reality to one of possibility, from linear to lateral, from prose to poetry, from fear to faith. I hear a tune in my head, can you? *You raise me up.*[1]

At home, I loved when my father would put on music, even though I couldn't sing too loudly because it would disrupt the focused, important, real-life work that makes adult people matter. Like talking business on the phone and making sure the house was spotless enough for everyone to be concerned about dirtying it—one of the only things I could do really well without much effort. It was at these moments that I promised myself I'd for sure marry one day, just so that I could have a house of my own in which to move around with an uncensored voice of joy—and keep it overly messy every now and then, actually more nows than thens. Indeed, I still recall some of Mrs. Ginberg's tunes, and when I do, I am transported to a rare oasis in time—in the same way a smell of potent perfume can have you traveling long-forgotten life journeys in the quickest of seconds.

It was Mrs. Ginberg who one day sat me down in the auditorium when my pre-class crying spell lasted longer than its usual cut-off at the ring of the first school bell at 9 a.m., once again making Brenna late to her sixth-grade classroom. Off to the corner in that large room which held rows of rectangular brown tables and benches enough to seat five-hundred hungry elementary girls at lunchtime, stood four foot eight-inch, eighty-year-old Ms. Kathy, with her toothless smile and bucket of soapy water at the ready. With her ever-present cigarette rolled between the edges of her thin upper and lower lips, supposedly to contain her overly fresh mouth, she scoured, "Miz Ginberg, you gonna be looong in hea? Gotta wash that flah, ya know." Kathy sure knew how to get that floor clean. And always nearby was Mr. Norris, the school cook, who'd bake macaroni with the curly, cheesy top and burnt underbelly that has never

---

[1] "You Raise Me Up," sung by Josh Groban.

met its equal since those days when lunch was served in school. Between the two of them, I somehow drew some life from both the divine smells and tastes of excessive carbs and from the fact that a dirty floor could be made clean by a mop in simple, but skilled hands.

"Shifra, why are you crying?" probed Mrs. Ginberg.

"I am scared," I whispered.

"Shifra, of what? Of what are you scared?"

"That I will be alone, that no one will come get me. I don't want to be alone." I wasn't sure she could understand that concept. After all, how simple is it to understand that a small child who is materially well-cared-for could be so utterly scared?

"I promise you that if you ever need me, in your whole life, I will come to get you. I will."

And for that whole day, I felt I was safe and that I'd be okay.

Many times, I replayed her reassurances in my head as a way of soothing the aloneness of my growing-up years. It was nearly two decades later when I saw Mrs. Ginberg at the graduation of my sister Rebecca who was born in the year that Mrs. Ginberg was my teacher and friend. She had long ago moved out of Baltimore, but was now in attendance for her graduating niece. Rebecca mentioned to me that she might be there and that, in case I didn't know, she was now a nationally-renowned educational mentor. Aside from taking a moment's undeserved pride that surely I contributed to her expertise along the way, I wondered if I'd recognize her all these years later, not bothering to ponder if she'd recognize me.

It was her smile from across the room that I first recognized; lonely hearts do not easily forget the smiles sent their way in the darkest days. When I saw it, that smile from eighteen years ago, I asked Zack to come with me to reintroduce myself and to introduce him, but mainly to thank her. Her thick glasses were now gone, leaving her with a pair of surgically-corrected eyes made even kinder and shinier by the intervening years.

"Mrs. Ginberg? It's been a long time; a really long time, I know."

She focused her gaze fully into my eyes, ten seconds in all.

"Shifra!" There it was—that welcoming voice that had enveloped me in her class through those sun-deprived, bone-chilled days of fourth grade, very much like my olive-colored fleece blanket offering me its extra warmth I crave on winter's blackest nights. I allowed her to take the few moments necessary to open that memory file and integrate a memo: young, heavy, anxious student has grown into a smiling young woman, and who is that friendly-looking guy next to her?

With a soft, smooth turn of her small-boned shoulder, she put both hands around my neck. Hers was a quiet, genuinely happy hug. Accepting that close connection while remembering her promise to always be there for me, I knew her hug would soon drop open into a conversation. I heard myself say, "I want you to know something."

I tried to tell her about what her kindness did for me, about the gift of the music in the back of her room, about the meaning of her friendship, but my words froze inside, and could only be thawed by the grateful tears that had to finish my sentence of appreciation never forgotten.

Young Faith Tested

Despite the solace and relief that these two friends, my thumb and Mrs. Ginberg, managed to provide me, my mind wandered a lot to one more friend whose presence was taken for granted until the day she did not return to school. Little Ellen and I had exercised our sensitive five-year-old imaginations for hours at a time, in the real-life doll house in our kindergarten room. We entered it together, making room for other little girls, too, and learned how to mother little babies with gentle cooing sounds that surely put them into sweet dreams.

One day, Ellen did not come. We, my classmates and I, wondered where she was. We asked our teachers and our parents, but no one seemed to be able to tell us. But what was left unsaid could be overheard. Ellen and her father were in a tragic car accident; Ellen had died. That was that. We were expected to go into the dollhouse, without Ellen, and continue to mother our baby dolls and inspire their trust in us, their loving caretakers. It didn't help when Brenna told me that I resembled Ellen with her cute, roundish face and angelic smile.

I did not know how deeply this hurt was stored until nearly forty years later, when I went to offer my condolences to Ellen's brother and sister who were *sitting shiva* for their mother. (Shiva, literally "seven," refers to the Jewish law requiring close blood relatives to mourn for seven days, during which they receive visitors who wish to offer comfort. By just showing up and even relating the importance of the person who has passed, the visitor has fulfilled the Biblical injunction to comfort the bereaved. It is a time designed to safely allow the mourner the full intensity of the mourning experience and the strength to begin to heal—as a resting place before easing oneself back into everyday life.) I began to speak, and suddenly the pain-filled memory rushed over me, leaving me with eyes too moist and a mouth too dry to speak. There were other speaking adults around me, but all I could hear was the small voices of little girls, my dollhouse friends. "Where is Ellen? Ellen, where are you? Why haven't you come to play with us today?"

To this day, I do not know if the mourners understood that their sister's memory was standing between us, temporarily leaving me utterly alone as the five-year-old girl in the play-house, bereft of her good friend Ellen. Perhaps this *shiva* visit did more for me than it did for them, as it was I who began to heal that day from that long-ago trauma of the unanswered question about Ellen, and the unvoiced lingering fear in our hearts begging to know: Are we safe in our lives? Having the opportunity to participate in her family's mourning this time around, I retroactively applied the current comfort to assuage that long ago hurt. While the adults could not answer us, time somehow had. Ellen lived. Ellen died. Ellen mattered; we never forgot her. And somehow we were okay, though it didn't always feel that way.

Facing Fear, Finding Faith

But there I was, left with a growing problem of too little faith and too much fear.

It didn't just start there in the empty dollhouse, of course. Where does a problem like that begin for us humans?

I am honestly terrified to talk about faith; it is not one of my naturally strong subjects. If I am not prone to feeling the faithful side of things as a first response, how in fact did it even get here on the page? Can it be that it is central to living a large life . . . not to mention intimately connected with money and mattering and friends?

Although this subject of faith is without limit, I can start with this: It is the profoundest of truths that our sense of trust is shaped at its core by our earliest relationships, usually with our parents who are proxies for G-d. Judaism posits that there are three partners in the creation of every human being: two parents and G-d. How G-d cajoles us humans into this vexing parenting partnership to begin with is testimony to His powerfulness. But parents (or guardians) do indeed become co-creators, entrusted with shepherding His prized human creations, and it is clear that the echoes of this relationship can build or disturb our sense of faith in G-d. What's hard to understand about that? *The way we feel about G-d is deeply shaped by how we experienced our relationship with our parents.*

How many grown males and females have desperately confided in me, a non-therapist friend, their gaping hole, begging for the adoring eye of a mother who values them regardless of how they look, or the validation of a father despite their capacity for making money?

Here's an excerpt of a heart-hurting text I received just the other day from a young woman in her early thirties whose path recently crossed with mine.

"I'm the victim of so much pain from my parents. Parents who steal the happiness of life from me are not worthy of the title 'parents.' All these things I deal with on a daily basis are holding me back in life. My mother told me once she dislikes me most out of all her kids because I remind her of her mother with whom she cut off ties, years earlier. All my father cares about is how much money I am making, and if it is enough to cover my bills."

I know she can't help but envy that sense of hopeful confidence, self-acceptance, and joy her well-parented friends display, leaving her lagging far behind in all three of those categories, through no fault of her own.

Having difficulty with trusting those closest to us sets us up quickly and deeply for not knowing how to trust G-d's love and compassion for us. And more fundamentally, we agonize over why G-d set it up this way; perhaps we cannot trust Him, either.

Family dynamics have huge spiritual consequences. For now, and for generations to come.

There was an ancient author who knew that. His name was King David, and he wrote a book of his own known as *Tehillim*, or Psalms, whose central focus was to find, foster, and feature his unequivocal faith in G-d's overwhelming, eternal, and constant goodness to His creations. "My father and mother have forsaken me, but G-d has gathered me in." (Psalm 27:10) Seems oddly contemporary, feeling forsaken and blaming our parents for it . . . except for the fact that his parents were none other than the extraordinarily devout Yishai and Nitzevet, a woman of rare moral caliber. I have learned that his intention was not to disparage them, rather to note the limits of the parent-child relationship. For all their love and noble intentions, his parents sent him out on his own after youth and adolescence, which to him felt akin to abandonment. But, says King David, he had no need to worry because G-d is the ultimate parent, the Chief Creator who never abandons His children.

What should others, like my friend above, say about the parenting they received that was not nearly as well-intentioned as that of King David's parents, and certainly very misguided? Perhaps King David's words can foster the beginning steps towards shaping a faith in G-d, that He can guide us through the shards of brokenness to shreds of wholeness.

I am among those for whom it is eminently true that we struggle from the get-go to trust that we will have what we need. How many of our faith systems are intimately wrapped around the notion that our Creator will provide our needs, to sustain us? Indeed, the Jewish concept of tithing, giving one-tenth of our income to charity, goes straight to the heart of this fear, redirecting it towards an act of faith. The Torah encourages us to bank on this, that G-d will replenish our funds when we demonstrate the requisite faith in taking less while giving to another, acknowledging that it is entirely His anyway. And that increasing our faith somehow activates the Heavenly flow of abundance. As with Rabbi Kahaneman, his heroic demonstration of personal faith evidently expanded his spiritual capacity to attract and hold more material blessing.

Upon the exodus of the Jewish people from 210 years of Egyptian slavery—gratefully celebrated every spring as Passover—G-d brought them to the Desert for forty years to have them learn one primary lesson: *Rely on Me.* He rained down food, known as the *manna* (literally portion)—which sounds eerily similar to another word I know, *money*—with the exclusive intention to nourish their sense of trust. Tangentially, the Hebrew word for belief in G-d is *emunah*, from which the word *amen* derives. (The word *amen* is actually comprised of three Hebrew letters which also serve as an abbreviation of three whole words translating as "G-d is a faithful King." Saying *amen* is a powerful way of exercising our belief in G-d's love and kindness for all of His creations.)

We humans are wanderers on our own journeys. And while manna sounds as heavenly as it actually was, we typically have to pay for our food today, and anything else we consume. All is still a miracle, just less overt. I have been in both situations where I immediately had what I needed financially, and where I didn't. And the prospect of not having is itself a terrifying experience, one that niggles at me as intensely as I allow it. It starts in my chest as a vague, downward tug on my sense of well-being, of something feeling intensely un-joyful, and gathers strength very quickly. Breaking into stormy, vivid imaginings of being left on the coldest of streets without food, and even more uncomfortably, without befitting clothes, my mind's refrain, *"what happens if . . ."* sucks me into the quicksand of the dangerous downward spiral I have fought ten thousand times before.

The experience of not having, uncomfortable as it is, can be a spirit-building one, offering us the opportunity to exercise our belief that G-d can and will figure out a way to support us. One of the smallest examples was the pre-Uber time when I walked out onto the street in a foreign city, needing to hail a taxi to an important appointment, but without even a penny in my pocketbook. I had no choice but to use the currency called faith. Faith presupposes that you will ask G-d to help, and that you believe that He not only can, but that He will. And actually He did on that day, by sending a private car whose kind, unfamiliar driver offered me a ride. (Okay, maybe my urgently waving hand had a little something to do with it.) Turned out my personal driver and I shared a mutual friend from my hometown, which might be totally beside the main point that G-d has many ways to fill our needs . . . or maybe it is part of the larger point that G-d even chose a specific driver to help me as part of this faith-building exercise.

Funding Friendships

"Buy for yourself a friend," the Torah (Ethics of the Fathers 1:6) advises us, making it clear that friends are an asset. As with other assets, friendships often have to be secured with material means.

If we were just unembodied spirits, we'd have no need for friends or food or funds, for any of this world's currencies. But once a spirit merges into a body and lives in this worldly experience, we have to concern ourselves with this world's realities. In human form, and via the human form, the spirit agitates to express and communicate its essence in a tangible way. *To matter is to concretize spirit.* Demonstrating a spiritual impulse, such as gratitude, regret, or hope, necessarily involves the appropriate transfer of a human currency. We must concretize spirit with whatever worldly currency we have at any given moment—including words of caring and concern, financial support, food, clothing, and other earthly goods that support another human being, including ourselves. (The Torah is called a "Torah of kindness," acknowledging that we humans activate our spirituality in many ways that have us extending ourselves to others in the most physical, mundane of ways.)

Hallmark has made buying and selling friendship its business. They have us believing that "What I'm really giving you is a part of me." We buy into it, don't we? Many, if not all, marketing campaigns endeavor to have us translate the unseen—but felt—emotional pieces of our lives into visible, transferrable energy.

If something matters to you, it must come into being. It must take up space and consume emotion. It must have a way of being seen, heard, felt, touched, and smelled. Yes, t*o matter is to concretize spirit.*

And the choices we make tell us, and everyone else around us, what matters. There is no other way to know that, other than by seeing the choices we make. And our human spirit endows each of us with the *inalienable right to make life large*, to imbue it with the wealth of meaning that is consistent with our spirit.

But I know how easily we can become *dis-spirited* . . . falling for the idea of spending an earthly currency such as money, *in exchange for counterfeit mattering.* Capitalizing on this human drama of being and becoming, the market does not always seize healthfully on our spiritual impulses. And sometimes it can actually bankrupt us in multiple ways. While "say it with flowers" or "express it with diamonds" seems loving enough, what about the endless stream of capitalist commercials designed to stimulate the baser side of the jealous, greedy, lonely, insecure human heart? These are "emotional idols" that we learn to glorify, unless we are taught how to smash them. *They will destroy us, if we do not neutralize them first.*

Because what is their cost to our mattering? Often, insanely high. It downsizes our dignity, suggesting we feel jealously small. It wears down our mattering, to the point of acquiescing to their covert demand for our desperate trust, otherwise known as our money, in exchange for their empty promises. Here, the buck never stops; it is the language of the land. And it can leave us impoverished.

Mastering Money

The Torah states that "Whoever has one hundred portions, desires two hundred." (Koheles Raba 1:13) If that is so, then we are being given fair notice: we will always be in a state of wanting more, leaving us with tongue-wagging appetites, no matter what we have consumed, if we depend on it for our ultimate satisfaction.

If you have a billion dollars, but spend a billion dollars and one penny, you are not only in debt, you are destitute. *Wealth is a ratio of what you have to what you need.* And wealth is always in the satisfaction, curiously often found in having a bit less, rather than a bit more. Protecting ourselves from excess anything is the wealthy thing to do, because wealth is not only in the having; it is in the being and in the giving. *Just like our mattering.*

While money can buy pieces of pleasure, comfort and convenience, even moments of mattering and friendship, over-depending on it potentially makes our empty holes bigger and the appetite more illusory. As with food, there is only a certain amount of emptiness that can be healthfully filled with things money can buy. *Enoughness is that exquisite balance where body and spirit peacefully co-exist, where they live and love.*

Spirits cannot be bought. Neither can trust. Economics was not a favored subject of mine, but one thing I remember well is the lesson that underlying the power of money is the trust people have in it as they move it around. Distilled to its simplest terms, our faith in the market can powerfully persuade or dissuade its success. We deposit our money into an FDIC-insured institution, banking on the faith-backed system that protects it. The minute people lose that faith, a run on the bank is sure to follow, like my father's savings and loan bank that went bust. The market is a remarkably sensitive barometer of people's faith, which in turn can manipulate markets. People are far more powerful than money itself. Indeed, generating trust between people is good business.

Ideally, money is our servant, not our master.

Kind Heart, Open Hand

Combined with friendship and faith, money can help us matter and feel loved when it is connected to an open heart. Hearts can love, but pockets of their own accord cannot. The Torah remarks that one who gives charity receives six blessings from G-d. Yet, the one who opens his hand *and* his heart by giving the money with a smile and a kind word deserves eleven. Clearly, extending friendship in the form of a sincere and priceless smile is considered an act of great kindness that can offer another person the support needed in the fall. It restores one's faith that he can rise again.

I know about that. I think back to Mrs. Ginberg, and her charity of warm words and soothing smiles assuring me that I'd be okay. Yes, she was a friend in the fall, and I hope she got the blessings she deserves. In hindsight, her attention went a long way to helping me matter, at least enough to opt into another day and another day, year after year.

And I cannot stop wondering: What would have happened if Aunt Rosalie had a Mrs. Ginberg in her life? Someone to notice her loneliness, to raise her in her life. To smile at her and to extend a heart's healing, to be her friend in the fall. Would she have been able to opt in more to her own life, day by day, to build her spirit—and her mattering?

Using one's material resources to express spirit expands our mattering. Abusing them contracts our mattering, and that of the people around us.

CHAPTER SEVEN

A Smattering of Mattering

*Determination, energy, and courage appear sponta-
neously when we care deeply about something. We take
risks that are unimaginable in any other context.*

—MARGARET J. WHEATLEY, Writer

"I F ONLY I had known that it mattered, I'd have done something even more."

Ever had that thought? These sentiments seem common
enough, and yet they also belong to three Jewish biblical personalities, one of whom was Boaz the Judge.

In each case, these three individuals did something
kind and life-affirming, but were unaware of the enduring
magnificence of their actions. In what I call *kindsight*, the
Jewish commentators teach that in looking back, G-d wishes
to testify to the wholehearted integrity of their thoughts and
actions, which incidentally were in the privacy of their hearts,
in non-public displays. And G-d wishes to reward them, too.

Kindsight

He was walking past his expansive grounds when he saw a
young woman in the corner of his fields designated by Jewish

law for the disadvantaged to come and take from the leftover wheat. Starving and dressed in thread bare clothing, it was her modest demeanor, rare among the people of the field, which caught his attention.

Here began the fateful relationship between the eighty-three-year old Jewish leader and judge of his generation, Boaz, and the forty-year old widowed Moabite princess, Ruth, the female Jewish convert.[2] It was toward the end of the era when the Jewish nation was governed by the Judges, a form of leadership that spanned roughly 350 years—following the death of Joshua until the establishment of the first Jewish monarchy of King Saul (968 BCE / 2792).

As the story develops, it becomes clear that *one's mattering is often subtle and quiet, while still gathering massive and unexpected energy as we move along the continuum of choices in our lives*. And as we do, G-d stands by us humans, giving us not only first chances, but second chances too, when He discerns our determination and courage for things that are important to us. He opens for us the door that we might not ever have dared to approach, or even knew was there.

Of Chance, Courage, and Commitment

In this case, Ruth had returned to Bethlehem in the land of Israel with her widowed mother-in-law Naami (mother of Ruth's deceased husband). A mere decade earlier, Naami and Elimelech, her famed philanthropist husband, along with their two sons, fled from Israel to nearby Moab. It was an attempt to escape his moral obligation to support his fellow Jews who were experiencing a severe famine. With his fabulous wealth, he could have sustained his nation for ten years. Instead, this family made the grave mistake of withholding kindness to an entire people, ultimately incurring the wrath of G-d, who killed

---

2 While Judaism embraces the convert, "Love the proselyte" (Deuteronomy 10:19), Judaism does not actively seek to convert non-Jews. Non-Jews are accorded righteous status when they faithfully uphold the Seven Noahide Laws. Parenthetically, it is a Biblical teaching that G-d does not withhold earned reward from any human, regardless of his moral or spiritual standing.

Elimelech and his two sons, who had married women from Moab, but died childless.

After this tragic turn of events, Naami wants to return to the land of Israel. Her daughters-in-law, the wives of her two deceased sons—both sisters and princesses of the royal household of Moab—pleaded to go with her. That, in itself, is astonishing; it's not the norm for a daughter-in-law to want to follow her mother-in-law, is it? Knowing how difficult this would be for them, both physically and spiritually, Naami works hard to dissuade them from doing this.

In a fateful decision that would forever mark the diverging destinies of two different nations, one daughter-in-law returned to Moab, while Ruth refused to detach herself from Naami who was facing the fate of an utterly hopeless future marked by poverty, and infamy over her husband's shocking disregard for his people's welfare. In a remarkable display of spiritual courage, energy, and determination, Ruth forgoes her predictably entitled royal life for something she deems eminently higher and more worthy. The inner nobility and depth of G-d's *Torah*[3], as translated through Naami's persona, captures Ruth's unrelenting admiration and growing attachment to Torah ideals, compelling her to make the exchange of an earthly prestige for a Divinely-inspired one.

And while we might not be able to fully articulate the scope of what motivated in Ruth this stunning display of loyalty to G-d, and while she could not have ever known where this would lead her, here's what we now know: that G-d ultimately shaped and elevated her uncommon conviction and commitment for doing kindness to a destitute relative—selflessly, with no prospect of personal reward—into a house of Jewish royalty, earning her the biblical title *Mother of Royalty*. A fitting reward, because royalty, in its ideal manifestation, bestows a vast opportunity

---

3 Literally "Guide," loosely known as the Jewish Bible. (The Torah consists of the Written Law—24 books including the five Books of Moses, eight Books of Prophets, and eleven Books of Writings such as Psalms, Proverbs, Ecclesiastes and others—as well as the Oral Law comprised of the Mishna and Talmud.)

and capacity to extend resources to benefit others, without the expectation or need for anything in return.

Small Choice, Huge Chance

Boaz was elderly, and had just lost his wife. It was at this time that he encountered Ruth in his field. After inquiring about her and learning her identity, he gave her extra food in a display of concern and kindness for her and Naami, his close relative, whom he had heard returned to Israel after the unspeakable suffering of losing her husband, her sons, and her monetary fortune.

It was this seemingly small action of giving her extra food that would earn Boaz an eternal shout-out: "And Boaz handed her parched grain, and she ate and was satisfied . . ." The Torah tells us that had Boaz known the import of his action, he'd have exerted himself to give her a more substantial meal of fatted calves. *If only he'd have known.* He originally held back his full measure of kindness for fear of reprisal that perhaps it was not the right course of action, that his noble intentions might be misunderstood by others as ill-intentioned or inappropriate. The lesson is made clear by the Torah: *When doing a kind deed, do so with a full heart, even if you are uncertain of its worth.* Because we can never really know. Yes, sometimes situations strenuously test our moral clarity, yet we can access the high ground of enthusiasm and a full heart to do our duty as we judge it. And if we err on the side of generosity, I am almost certain G-d knows how to forgive us for that.

Ultimately, Boaz performed another great kindness by marrying Ruth, in fulfillment of a little-understood commandment calling upon the closest relative of a deceased male who died childless, to marry the wife of the deceased so that she might have a child. This was considered a great kindness to the departed. Boaz died the morning after they married, leaving Ruth to mother his seed, which would birth the progenitors of King David. She was a great grandmother when she saw the blessing of royalty take shape. Human loyalty that is given lovingly to G-d births royalty. Actually, what is love, if not loyalty? We don't know what we love until we see what attracts our loyalty.

Both Ruth and Boaz located in themselves a deep loyalty to doing the honorable action, *at high cost to their convenience and comfort*, a price they were willing to pay for the value they perceived. Again, what could be more fitting than the reward for their descendants to be privileged with Jewish royalty, the opportunity to serve as premier emissaries for G-d's honor on this Earth, which was in fact the primary responsibility of a Jewish king. Although Torah law limited the amount of "wives, horses, and silver" he could personally have, a Jewish king was endowed with exceptional resources in support of his G-d given authority to protect and assist his people. And while he was obligated to humble himself before G-d in prayer more than his subjects, the Jewish king was gifted with the extraordinary merit and opportunity to influence and impact on a mass scale, to leave his individual mark on his people and on history in a most prominent way.

I listen to this story, and all I can do is wonder: How could the worth of one's own deeds be unknown to oneself? Don't we know if and when we are doing something good, sometimes even letting others know of our not-so-secret goodness, too?

It occurs to me that maybe this question of mattering is more central to us humans than I realize. If the moral greats suffered this feeling, what should I think? While small things, often matters of the heart, count so greatly, we humans may have a hard time recognizing them. We aspire to the louder and the larger, but it is so often the quieter and smaller that brings us along on the continuum towards bigger and greater.

In this account, it was the accumulation of the small, steady kindness of Ruth towards her mother-in-law, and of Boaz towards Ruth and Naami—the smatterings of mattering—that ultimately conglomerate into the bigger mattering that we aspire to, that we can recognize and feel.

Moments of Mattering

Do you have any idea when was the first time you felt you had a big life, that you mattered? How did it feel to matter? And most important, who are you when you matter?

As I experienced it, spirits need a body to contain them and carry them around in this life. My spirit chose as its partner a decidedly un-American ideal: a larger body. Being in a larger body did not mean I was living a larger life; just the opposite. American appearances dictated worthiness based on a smaller body. In fact, the bigger I was, the smaller I felt as a person.

So, if you asked me when the first time was that I felt I had a big life—that I mattered—it was when the Diet Workshop scale dropped me to one hundred pounds. I was three months shy of twelve, and now I would fit into real clothes. I had a real body, a defined shape. How powerful my clothes were; instead of shaming me as in the past, they now hugged me with great applause.

Skirting the Issue

This newfound mattering was just in time for my becoming a *Bat Mitzvah*.[4] This was the first occasion in my life (that I could remember) that I would own a two-piece outfit, my first skirt and blouse bought from a clothing store, to be worn at a Bat Mitzvah celebration in school. No standing on tables to be measured, just directly and instantly approaching the rack, removing it, trying it on with confidence that it would fit. Yes, off the rack . . . what tailor-made joy. I mattered.

Parenthetically, while a boy reaches his Bar Mitzvah— literally, "the son of commandment"—at the age of thirteen, interestingly, girls beat them to maturity by one whole year, as they reach that occasion at age twelve. It is worthwhile to note that for the male becoming a Bar Mitzvah, the formal celebration is often more public, if not more lavish, seeming to translate into more overt privilege and responsibility. The young man

---

4 Literally translated as 'daughter of commandment,' suggesting that she will now begin her personal, individual relationship with the Torah wherein she will assume more privilege and responsibility.

now may join in the synagogue services as a participant in the *minyan*, the quorum of ten people necessary for a communal prayer, and as the leader of the services. I am not one for public displays, and I did not mistake the extra pomp for more joy or importance. Or for more mattering.

While Judaism places the male in the external, public domain of the synagogue, the woman is ensconced in the safety and security—and spirituality—of her home. I actually find that convenient; I don't like being told where and when to go, too much of the time. But if her voice sounds quieter to you, listen again. She is the heartbeat of her home and her people. Hers is the voice that resounds and resonates well beyond just the walls of home and synagogue. Even beyond her generation. As with a healthy heartbeat, she gives life to the whole body. Her well-being is the center of it all. And while it sometimes seems to me that we make a bigger deal about boys growing up, celebrating their births and Bar Mitzvahs with pre-arranged rituals, I half-jokingly wonder if his voice bouncing off the public walls is so that he, above all, can hear himself.

I wouldn't say Judaism is a women-centric religion only, as I think it favors the needs of each gender in remarkably wise ways. But I was taught that women play central roles in life, whether or not their faces and accomplishments are on physical and public display (and sometimes especially when they are not.) When G-d instructed Abraham to hearken to the voice of Sarah (Genesis 21:12), He was paying tribute to a woman's profoundly capable spirit that animates her world and those in it. And beyond it.

Prayer and Pizza

In reaching this age of *Bat Mitzvah*, I anticipated two celebrations—one in school and the other at home. In school, my friends and I performed in a cantata at a group dinner held for family and friends. With each girl dressed modestly in a dark velvet skirt and white blouse (mine newly bought from the store), and stockings and heels of varying heights (yes, mine were the highest), she was ready to march in a graceful line to the stage to speak her part in a script designed to communicate messages of the nobility of the Jewish woman. The lovely qualities of our four matriarchs and other female personalities would be lauded as a way to prod us along a similarly noble path. After that was done, each of us would be called individually by name to come forward and accept a gift—a prayer book known in Hebrew as the *Siddur*. Engraved on the Siddur was our name in Hebrew lettering. Inside the front cover was a small hand-written message mixing a celebratory note with a hopeful one for future success in our various roles—none more prized than that of a Jewish mother furthering a link in the unbroken chain of "royal daughters," as we were called.

That "r" word was being used, and I *loved* it. Royal or regal, both worked. I rolled it around in my heart; I began to think that this was what I wanted to be when I grew up. Yes, I wanted to be a royal or a regal, whatever the actual entity was called, and whichever one of those positions would open up for me.

Instilling a sense of dignity, joy, and possibility for this new Bat Mitzvah girl was pleasantly done. Deliciously, too. While I have no clue where that Siddur is today, since it has been replaced by others, I can readily savor the memory of the corn-flake-coated chicken, baked with the caloric skin still attached—a rarity for the girl who had just dropped a quarter of her corporeal being.

On the home front, the celebration was much less formal. My mother dared a surprise party. Unbeknownst to me, she invited my whole class to our house right after school finished that Sunday at 12:30. (Yes, school consumed six days of our week, although Friday was a half-day devoted to secular studies, and Sunday's half-day was exclusively for Jewish studies, with the rest of the days being divided into Jewish studies in the morning, and secular studies in the afternoon.) My grandfather picked me up late so my friends would be able to settle themselves in my house before my grand arrival. Considering how the surprise party my mother tried on me in fourth grade turned out (I promptly fled, and did not return until my friends had finished eating my birthday cupcakes), I am still surprised that my mother attempted this. She must have counted on the food factor—that the smells of the pizza would assault and overpower any stubborn anti-social inclinations I may have had on that day. Upon walking through the front door and seeing my classmates there, I headed straight to my bedroom. With hungry stomachs, family and friends all waited. "Is she really going to pull that on us? Is she going to stay locked up in her room ungratefully, and ruin the party we are making for her?" I cannot remember why I just decided to place my books down on my bed and emerge cooperatively as the happy birthday girl everyone needed me to be. It must have indeed been those over- whelming smells of the pizza that I had not tasted in more than a year because I had been on that diet, leaving me thinner than many of my naturally thin friends. My clothes fit comfortably, but those pizzas still had a pull on me. There is no robust way to describe the naughtiness of devouring a corpulent slice of hot, cheesy pizza followed by the next, both allowed by my mother. Yes, this was how birthdays should be celebrated . . . although I am virtually certain I would have preferred to have the entire pie, for and by myself. But, when it came to pizza, I would take it any way they'd give it to me.

Womankind

Becoming a Bat Mitzvah enlarged my life; it gave me more mat- tering. For one thing, it conferred a formal declaration that now I'd be privileged and obligated by Jewish law to keep, or at least try my best to keep, the Torah. There are many commandments known as *mitzvot*[5], 613 to be exact, although no person has the task of doing them all.

Of all that would pertain to me, I had been taught that there were three most cherished by women: lighting *Shabbat* (Sabbath) candles each week before sundown on Friday, baking

---

5 The root word is "tzavtza" which means to connect. Mitzvot are designed to connect us with G-d. By aligning ourselves with His will, we'd be connected with our highest selves, in accord with His intentions for our greatest good.

the weekly *Challah* bread for *Shabbat,* and observing the laws of "family purity," popularly known as *Mikvah,* or ritual pool. Each one is its own subject, of course, and would be lovingly taught and understood in due time. I gathered that the influence of the Jewish woman would be amplified by committing to these in particular, no matter what the external structure of her life looked like. No matter her career choice, mothering choice, or relationship choice or circumstance, she'd have a ready, individual, undeniable source of mattering to herself, to G-d, and to the world. Each of these particular mitzvot expands a component of her womanhood. At its most basic, bringing light to the world (Shabbat candles), offering sustenance to others (baking bread), and generating purity (Mikvah) are all in the domain of the woman at designated times in her life. And their import is far-reaching, even though, like Boaz and Ruth, we cannot necessarily know it in the moment. *If only we could know. And feel it too.*

Mattering, or at least a part of it, might not be a question of who is loudest or who is seen the most. Nor might it be rewarded instantly, which could prove challenging and even unfair. But, it would always be accessible through Divinely-designed portals. Just as the home, not the synagogue, is the heart of the Jewish nation (evidenced by the Biblical directive that the building of a *mikvah* takes precedence over the building of a synagogue), women are paramount to keeping humanity going. These domestic affairs, private as they may be, yield enormous influence for the woman personally, her family, her fellow humans, and indeed for the whole world.

> *If power drives the outer world, her influence drives the inner. Power controls, influence compels. Power pushes, influence pulls. One is external, the other internal. And eternal.*

Queen-sizing Our Lives

I know all of this, and I even believe it. And yet, I have a question, a longstanding one: If womankind is at the center of the world, *what is at the woman's center?*

And I cannot dismiss the word that keeps pulling on me, ever since I heard it at my Bat-Mitzvah school celebration. It's that "r" word again, and it insists on being part of this answer. It seems like such a large word. Royalty. *Royalty is at the core of her being.*

This word has long been a favorite descriptor when I think about what makes life worthy. If you are royal, you matter, right? The world will tell you that your value is extraordinary, that you are not exchangeable. Your status is enduring, cannot be taken away. You are adored, valued, deserving, and important; treated well in this world, better than others.

I press on: What makes a woman royal? Or at the very least, adored? The admired women I knew in my life growing up were considered attractive, well-dressed, courageous, determined, and selfless of heart with a developed capacity to give a lot of themselves, to demonstrate responsibility for oneself and others. They were warm and personable, often with a simple acceptance of things the way they were. They had the capacity to work hard, very hard, in pursuit of a goal they held dear. They didn't have to be very tall, though they were usually thin. But that wasn't enough.

I think of my maternal grandmother, who led to the stage her graduating class of eight hundred students, not because of her academic stature, but for her physical one, all five feet of it. The family picture, seven and a half decades later, captures the royalty of this woman walking down the aisle of her grandson's wedding, escorted by the groom's brother, 6′ 8″ in all. The sense of regality that her carriage exuded was not coming from him, nor was it borrowed from the fitted, sequined pearl-grey gown she wore, or from the fashionably swept up-do with curly wisps dancing around her sparkling, proud grey-blue eyes.

It was in the way she held her heart: with a combination of gratitude, fortitude, and privileged attitude for being a grand-mother, the one she always wanted to be, the one she never had. She wore her sense of personal mattering for all to see. And that translated into a composure that I associated with royalty.

A sense of mattering that could not be taken away from her or compared with anyone else.

And then I think about Aunt Rosalie. I once helped her shop for a dress to wear to a wedding she wanted to attend. After having her thick, black hair professionally blown and combed smooth, she put on the dress, her thin figure sliding easily into the aubergine, silk chiffon cloth draped in soft ripples across her waist. Her smile came out that day, and she even put on her two-inch silver pumps, along with a glittering attitude meant for dancing. A few minutes before I was prepared to drive her, she said she could not go. As she took off her adornments, she tried to explain repeatedly, "Too anxious. I don't really belong there. Just don't belong there. Not gonna hurt nobody if I don't go."

I pitied her for that sad turn of emotions. But I busied myself with wondering if she could be considered royal, especially as beautifully appointed as she was. I knew she couldn't be, because sadly, she didn't have any personal mattering to call her own. No one had given her any, and she didn't seem to reach for any of her own accord. How does that happen to a person? It frightened me deeply, to be so devalued that you have nothing others could appreciate about you. And if she couldn't be royal, then I knew I couldn't be, either. And besides, I wasn't thin. No royalty for me.

This queen-sized question of who gets to matter loomed large and steady over my existence, like an ever-shifting shadow that jumps ahead and behind you, trying to adjust to your position and accommodate your gait.

Just the other night, with the blinds fully down as I drifted into a badly-needed sleep, a popular dream of mine began again. I was sitting in a very large residence, one I have only seen when I am sleeping. There are many rooms, but I do not see anything clearly. I am inhabiting something beautiful to me, something big; I am content. And then I was awoken by thoughts that had me deliberating Princess Kate's fate and Meghan's sparkle, two contemporary, formerly non-royal women referred to condescendingly as 'commoners' whose marriages to princes now confer upon them royal status. And upon their children born to them. Kate is a queen in waiting, a wife and mother of future kings. Turning their burdens of public service into royal privilege: Is it as large and important as I envision? I wonder, because I know that the British monarchy is all figurehead—largely a show of pomp, with no reality or relevance except for what the British people are willing to keep giving it.

And the bigger question I am asking: What strength of character did they have to exhibit to earn that privilege, other than agreeing to marry their husbands (I am not minimizing that feat) and to agree to appear at all public times calm, collected, and stay slim (I'm definitely not minimizing that, either). And this is perhaps the biggest qualifier of all: Their clothes must be highly distinctive, not in a crazy, cheap celebrity way, but in a dignified, classy way that reveals their noble status, stockings and all. There I go again with that clothing thought: The clothes make the (wo)man. They tell us who she is, enough to draw out that phrase, *How royally splendid she looks.* (Show me her clothes, I will tell you who she is.)

I don't mean to be interfering in how G-d positions people, passions, and purposes. But I do want to know *if they should be defining my sense of royalty, the core of my ideal womanhood?*

Defining royalty would become a stubborn, life-long question for me, so far removed was I from its official corridors of impact and influence. And so enamored was I of Kate and Meghan's deceased mother-in-law, Princess Diana, whose royal charm seemed to have so obviously radiated from the inside. For all her supposed moral and emotional failings, what I saw was something bigger than her title and her elegantly-clad body. It was how she cast her eyes downward and kept her voice soft, all so unassuming. There was a heart that beat to others, maybe a troubled, broken beat, but human, vulnerable, and real. I remember her interview (with Martin Bashir of BBC, November 20, 1995) wherein she acknowledged that she "led from the heart" and stated, "I'd like to be a queen of people's hearts, in people's hearts . . . someone's gotta go out there and love the people and show it." *It was mostly her disposition, not her position, which made her royal.* What an uncommon touch, and the world absolutely adored her.

So I ask myself: Is there mattering outside of royal titles and residences? I know women who do not live in royal palaces, but royalty resides in them. They bear their burdens with a purposeful privilege. Helen Keller said it so well: "I long to accomplish a great and noble task; but it is my chief duty and joy to accomplish humble tasks as though they were great and noble." They are royalty waiting to happen. You can see it in how they comport themselves, amongst others and towards G-d, like I discerned in my "queen" grandmother. It is mostly in their carriage, not their clothing. But not everyone can be royal, *or can they?*

I recall some lessons I had learned about Jewish royalty . . . about Ruth, the convert and mother of royalty, and Esther, Queen of the Persian King Ahasuerus (Achashverosh in Hebrew). Like that of my grandmother, their regal grace stemmed from distinctive *inner* qualities, the force of their beauty connected to the strength of their characters—humility, modesty, and kindness above all. Enduring particular life hardships including widowhood and orphanhood, they summoned a loyalty to others and G-d. I wanted to know more about them.

Sacrificial, not Superficial or Artificial

And I would do exactly that in the years to come. I'd learn about the sacrifices that they'd make in the name of their highest selves, in their G-dly service. A sacrifice in the best use of the term, not in the resentful, martyred way that leaves one diminished—and those around them. They were willing, even wanting, to be used up, spent, in fulfilling a higher purpose or function. There was a selfless quality, an ability to live beyond themselves, for the benefit of the other. Whatever extraordinary privilege and opportunity fate had handed them, they employed in the service of others. Both of these royal personalities were models of sacrifice, not necessarily in comfortable and convenient ways, but in authentic, timely ways, answering the call of their beautiful, understanding hearts that shaped their life's purpose. And they showed up to inhabit their fate, which became their destiny. Royal, in the deepest sense of the word. And their lives still reverberate throughout the generations as relevant, and very admirable, at least to me.

But for me now, as that Bat Mitzvah girl who was just coming into all of this new mattering, the important thing for me to know now was that I could grow into these qualities by learning the laws, appreciating their purpose, and *believing that I would never outgrow their depth.*

Having been born into a family where traditional loyal adherence to Torah observance was paramount, I had been given a positive "heart" start with the spiritual side of life. While the growing got rough many times on the interpersonal front between family members, the connection between G-d and us was still kept uppermost. And even though it could not spare us from the tests of difficult relationships, a close connection with G-d could encourage us to slowly work through them, because ultimately any default between man and his fellow man disturbed one's personal connection with G-d. Wow, relationships would matter and we'd need to work on getting them right; how's that for a royal pain?

As with the people in my life, there was plenty of room for failure here—with G-d, too—and for success. In this G-dly domain, we were allowed wide appetites to consume and imbibe the workings of a Torah life. We were fed a satisfying menu of inspiration about goodness and greatness, and we dined on stories of our great leaders—both past and present. Each week, as we were treated to special foods for the Shabbat dinner and lunch meals including chicken matza-ball soup, *gefilte* fish, chopped liver and the meat, potatoes, and bean stew known as *cholent,* we were also served tantalizing thoughts about the weekly Torah portion that was read in the synagogue on that Saturday morning. This was particularly gratifying for me as I would answer my father's questions at the Shabbat meals, which he'd ask to stimulate our thirst for spiritual and intellectual growth. My efforts would usually attract his enthusiastic sing-song refrain, "Shifra knows it, Shifra knows it."

Clearly, I mattered in the Divine scheme of things, i.e., I knew that I had intrinsic worth as a human being, in particular as a growing Jewess. But that was not always satisfying enough, because it wasn't specific enough or individual enough to make a difference in this world. And it didn't carry royal entitlements.

As a non-queen, where was my core mattering? *The question kept me in its clutch, leaving me once again to feel so hurt by the core pain, the smallness of my being.*

Just not enough mattering to make life feel worthwhile. And this sucked the energy of many days, years really. As I grew older, I watched many of my acquaintances find ways to matter. They didn't marry into royalty, but they found ways to make their lives count. And while many women I knew drew energy from keeping up their appearance, most needed something more enduring to keep their lives engaging. Many felt strongly that raising their children, even if they were also holding down a moneymaking job, made their lives greatly matter. Others identified their purpose and worth, majorly or even exclusively, with their professional accomplishments in careers of medicine, mental health, law, technology, education, business, arts, and politics. With all the generation's ongoing guilt-inducing conflict swirling around these choices, known as the "mommy wars," I always thought work that is meaningful to you, that makes you feel your life matters, whether on the home front or outside of it, or both, is a huge gift, not a crime. Something to be celebrated, not condemned. In fact, I don't really understand how people thrive, or even survive, without some of that in their lives.

As for me, I could not think of any mattering to choose. And none was choosing me, either. I tried so hard over the years to understand how to have purpose, how to find it and feel it, but just as for Aunt Rosalie, the doors to personal mattering seemed to be closed. I knocked on the doors of diverse opinion-givers, such as career guides and spiritual mentors—male and female—of assorted religious bent. Very hard to say this, but few could lead the way, and some even obstructed it. No one was able to help me specify what I had to offer; some just told me to stop trying to be "special," just accept "ordinary." Keep your house and kids clean and fed, and call yourself a success. But cooking and cleaning weren't my interests, not to mention my skillset, leaving me at a huge disadvantage if my mattering truly lied there. They saw the same limitations I felt, but could not offer any clarity or hope about finding more of my purpose. Like the sales lady in the dress store who sized me up at age sixteen: "Hon, I am really sorry, but I have no idea how to dress you well. You are a hard fit." A trail of despair, shame, and hopelessness, *again*.

Could it be that I was asking too much of others? Can others really tell us who we are? I'd come to realize that many of us have no choice but to do it for ourselves. *We cannot depend on others to know our truth*; how hard is it for us to discover it for just ourselves?

And hard it was. Any purpose or profession conferring lots of letters before or after one's name would surely en"title" me, but when honestly considered, felt more like an attention-get-ting dress, showy with bragging rights, but that did not fit quite right. I knew a lot about ill-fitting clothes, particularly ones that were too small. If they didn't feel right, they wouldn't look good either. They'd ultimately cause more harm than help. And as far as I knew, one could not train to be a queen if they were not called into it. Or could they? *Could our choices build what circumstance didn't, and what might that look like?*

The questions kept recurring: How much mattering is enough? And where must it come from to register in our psyches as real and worthy? Would Ruth-like loyalty to G-d really confer a sense of royalty, of stature, of enduring value? And if it does, why doesn't it look like the royalty we know, that captures our hearts, striking us as large, though we know little of its true demands? Where we are called into service, with outward glamour and honor, all in the public eye? More, what happens if the mattering that is offered to us is different from the one we deeply wanted?

And maybe biggest of all, what right do I even have to ask these questions? Maybe I should just get on with life like everyone else? I would have, I really would have . . . if I could have gotten out of bed. These answers, I knew, were important to my well-being, to my mattering. *To my survival, even.*

CHAPTER EIGHT

The Soul
of the Matter

*I can say with conviction that the struggle which evil
necessitates is one of the greatest blessings . . .
It lets us into the soul of things.*

—HELEN KELLER

A Nation that Matters

I was told I belonged to "a holy nation" (Exodus 19:6) commonly known as the "chosen people." I'd come to understand that being a member of the "chosen nation" meant that I would ideally carry more moral, ethical, social, and financial responsibility than others, and for others. *It was a title, but never a free entitlement.*

Chosen. It is 2020; that word is hard to write, but not that hard to explain. To understand Judaism, and specifically the concept of chosen in this context, here is one Hebrew word: *Kedusha*, translating as holiness. It is around this concept of holiness that Judaism—and chosen-ness—is constructed.

By holiness, I mean that the Jew was chosen, designated, asked to be separate, consecrated for the particular purpose of keeping the Torah. Tasked with following this structured discipline for living a moral existence[6], the Jew commits to a G-d-centered existence around which his thinking, feeling, and actions are intimately directed. I had been schooled that G-d actually created His Torah—containing His Divine will—before He even created this world. In so doing, He intended for this world to be powered by the spiritual energy of the Torah. When the Jews accepted the Torah, they accepted to uphold the will of G-d as expressed in it. Love of G-d would have to equal loyalty, unequivocally.

Accepting the Torah would also mean we accept that this world is the corridor through which we pass to the next world, which is the true, eternal, and enduring one. Simply put, that is where the real palaces are, although I cannot tell you what they look like because I don't know.

But honestly, since I needed a nice place to live here in this world, I had to wonder: Was it possible to matter in both worlds? Whose status could be enduring and non-negotiable in both worlds? Couldn't be voted out or taken away? Specifically, is it possible that Aunt Rosalie didn't matter greatly here in this world, but matters there in the next? Could it be that some people matter here, but do not matter there? The Queen of England matters in this world, though have you ever wondered why a whole country of people agree to allow her the desires of her heart while she gives them nothing in tangible return (although she has decided to pay taxes, and the royal industry does bring in huge revenue to the country)?[7] What then to make of fame and fortune and status in this world? Is it all one big mirage?

---

6 Specifically, the Torah lays out both a system of beliefs and an intricate code of actions referred to as *Halacha*. Halacha, literally translated as "the path that one walks," is the collective body of Jewish religious laws derived from the Written and Oral Torah. Our Talmudic legal scholars, known as *Poskim*, spend their lives studying the Torah and guiding the Jewish nation in adhering to these G-d-given laws, His inner will for our lives.

7 And yet the Torah instructs us to say a blessing when one encounters a gentile monarch who rules lawfully, but who cannot be overruled and who has the power of life and death. "Blessed is G-d who has given of His glory to human beings."

It appears that humans are hard-wired to see and want with their eyes; it is the wiring of the soft, sensitive heart that allows one to see beyond, to have what is called vision. While man sees with his eyes, we are taught that G-d looks to the heart (I Samuel 16:7). That which the external I/eye beholds—the realities and currencies of this world—is the Divinely-designed veneer that convincingly lies above the "spireality" (my personal concoction describing the combination of spirit and reality).

It is the internality, however, that essentially defines us as humans. And if it is the spirit that bestows our worth, then I might have to rethink the question about my mattering, and my American ideas emphasizing image and façade, including outer measurements. For all this "thin is in," maybe thin or fat was not where it was at. I did know that the Hebrew word *middot*, character traits, also translated as measurements, suggesting a novel idea—that the measure of a person is his/her character, not physical dimension. Like the King (Martin Luther) eloquently expressed, *let people be judged not by the color of their skin, but by the content of their character* . . . Yes, I have a dream, too, and part of it wonders if we even should be judging others at all.

Diffusing this tension between opposites—the mind and the heart, the body and the soul, the external and the internal, the ephemeral and the eternal—demands the skills of a diplomatic negotiator. Each claims its right to be admired, to be dominant, to matter, to drive us.

This much I was starting to now know: If I cared to train in this art of diplomacy, I'd need to commit to G-d's wisdom as expressed in the Torah. The Torah would instruct me how to appreciate the tension, to give each its due, ultimately blending two disparate entities into a harmonious whole. Friction would turn to fortune, pain to purpose, ordinary to extraordinary, and mundane to magnificent. *What is to give light must endure burning*, said Viktor Frankl.

I was beginning to understand that there is a way to matter in both worlds. Or more simply put, to make both worlds matter. And while I cannot understand the British people's rationale for handing all that mattering on a silver platter—or is it a gold one—to their queen, I'd take some cues about mattering from my own people. And here I offer it to you.

Consecrated Ground

The theme of mattering was now playing out in a bigger arena outside of myself. I was acutely aware that the Jewish people both mattered and did not matter. This was an idea very close for comfort. Historically, they were a people who were alternatively privileged and persecuted. They were a people who, by the rights and rules of this world, should not have mattered, but they did. A nation small in number, poorly treated for much of history, beginning as slaves in Egypt—and yet, as mentioned above, they are called "chosen."

I came to think about the Jewish people as the firstborn among G-d's family of nations. Maybe that is why they are charged with being a "light unto the nations" (Isaiah 42:6). You know this already: I am not a firstborn; thank you, G-d. But I know from watching my brother Aaron and Brenna, each a firstborn in their gender, that they seemed more closely connected to the will of our parents. They were certainly watching over us siblings, and in their good moments, were very kind and accountable for our welfare. They were responsible to channel wisdom and well-being to us. (After all, it was Aaron who relieved me of my crib harness, giving my free spirit the space to breathe and toddle. And Brenna who supported my fourth-grade crying spells at my locker until the bell rang.) We—our parents and the other children—held them more accountable when they disappointed us because we expected them, fairly or unfairly, to be more evolved than the rest of us. In their ideal state, firstborns are depended upon for their principled and loyal upholding of their parents' will. They are doubly accountable, both to their parents and to their siblings. And because of that, I could agree that they deserved the privileges they had—such as getting a driving license first and having a credit card of their own. But when something goes wrong, the other children instinctively and guiltlessly lay blame at their feet as they are held up as an example for the others.

As part of this nation, I'd have to be willing to remain apart in certain ways, not as an elitist, but as an *idealist*—not looking down at others, but setting my sights upwards. I would learn that the highest contribution my people were invited to give the world was in the realm of morality. *The essential beauty of my nation is its soulful heart, which radiates beauty from within.* With three defining characteristics listed in the Talmud—modesty/inner dignity, compassion, and kindness—the Jewish nation is equipped to bequeath the world its first-born sense of justice and uprightness based on G-d's Torah given at Mt. Sinai.

And evidently it has. American scholar (of Irish descent) and historian Thomas Cahill writes in *The Gift of the Jews: How a Tribe of Desert Nomads Changed the Way Everyone Thinks and Feels,* "The role of the West in humanity's history is singular. Because of this, the role of the Jews, the inventors of Western culture, is also singular . . . theirs is a unique vocation. . . . The Jew started it all—and by 'it' I mean so many of the things we care about, the underlying values that make all of us, Jew and gentile, believer and atheist, tick." He credits the Jewish concept that men and women are individuals with unique destinies, as the one that informed the Declaration of Independence. That indeed, Western society is built on many of the moral principles first found in the Torah, undergirding our democratic sensitivities and rights.

And if this is true, that the Jew has a mission statement that has uniquely influenced the world, might it be true that all peoples of the world have one, too? And that, indeed, every person can search for, and find, his special qualities vital to developing a life that matters. Isn't it worthwhile to reflect on our individual and collective defining qualities so that we can all contribute purposefully to the world at large? To build ourselves and each other into large worlds.

Not always easy. Upholding this mission and status of the first-born evidently does not happen without cost. History has placed the Jew at the center of a harsh reality of double standards, and sometimes impossible ones. I have learned two things witnessing Jewish history. First, Jewish people aren't perfect (does perfection exist?) but Torah is, and will lead us as close to the Divine mandate of human perfection as we allow it. Second, on many occasions, we'd have to suffer and bear patiently this separateness in many harsh ways. This is not a treatise on why Jews are often the victims of hate—somehow evoking fear, ill will, or dislike in the hearts of others—for I am not able to speak for other nations; I can barely speak for mine. But it seems to me, that where Jews are concerned, the world's job is to remind the firstborns who they are—in case they manage to conveniently forget.

How and why would Jews forget who they are? Why would any human being forget who they essentially are; that G-d breathed a piece of Himself into each of us, a soul? And that therefore, *it matters greatly to be human because our lives have a Divine purpose and, if recognized and honored, a promising future. For all humanity—because we are all family, children of G-d.*

Actually, is it really that difficult to understand why or how we might forget? If we never adequately understood our purpose, how could we fully connect to it? Or maybe we override it for more compelling reasons, like momentary lapses of not feeling or finding our purpose? Or just maybe, there is a safety in feeling powerless to change, relieving us of the heavy burden of being responsible to our missions of humanity? *But being Jewish, or human for that matter, isn't a disposable piece of identity.* Like my clothes, it may not always fit well, but I guess we have to figure out how to wear it well, or it gets figured out for us by G-d through His other children, who sometimes know better than we what He wants from each of us, including His oldest.

There is a story told about a painter who was working day after day on his artistic masterpiece, up on a mountaintop. His friend accompanied him there, sitting quietly off to the side as the painter did his work. One day, the painter stood up to take a good look at his portrait, stepping further and further back to assess and admire it from all different angles. His friend suddenly charged past him, ripping the painting to shreds, which ignited in the painter a surge of painful outrage towards his friend.

"What have you done? You have destroyed my life's work! Why?" he cried in pain.

"My dear friend, I saved your life. Because I value you," whispered his friend. "Had you taken one more step back, you'd have fallen off the edge of the cliff."

G-d saves us, sometimes even from ourselves, when necessary. Because we matter to Him . . . and our lives are the masterpieces we are creating.

Shabbat and Smilestones

Speaking of consecrated ground and masterpieces, keeping the Shabbat is just that for the Jewish people: a holy space of time honoring G-d's supreme achievement of creating the world in six days, and then creating something called "rest" on the Seventh. The Shabbat is famous throughout the world as the day of the week that the Jews "can't do anything." No electronics, no cooking, no driving, no work, and worst of all . . . no shopping.

"The Jewish Sabbath is, on the far side of its tough disciplines, a day of ennobled pleasure; that is hard to achieve but worth all the efforts it calls for. In our religion, it is the keystone of the arch of symbol through which we pass to seek the great truths."[8]

In actuality, it is a *holy* day—chosen and set apart for something different. Saying "no" to those other activities allows us to say "yes" to the blessings of plugging in and recharging to something other-worldly. Remember the two worlds, this one and the next? On this one day each week, we consider how to function in our lives with more spirit, as we stop undistracted to consider a bit what the next world might be like. We sample

---

8 *This is My G-d*, by Herman Wouk p. 52.

it in accord with G-d's will for what we can do and shouldn't do, much of which we can grow to understand and appreciate. We sample concepts such as: What will it be like to have our work finished, when we can just luxuriate in the expanse of our spirits, in a G-dly presence, with souls being the dominant force, not bodies? With *mitzvot,* not money, being the currency? With our mattering being a foregone conclusion, not an ongoing conversation?

There are many ways for us all to bring light into this world, because there are many acts of spirit we can do. As a woman who lights the candles ushering in the Shabbat, this is one of mine. And when I do touch fire to flame, the light beckons me into the royal palace of Shabbat, where G-d resides in close proximity. (It is axiomatic that G-d is most comfortable choosing holy places to frequent. Shabbat is a space in time that attracts G-d's presence because of its sacred, set-aside nature.) And yes, it enlarges my life.

There are many ways to honor the Shabbat, such as the previously mentioned consumption of special once-a-week foods. Wearing fine clothing is another valuable way, which for me usually means wearing a long, free-flowing silk or velvet robe, leaving me comfortable enough to think about G-d, and not my tight-fitting waistband. And in my family, we had a home-grown idea that I don't think upset G-d in any way: we'd wear a special dress-watch that was gifted to us when we turned twelve. Upon the occasion of our Bat Mitzvah, our first major *smilestone*, we were invited to the jewelry store to choose a dress-watch of our liking. This watch was to be worn in honor of the weekly Shabbat, the holidays, and other special occasions.

Choosing my watch for Shabbat was more complicatd than I would have liked. This was not the first time I had been inside a jewelry store. On occasion, I had been allowed to accompany my mother when she'd decide it was time for her to adorn her long, slender fingers with a new ring. It usually came after a stint of steady, hard work in her office. A new purchase would offer her the chance to indulge her elegant side while prodding her back to her desk to begin anew the rigor and discipline of making numbers match up. Her fingers must have ached beneath the tasks of constant typing, calculating, and computing. What better way to massage those weary fingers than with a new friend that sparkled while she worked? She held out her options, in front of the gold mirror strategically sitting on top of the showcase, to the admiring "oohs" and "aahs" of a staff eager to fill their weekly quota in one hour by encouraging her to treat herself to a few rings. Meanwhile, I took the time to familiarize myself with the lonely stones not being eyed. As the saleswomen, coated in heavy Dior perfume, moved their crimson-painted nails laboring under heavy jewels of their own, I amused myself by learning to differentiate between the pearl, the diamond, and the emerald. But opal was my favorite. With an opal, I didn't have to decide on just one color because it was a stunning combo of blue and green, streaked with salmon and white and other colors, depending on how the sun caught its center.

Actually, there was one other stone I liked well, and that was because it was in my first piece of jewelry. My maternal "queen" grandmother made it her practice to buy for each of her granddaughters a birthstone ring at the age of nine. That was how I knew early on that I was a Scorpio, beginning my lifelong affinity for the color of intense topaz. The thing about jewelry I had not yet known (but would learn numerous times over the years, especially after marriage) was that you have to be really careful with it, because somehow these pricey colored stones tend to get more easily lost than found. It didn't take long for my first topaz to meander down the bathroom sink drain, ultimately being retrieved by a spare hanger—much to my relief, and everyone else's, too.

A Holy Problem on My Hands

So when it came time to select my Bat Mitzvah watch, the lady pointed to the showcase. It was a fairly quick process at first; I narrowed it down to two possibilities. The first watch wowed me with its unconventionally oblong, elegant, brilliant topaz face held together by a showy gold strap. The other calmed me with its warm, playful round center, set in the emotionally strong color of coral and secured by a band of interconnected links. I was acutely aware that the gold band would attract the admiration of those whom I'd make sure would see it, while the other would hug my hand close, loyally, without undue attention.

It was here at the showcase, looking longingly at the two faces lying in my hands, that I became aware of a big problem: How would I ever decide on just one guy to marry? They both suited me well, their fit closely aligned with my tastes and preferences. How did all the married people I knew make that decision, and then seem happy with it? (I remembered that a "holy" life would mandate loyalty to one spouse; remember that holy means set apart, designated for a particular purpose.) Would it really be possible to decide on one, without thinking back to the other? What part of me would I be forced to leave behind?

To circumvent discomfort on that day, I promised myself that while I'd buy Mr. Elegant to wear on *Shabbat*, I'd soon enough buy a simpler one for the weekdays, similar to the one I was leaving behind. I must have known that husbands wouldn't be interchangeable by the days of the week, but I decided to revisit that in a few short years—at the age of eighteen.

Choice Decisions

Decisions move our daily lives, from moment to moment, day to day, stage to stage. And we all need to make them. They are sometimes painful to make, but we cannot opt out. *And it is our decisions that show what matters to us.* It was in the jewelry store that I learned something valuable about decision-making: Often in life, small and big decisions are not made in favor of what you like best—for it is often hard to directly know that. They are made by ruling out what you don't like until the happy moment of clarity shows you what you do. Like a sculptor's work, one has to cut away what does not belong, what does not matter, revealing the image that does.

Like Ruth who turned her heart on her father's royal home to embrace her individual mattering—chiseling away at her life's work which would grow into a royal home of enduring eternal worth—we all have the opportunity to create masterpieces. And yes, each journey is completely distinct. As Martha Graham said, "There is only one of you in all time, and this expression is unique. And if you block it, it will never exist through any other medium, and it will be lost." Biblically expressed, "One man's kingdom cannot encroach upon another, not even a hair's breadth." (Babylonian Talmud Brachot 48b)

Incidentally, if you wish to glimpse your kingdom, look at your name. The Torah tells us that parents are divinely inspired when they bestow a name on their newborn child. And that a name can tell us much about our mission, because G-d calls each of us by name "like the stars He sets forth." (Psalms 147:4)

Each soul has a kingdom of choices to make, to rule over, to arbitrate, and to answer for. And to celebrate. Separate from everyone else, holy in that way. And in my book, I call that *royal*. If life hasn't yet given you the big circumstances, you make the big choices that will transform fate to destiny. *Fate is small; destiny is large.*

And by the way, did I mention that my name, Malka, means "queen?"

CHAPTER NINE
Riding the Loneliness

At the innermost core of all loneliness is a deep and powerful yearning for union with one's lost self.
— BRENDAN FRANCIS, poet

OUR INNER KINGDOM—it's a large place. Lots of riches live there, amidst multiple feuding entities, enough to last our lifetime. One such entity called *loneliness* lives there. Even if one has all the mattering this world has to offer, it still cannot protect us from that feeling of loneliness that intrudes like bursts of willful, dark clouds puffing across a gold sky.

Finding our mattering requires strength, strategy, and stamina to capture our individuality, and to recapture the largeness of who we are. It is often a lonely sport . . . other people may not care, and even if they do, they cannot give us a specific road map.

It was becoming clear to me that loneliness was taking me to places that were not healthy for me, in my relationship with food, and, as it turned out, with boys. I'd come to understand how loneliness—and its twin, emptiness—were leaving me vulnerable and bringing me to a place that was morally compromised, emotionally too.

To be human is to be lonely. In the words of the American spiritual teacher Ram Dass, "We're all just walking each other home." *We travel through life together, alone.* Not always a bad thing. It has been said by poet May Sarton that *loneliness* is the poverty of self, *solitude* is the richness of self. It is how we use the experience, how we fill that inner space that will allow us to weather the unwelcome, but inevitable, inner storms. I'd learn a few things about this soon enough.

Timely Message?

When my parents gave me that watch for my Bat Mitzva, I don't think it was with the intention of teaching me how to make decisions about marriage. So why did they give this to me? Besides adorning me with a concrete way to honor the Shabbat, I surmised it was a subtle message that as we were growing into young ladies, we were becoming more accountable for our choices. Using our time wisely was certainly one huge choice in growing a worthwhile life.

Teenage years are notorious for finding ways to misspend time, and while I certainly enjoyed wearing my watch, I got its timely message later than most girls I knew. My teenage years were dotted with activities that were not meant to be part of an Orthodox girl's formative years. But I was in a restless class, the likes of which my school administration had admitted were the brightest, most willful, limit-testing bunch of middle school girls that they had seen in years. The ease with which some of us found things to do outside the accepted range was a growing class-wide problem.

In truth, school was designed to leave us with little spare time. With a dual curriculum that kept us at our desks from 9 a.m. until 4:45 p.m. four days a week, and half-days on Friday and Sunday, not much discretionary time was meant to be ours. Doing our homework, and maybe offering an occasional, begrudging, helping hand in the home, busied us at night. Add to that extracurricular involvements such as volunteering in nursing homes and hospitals, taking a weekly music, art, or dance class, plus generous doses of mall shopping for modest but stylish clothes—and our teenage calendars should have been happy. Frequenting Sunday baseball games downtown at Oriole Park (later Camden Yards) was a personal favorite pastime—once even having my eyeglass case signed by Hall of Famer first baseman Eddie Murray and colleagues.

Summers sent most of my friends to sleepover camps, located six hours away in the Catskill Mountains. But not my siblings and me. Not one of us wanted to leave home, although I have no one clear reason for explaining why not. Was it that our housekeeper would not be coming, leaving us with the unthinkable responsibility to clean our own clothes and make our own beds? Maybe it was because we did have a great deal of independence, a fringe benefit of having super busy parents. We kept our own time clocks, sleeping and rising as we desired. This welcome lack of structure allowed me to megadose on food, sleep, and television, which kept me busy, if not content. Why pay lots of cash to give away your summer freedom to a faraway authority that mandates your daily schedule with rules, limits and consequences?

Hard to believe, but I also signed up for summer school, as if the rest of the year's academic misery was not sufficient. Taking Mark Twain's advice to never let school stand in the way of learning, I took the opportunity to sample more learning without the rigors of competitive testing and the grueling structure of the regular school day. Truth be told, if I ever did learn how to write a decent paragraph, it was at this preppy summer school that taught me the Latin roots of words and the more relevant sport of bending words to my liking. I also came to admire the conservative, understated attire that my academic-minded, Ivy-educated teachers wore, especially the sporty Lacoste polo shirt with the green crocodile logo, the hallmark of the classic preppy uniform.

To be sure, I still had lots of spare time to do plenty of pleasure-eating: leftover cheesy macaroni, pistachio and chocolate ice cream, and creamy candy bars sitting impatiently in our friendly breadbox. Additionally, I did some volunteering at the local health clinic, a position I abruptly ended after two days due to a developing foot problem. Technically, it was a "vain" problem: specifically, my new, stylish three-inch clogs impeded the stance needed for volunteering.

And of course, all year round, I maintained a diligent schedule of watching television. Summers had me hooked on *General Hospital's* Luke and Laura loving it up, with the show's writers often leaving me anxiously hanging for the night, to find out the inner workings of their never-lukewarm romance. Then I had my basic lesson in "social studies" from the evening dramas of *Dynasty* and *Knots Landing,* which featured the lesser side of humans whose relationships were fraught with disloyalty, angst, and hurt. I did this relationship-training solo; I don't know why my siblings didn't join me in savoring these valuable life lessons in how to hurt others and go astray. Brenna just sat on the red velvet living room couch in a consistent and conscientious trance, doing her homework while cracking her gum as if it were the guitar strings she had learned to pluck. Though I have tried my whole life, I have not been able to play the chewing gum beneath my teeth with her same musical tenor and balance. Aaron had no homework; remember, he didn't go to school. (Not to worry, he woke up in time to attend law school.) As for Sima, I am not sure if she did her homework. But if she did, it was on her bed, with the phone cradled in one hand and a bag of candy in the other.

Lonely Hearts Attract Daring Friends

Watching people mess up their lives could have helped me clean up mine. But it is pretty clear that we humans have to make our own mistakes, generously called "experience," in order to grow and develop.

For parents who were real estate professionals, mine realized a bit too late that in my case, *location, location, location* was not a good sell when it came to their daughter keeping herself on the straight and simple path . . . if such a path did indeed exist for me. For my dream life, I was in prime location. We lived right down the street from a boys' dormitory that housed twenty-five teenage boys who themselves had extra empty time on their hands—more than enough to strike up relationships with my friends and me.

And that was how inevitably it happened that my curious teenage path meandered to dorm room #105, wherein resided the school's coolest guy, by my friends' estimation. Leo was a high school junior, three years older than me, with streaky blond hair and cloudless, sky-blue eyes whose brawn and vulnerability co-existed in that elusive, but irresistible energy called charisma. He was present when I spoke to him, often smoothing out my fears with his two hands, held the way an orchestra leader closes out a song, "Don't worry, it will work itself out." He knew how to give a compliment easily, without overdoing it, "Shifra, you are looking happy today. Pretty, too, in that color." He suffered from no lack of confidence, which was especially evident when he'd slow down his speaking, knowing that others would want and wait for his words. And most alluring for me, those eyes, with a subtle and mysterious twinkle, held his heart in them. That was how I could know what he was feeling. And by the look in his eyes, I knew he liked that about me.

The age difference between us, a junior high and a middle-schooler, did not strike me as inappropriate, though looking back, it tells me much about my decision-making when I was lonely. What I knew was that his full, soft-looking lips spoke soothingly to a girl who was lonely and unsure how to be and not to be, at the same time. Showing up in his life gave me a place to be, though I wasn't sure what to do there. Not sure where I fit into the life of a compelling, energetic male always in search of his next thrill. But he was there to teach me how to hold a cigarette between my lips and inhale just deep enough to release teenage tensions into the giddy night air, and to receive my handwritten notes of admiration. My notes told him, "How lucky I feel to have you in my life," "I admit I am a bit intimidated by you because you are just so cool," and the big one, "Do you still like me?" I was slightly aware that he had an eleventh-grade girlfriend in my school, but I was a close second (if not a distant first). Meaning, he had a place in his heart for me, and I was happy to take it. Lonely hearts make accommodations when necessary.

The month of November belongs to Scorpios. And this Scorpio belonged to Leo.

One night, as I slipped by the dorm's hired guard who was sleeping, drunk, or just paid off by the guys to look the other way, I got to see up close the inner workings of a teenage boy's habitat. First, let me just tell you that the inside of a boy's dorm is loud, playing jarring noise they called music, meant to stir them to adult places they are not at all ready to responsibly go. It is also unkempt, and meant to impress no one. Perched on the edge of his unmade bed, I delighted in watching Leo smooth a cucumber scrub mask over his face to keep his light complexion cool and clear.

"I thought only girls did that kind of vain stuff," I remarked.

"No," he stated. "Boys also look in mirrors."

I was glad males looked in mirrors, too. It made me happy to know that boys also had to concern themselves with appearances, that it was not the exclusive burden of the girl.

Grease had been the musical in my eighth-grade year that captured America's collective heart, and the song "Hopelessly Devoted to You" was my thirteen-year-old refrain. There was something of that shy, straight, waiting-to-happen Sandy character (played by Olivia Newton-John) in me, while Leo embodied the wild, but sensitive energy of Danny (played by John Travolta). I lost count of how many times we watched that movie, substituting ourselves as the main characters in our own drama. Like Sandy, I had to make the choice to embrace the braver, edgier part of myself that I knew Leo saw in me, and wanted. It sure felt better than loneliness.

Warm Heart, Cool Head

While my chilled, wise father invited dorm boys to join us at *Shabbat* lunch meals, Leo somehow never made it onto the guest list. I would just have to handle my own invitations, I realized. I remember the night I skipped out to see him, under the pretense of visiting my "birthstone queen" grandmother who lived eight houses away. It happened to be my birthday. When I returned, my parents—sitting on that same red velvet couch in the living room that had already absorbed years of family drama—asked me where I had been.

"Just visiting Grandma. She sends regards."

My father said, "Just hung up with her. Funny thing, she told us she has a birthday card for you; to please come get it." Realizing they must have checked their suspicion with her, I resorted to one of my favorite "social studies" lessons from television—the right to remain silent. That tactic must have inspired a wise silence in my father, who said, "Shif, Happy Birthday." With that, I considered myself to have had a lucky, if not happy, birthday.

Staged as random, coincidental meetings, Leo and I would frequent the Pac-Man arcade machines tucked away at the rear of the nearby pharmacy where one could not be as easily seen. For the uninformed, i.e., anyone younger than thirty, Pac-Man was the pre-Internet game developed in 1980 that reached unparalleled fame by the 1990s. It was named after the legendary video game icon stemming from the Japanese word, *pakku*, to chomp. According to its creator, Toru Iwatani, his brain was entrepreneurially stimulated when noticing that his cut-out piece of eaten pizza looked similar to a head with its mouth open. (Who eats pizza slowly enough to notice the shape of the as-yet-to-be devoured piece? But I guess that's what separates the entrepreneurial from the epicurean.) For twenty-five cents per game, we were *pakkuing* for hours until Pac-Man ate up his dots, along with globs of our time and money. But we had to help Pac-Man race around the maze while eating his supper, before he would be eaten by Blinky, Pinky, Inky, and Clyde.

Secretive phone calls and low-profile, in-person meetings with my new friend moved along my first months of eighth grade very happily, if not naively, on my part. We had a growing friendship as we shared our school woes and absolute admiration for Baltimore's dazzling fall foliage, which looked like someone had taken a box of magic markers to color the leaves in striking hues of orange, red, yellow, and brown. And even though the age difference between us was three years, I don't think it bothered me. I had often chosen to strike up a conversation with people older than me—a skill I learned from my Diet Workshop days when I was always the youngest in the group. Or maybe I just chose not to care. What did age have to do with anything when you genuinely felt a connection to someone, and it seemed mutual? So what if he had a driver's license, while I had just celebrated my Bat-Mitzva within the past year? But, ultimately, we were on two different emotional wave-lengths.

On one late November night after our nightly stroll and smoke, Leo and I settled ourselves down on a hill not too far away from my backyard to talk things over. A budding relationship needs discussion, doesn't it? His beige cable-knit sweater had these round, light-wood buttons that were begging to be slightly undone, if only to allow me to lean in a bit closer for this face-to-face conversation. As I reached just to undo one, he took my hand and got us moving again to a nearby bush. He was done talking. Stylishly cupping my chin, holding my teenage naiveté with his experienced hand, he had a message of his own he wanted to communicate. His lips invited mine to continue the conversation a little differently than I had anticipated. He had the upper hand, but I had the final say. Not ready to be dominated by his desire, I ran home, abandoning him to the sudden bite of an unseasonably cold Scorpion night.

It was then that I figured out my first lesson in romance: You cannot be touched until you are ready. And that would not be with him, because just a few days later he was inexplicably expelled from school, and although someone slipped a letter to me that told me how much he'd miss me, I never saw him again. I never did find out conclusively why he was "let go" by the school, but my guess is that his extracurricular involvement with girls and other distracting activity I didn't even know about disturbed the administration, who decided they could no longer overlook his infringements on their "no relationships with girls" policy.

After running away from him, I wondered why I, hyper-alert to every shadow of danger, had not anticipated that matters would come to a head. For a religious girl whose duty it was not to mix with the opposite gender and certainly to keep away from any physical contact, I knew this was called a transgression. Why did I allow it? It should be obvious by now, and not the subject of too much internal debate: I was lonely, and I needed more to fill my life. Leo found a way to bring me along in a continuum of living and learning, moving steadily along the edge of danger where he walked all too easily. With three years to his advantage, Leo didn't expect me to have his know-how, just a willingness to be shown how. And I was willing. Any reprieve from the intense chill of a lonely heart was welcome.

Minding My Mistakes

Not all school lessons are created equal.

Using Torah texts as a basis for their lessons, our Hebrew teachers had spent a lot of time teaching us about the lives and lusts, strivings and stirrings, victories and vices of our Biblical ancestors. Just as soldiers study past wars to prepare for combat, albeit on different terrain, we explored their moral victories and failings so we could become warriors of our spirits. We would learn from their mistakes; why repeat theirs, when we could have the drama of making our own? I'm not saying we'd never repeat their mistakes . . . always a possibility. But it was nice to innovate our own failings, too. And to even repeat them, as necessary.

I knew that it was okay to err, that greatness lies in facing your mistake so it can lead you to higher ground. Although I was blind to the fact that food was filling my void, I was able to begin to connect that my loneliness was moving me to form inappropriate relationships with boys. And that it might not be healthy for me to continue with this. Brenna knew that Leo existed in my life, and had alerted me months earlier, "He is going to try to kiss you. You better stop this." I laughed at her concern, knowing full well I had no intention of stopping this friendship.

Aside from Brenna, our teachers had begun to discuss with us that touch can superficially induce the illusion of a connection. Similar to the phone texting and media socializing we do today, we often create pseudo-bonds of intimacy that allow us to think we are connected to others more meaningfully than we really are. Leo and I would become bonded, but not properly secured. Like Super Glue that can join two pieces of a broken plate, restoring it to a whole, it can also dangerously stick two fingers together, impairing the function of both. Super Glue bonds instantly and indiscriminately.[9]

So in my post-Leo life, where other boys flirted in and out, I had boundaries that I kept: no physical contact. With the #MeToo movement, the world has woken up to this concept of the importance of creating physical boundaries to protect men and women. If only my friends and I had appreciated this sooner.

Pushed to the Edge

Ironically, mono, the kissing disease, came along that summer, courtesy of a non-sterilized mannekin in a CPR class. Uncomfortable as it was, I was glad I made sure to get it in the summer, so I would not fall behind in schoolwork at the start of the new academic year. There were days of working incredibly hard, so beyond my limit, that my geography teacher Mrs. Pulsar—known to happily push any student to the edge—documented her concern for me in a progress report: "There were times I worried that Shifra pushed herself past the point of healthy ambition. Excellent as she was in her studies, I was not sure she could differentiate when to push and when to pull back with herself and, frankly, with others." Thanks, Mrs. Pulsar, for that subjective lesson in the lay of my land. That little assessment

---

9. *The Magic Touch*, Gila Manolson, Targum Press, Israel, 1999, p. 25-26.

notwithstanding, she was one of my two favorite teachers on account of her preppy clothing style—brown leather penny loafers, burgundy polo sweater, and navy blue blazer with three flat gold buttons on each sleeve hanging over her chair—and her energetic, organized teaching manner. I insisted that I'd never become a teacher; they clearly were too desperate to be heard. But if I did, I'd want to be like her, loafers and all.

After crash-studying for test after test and writing up lengthy essays and lab reports, I'd routinely fall asleep at my desk between midnight and 2 a.m., which left me with a lingering, head-hurting tiredness upon awakening at seven in the morning. This was accompanied by bouts of intense coldness that one or even two hot baths before school could not wash away. It was excruciatingly difficult to leave the intense, comforting heat of the early morning water, but school was waiting for me and, somehow, that mattered. I gave myself no choice. (To this day, hot baths are my first refuge from the coldness of life, even though I have mostly relieved them of the excessive burden of comforting me. They do a good job warming me, but sometimes just a good rest in there, in the hum of the womblike swish, is all I need to feel safe, un-lonely, and very content. Yes, the idea of returning to the cozy in-utero waters of the pre-birth state of life is sometimes compelling. I cannot remember from so long ago, but if I must guess, I'd say the fetus is very content not having to share its space or food with anyone else. No loneliness there, except for those few who do feel lonely and then just order a twin.)

Loneliness persisted. My high school years were spent alternating between my desk and the scale. My desk was producing the A+s I desperately sought, but the scale would not bend to my control. Weight gains, weight loss, and weight regains were constant companions as I went in and out of dieting plans, none of which I could figure how to make work for me. My eating got less logical by the day. Breakfasts consisted of that now defunct Alba chocolate-powdered drink, to which I'd just add a bit of water to make a thick paste that I could finger-spoon into my mouth. Lunch usually featured one or two sugar sweeties, *pleasure pops* as I called them, from the canteen, and an apple that one of my friends knew to save for me to stave off my dieting hunger. Diet Cokes refreshed me at the 3:00 bell, keeping me alive until our 5:00 dismissal. There were days when I had total control of my eating, tempting me to believe that I finally sampled the taste of dieting success, that I was well on my way to the smaller size. And then, I'd hit a troubling thought or an anxious moment, and my fingers instinctively, subconsciously, put my work pen down on my desk and found refuge in the kitchen. I would grab something, anything, to stop the downward pull. By the end of many school nights, jars of peanut butter, bags of Kit-Kats, and boxes of chocolate chip cookies lay empty and eerily quiet, at my side. These were my friends who objectively restored the delicious balance undone by the pressures of unending, demanding perfection in school while miserably failing to matter at home.

The fatter I became, the heavier my non-mattering weighed on me. Unentitled once again to nice clothing, I fell back into the small life of dividing my days into two categories: the dieting days and the bingeing ones. And my selfhood was segregated between gaining weight and losing it. I was being sucked into a lonely black hole from which I had no way of getting out. In a state of feeling remote from myself and from others, I was living between the numbers on the scale and the letter grades on my school papers.

Unbecoming is a perfect word to describe my life at this time. Unbecoming suggests an ill fit. When my grandfather and birthstone queen grandmother made a cross-country road trip to bring me back a light green and brown floral bikini from the California land of stylish bathing suits, I eagerly tried it on and heard them approve, "Oh Shif, this is so *becoming* on you." They were remarking on its congruence, on the rightness of fit for me. It fit everything about me at that time, including my body and my personality. It looked right to them, probably because it felt right to me.

Unbecoming is a lack of congruence, a lack of rightness that is not only unflattering to the outside eye, but badly wounds one's inner core which cannot grow and become. It is stunted, or even adversely undone. When that happens, a great loneliness finds its way inside the spirit. And when loneliness settles in, healthy boundaries have a way of getting moved around, often inappropriately. Unbecoming and loneliness fed off each other, making it a cycle that kept me going in circles of despair with no exit in sight, once again.

This was a pattern I had seen in Aunt Rosalie—the more rejected and lonely she felt, the more her boundaries became distorted, allowing her to disturb others. She didn't retreat quietly, but instead exhibited combative and crazy-making behaviors that would have others take in deep breaths of frustration before finally lashing out at her.

Testing Limits

Bouncing between limits and no limits in my dietary life was leaving me in a battle-fatigued zone of non-mattering, having to fight for the right to matter, to believe that I could make it, and that my life had value. Overeating, overworking, and under-mattering were the natural order of my life. My friends didn't seem to be suffering these great tensions. The overwhelming majority showed up to life with bouncy confidence, nonchalant attitudes about their grades, and cooperative, smaller waists. My mattering came at a high cost, pushing for excellent grades and starving to drop weight, an attempt that was as erratic as a non-sober driver weaving between lines he can hardly see.

Always having to push back against the deficit of hope, I was prone to carrying a surplus of fear. Battling my nature of easily giving in and giving up depleted my emotional energy, often trampling on my own healthy boundaries for self-care and compassion. Too many times I resorted to using condemning, hate-filled language towards myself, and sometimes others. And again, this made me think of Aunt Rosalie, whose own *unbecoming* so often could be seen in her pushing past the boundaries and limits of others. She didn't seem to be moving forward or upward in life, but rather backward and downward. She could safely drive a car, but she sure weaved in and out of people's emotional blind spots and comfort zones, leaving them angry with her for driving out of her space and trespassing theirs.

I think I understand something about her . . . that when we are out of balance, it is hard to consider or care about others, or even ourselves, in the optimal way. In her lonely and rejected existence, she could not always function in a way that was deemed reasonable and respectable to others. She often could not properly estimate those spaces in others, because hers had become so blurred. For example, listening into others' conversations was a customary and casual habit of hers, but a definite intrusion on others' privacy. Reflecting on my relationship with Leo, I could see how this played out similarly for me. My own healthy boundaries were overwhelmed by my lonely and empty inner spaces which grew and overtook my moral sense. And emotionally, I allowed a relationship that wasn't in my best interests to bring me a false sense of fulfillment.

Harboring Hope for Freedom

Leveraging our highest ground in the face of the overwhelming downward pull of emptiness is no simple matter. We have little choice but to continue to try, and to hope that we will crack the code of our loneliness leading to our personal freedom.

As I continued groping in considerable adolescent darkness and confusion, I understood how much I was at the mercy of my own untrained and, at times, unrestrained, impulses. I had little idea how to circumvent this emotional gravity that had me on the roller coaster of mattering and not mattering, all precariously riding on externally driven tracks.

CHAPTER TEN

Driving Away the Emptiness

They cannot scare me with their empty spaces
Between stars—on stars where no human race is;
I have it in me so much nearer home
To scare myself with my own desert places.

—ROBERT FROST

GETTING MY DRIVER'S LICENSE, I was sure, would prove helpful to this inner condition of loneliness—and its concurrent feeling of emptiness. Doesn't every teenager wait for that first morsel of real freedom? I was certain this freedom would pave the road to bigger freedoms, and specifically to the feeling of fullness for which I was hungering. At the very least, I could now access more recreation and food with greater ease and speed—and secrecy. Maybe I could also finally somehow figure out how to feed that recurring emptiness and loneliness. Both were sad, unwanted states of feeling: empty, in that I contained nothing of inner worth, and lonely because I couldn't share anything of real value, making me unwanted, unneeded, remote and disconnected from the world of purpose and meaningful accomplishment. And no hope danced on my horizon. Since freedom by design expands possibilities and choices, I reasoned it could offer me relief from those spasms of emotion that were paining and draining me too much of the time. At the very least, freedom could drive me to distraction, a short term destination called relief. Whether or not it could take me the distance to totally alleviate it was a test-drive about to happen.

Master Key to Freedom and Fullness?

As Driver's Ed was the first step towards getting that license for freedom, I engaged the services of Mr. Wyman who had taught Brenna how to drive. She managed to get her license on the first try, and in my estimation was faring quite well—having only taken off one side-view mirror from our Buick Estate station wagon, as well as the bumper of another car in an undramatic fender bender, in nearly two whole years of her driving.

Early on, Mr. Wyman let me know he could see that teaching me wouldn't be simple. Not sure how he could know that, but I guess things looked a bit different to him from his perch in the front passenger seat where more than once he surely convinced himself he'd die trying to teach me. Come to think of it, it may have been right after he spent a long time telling me we'd be entering a big intersection. It was a four-way deal where you patiently waited for your green light, but when it came, you had to go through it—traffic and all. I assured him that I was cool with that. Except for one little thing I forgot to take into consideration: my pervasive fear. The light decided to turn green and there was a lot of traffic, about fifty cars more than my liking, so I pressed on the brake, bringing us to a stubborn standstill right in the middle of this impatient intersection. Hearing his command, "When I tell you to go, you do," I did finally manage to pull us through this, trying to get him to admit that it was better that way than speeding, which would have just gotten us a ticket. If only Mr. Wyman would see me now . . . I routinely press on that gas pedal as yellow becomes red, and maybe even a moment or two after that.

If only he would have had the confidence in me that Grandma Lolly did. She started us all behind the wheel in a

Richmond parking lot at the good age of thirteen or four-teen. In between her pack of smokes each day, she had ample time to extend this Southern hospitality on our visits there. But how much trust could you ask of a driving instructor terrified for his life? By the time we were done, he'd made it openly clear that I was the most difficult student he had ever taught; why wasn't I surprised? This admission came after he tried explaining to me the logic behind a three point turn and oh, yes, the parallel parking nonsense. If only I could have driven the island cruiser I once had on vacation with my kids in Chincoteague Island, Virginia. That Fred Flintstone model could only go forward on its front legs. If it should happen that you needed to turn around, like to pick up one of the kids who fell out of it and was lying on the street behind, you needed to get out and turn the thing around by hand. That was much more my speed, mechanically speaking.

Finally, the day of the test arrived. Mr. Wyman had succeeded in getting me to realize that all I really had in my favor was my morning prayer in which I fervently said, "Dear G-d, let's surprise Mr. Wyman. He tried so hard to help me, and although he might be secretly praying to You to fail me so I stay off the roads for his safety, I think he'd feel even better about things if he knew that he managed to teach even the hardest of students (without killing them or being killed by them)." It was an unearthly 6:00 a.m.—after my first and only hot bath of that morning—when I ran out to the car in which Mr. Wyman was to drive two other students and me to the test. He promised us that he'd treat us to McDonald's if we passed. And I did, by the grace of G-d which was in overdrive that morning, gently guiding the car off the curb while I was demonstrating my prowess as an unparalleled parker. I told Mr. Wyman he could have the non-kosher hamburger; I'd take the license.

Test-Driving Loneliness

With my newly-earned legality in my pocketbook, the very first place I went was . . . school the next day. I was not alone; I had my mother's carpool kids inside the family Buick Estate wagon, which seated seven children younger, and noisier, than myself. Yes, a bit hard to believe that my parents had so much trust in me, but don't you know how much a parent's desperately hectic schedule—relieved by a roadworthy daughter—could engender trust in the parent-child relationship?

Beyond school, the car took me to plenty of suspenseful movies, flavorful ice cream stores, and more stints of every diet program that Baltimore in the 1980s had to offer. A few casual friendships developed and fed themselves on my dieting life, as I engaged in fruitful conversations with several classmates who wanted to drop "a few pounds," and who'd patiently listen to my wins and my woes about my endless struggle with food. That, and my twin passions for schoolwork and baseball, were the cards I dealt in "playing" friends, though they weren't the kind of friends who could relieve my persistent feelings of emptiness. I didn't have any of those, the kind who could understand the complexities of being me. I had a hard enough time figuring myself out; I didn't think anyone else should be unfairly recruited to assist, even in the name of friendship.

In truth, getting my license wasn't the EZ-pass towards the freedom that I had assumed it would be. Feeling empty and alone with no one to understand my inner world, I could not manage to shake the recurring deficit of hope and the excess of free-floating fear. Did all humans encounter this, I wondered, or was I particularly prone to these intense thoughts? And how does one break free from them? These thoughts had a way of seeping in through the cracks, my cracks, and flooding me with the feeling of overwhelming disconnection—from my body and from my spirit. What would ever become of me? And often, my mind would picture Aunt Rosalie in her striking repose of non-mattering: a sad, small smirk of her mouth that was bent into a cynical, hopeless commentary about life, but mostly about herself. Her interpretation of life: lonely, unloved, and lost in her own world.

Still lonely, at least having my driver's license made my driving legal. Small confession here: There had been times when I drove alone without my license. Not sure if I even had my permit yet. It was on a Friday afternoon when no one was available to take me to the store that I figured I could manage on my own, easily taking the car keys from the glass table in the living room. No one would have known if not for our housekeeper who thought it her responsibility to share this unimportant news with my parents. I should have been more careful because the time before this, no one did know. My parents had driven Brenna to New York's Kennedy Airport to see her off for a year of study in Israel. School was starting for me the next day, and I was still without school supplies. I settled myself in our car, promising myself I would just drive the familiar back roads to the store. I made sure to sit tall, look confident, and not to speed—all good things to do when you shouldn't be doing something.

I should tell you something else: Taking cars without permission runs in my family. When my son Daniel took our car without permission, though he had his license, I wasn't exactly surprised. In fact, while I secretly admired his unbridled daring, I told him I ought to call the police, but that as his mother, I would just suspend his use of the car for two weeks. Moms make for lenient judges; it was not the first time I had noticed that.

Backing up the story a few weeks, when I took my son for his license, I had no doubt he'd pass superbly. Mr. Wyman wouldn't have believed that Daniel and I shared the same gene pool. He got into the driving instructor's car as if he owned it, and ten minutes later, he emerged with his sure-footed smile. I told him, "Dan, this is a bittersweet moment. Sweet, because you got your license; bitter, because you have your license." He texted his friends who were already into the first hour of their school day that they should prepare for him a hero's welcome, which they did.

•

Making the Grade, Missing the Mark

Now weighing nearly two hundred pounds in twelfth grade, I anticipated my high school graduation that was on its way. As in our previous elementary and middle school graduations, two students would be chosen to deliver speeches on behalf of the graduates. Typically, these were the girls with the highest grades in the class. On both occasions, I was one of the two who delivered the speeches my mother wrote for me. (Known for her eloquence at the mic, I trusted her to write my thoughts, or at least for me to say hers as if they were my own. The only line I insisted on scratching was "with deep humility I stand before you"—since I wasn't sure how humble it was to tell others that you were humble.)

It was generally assumed by everyone that I would be selected once again as one of the two senior valedictorians. Only I knew that my grades were not as perfect as my classmates imagined. I was still working hard, but I had not pulled straight A's. Aside from Pac-Man eating into my success, computer science class was the culprit. I could not write the programs Dr. Smith was teaching us, and there was no Internet or Google to teach me how. Computer science was the time of day when we made serious fun in class, because my hardship was shared by many others, too. It did not take long before my full frustration kept me from even bothering to show up. It is hard to pass when you don't show up, so I didn't. But this setback was computing somewhere on my radar screen, because every time I thought about graduation, I found my head in the breadbox digging for the strength to not care. To fortify myself against the calculated, objective grade point average that showed no favor or emotion, I began to prepare for yet another lesson in failure and its ensuing trail of emptiness and shame.

Let's remember that Brenna was valedictorian, as was my mother, in the very same school. Besides the expectation from within my family, it was clear from casual conversation amongst my classmates that they cast their vote for me as valedictorian. Only problem was that my teachers didn't quite calculate it that way. They had the hard, unemotional numbers to guide this weighty decision. On that decisive day, the numbers came out in favor of two girls, one of whom was my closest friend, Sarena. Sarena and I shared that competitive inner drive to push ourselves in the pursuit of excellence in school, and that marked us as kindred spirits from the eighth grade onwards. And even though we didn't hang out a lot outside of school, we were on the inside of each other's lives on a daily basis, both in school and by phone at night. We'd wrap our connection around our compatible spirits marked by inquisitive, curious minds—hers the faster—unraveling the mysteries of both American and Jewish history, with science and math in between.

When she emerged victorious from the principal's office after having been notified of the selection, the two of us ran out of the building because we knew we had a little situation on our hands. In truth, I was genuinely happy for her, and she knew it. For many reasons, she was the more worthy recipient of this honor. For one thing, her numbers were higher than mine, if only by a fraction of a point (insider information). She had an incomparable grit that pulled her through the stroke of her young mother and its accompanying hardships, during our high school years. It would eventually propel her through medical school, her lifelong dream. When Sarena married at the age of thirty-six, Zack and I—pregnant with our youngest—attended her wedding. She now has six daughters under the age of my youngest. She is a winner who had earned every bit of that valedictory.

Hard to believe, but I was also happy for myself that I was *not* named valedictorian. There was something in me that was profoundly relieved to have *failed*. To know that my breath would continue to rise and fall, even in failure. To feel a smile on my lips, even in failure. Failure is often an intense taste, flavored with a host of feelings that I knew very well how to just eat away. But learning to feel them—slowly, so that I could tolerate them *without breaking*—would help me find my way back up. I saw that I could survive; that indeed I was. Even decades before

I met my current spin teacher, I knew how right she is when she reminds us as we desperately try to keep pace: *Failure is an option, quitting is not.*

Experiencing failure, it is now clear to me, is vital to actualizing our potential and living life well. Trusting that *every downswing will bring, in due time, its upswing* is a lesson I never stop learning. Following this pattern, happy and huge things have happened in my life; details to follow. My only concern now was facing my friendly classmates and how they would handle this disappointment on my behalf. Most of them did just fine. After seeing my real joy for our friend, they turned their attention back to how their hair looked that day and if what they were having for lunch would make them look fat.

There was, however, one person for whom this failure was disappointing, and I bless her for her willingness to let me share it with you now. Standing in our orange and yellow wallpapered kitchen, I can recall the conversation, though I am not sure how it got started. My father was at the table, reading his nightly paper, and my mother said something to me like, "You could have been valedictorian." Somehow, I cannot recall the rest of the phrasing, as I must have put a block on it like the library does on my card with unpaid fines. I do, however, remember that my father, in a rare show of opposition to my mother, silently shook his head, signaling the end of that conversation. I did understand how important my success was to my mother who had fully invested herself in all those endless homework nights. I was painfully aware how much well-deserved honor it would have brought her. After putting up with me all these school years and having shepherded me to my senior year, she really did deserve that pleasure. And maybe she was right; if I would have pushed just a bit harder, I could have tasted that victory she knew would make me happy. But I couldn't deliver the grades. Given that reality, I would have preferred that together we could rejoice in my friend's victory. It certainly would have been a lot less fattening for me, too, as I was left to sweeten the bitterness of my non-achievement.

Right on the Mark

Valedictory or not, it sure had taken long enough to get to the finish line in school. And really, the most important thing I took from it was the piece of paper that still sits near my desk to this day. Nope, I am not referring to my diploma or even to my award for excellence in Hebrew studies. Rather it was a gift from a famous thinker whose words touched me: "Is it so bad then to be misunderstood?...To be great is to be misunderstood... Envy is ignorance, imitation is suicide . . . Whoso would be a man must be a nonconformist. A foolish consistency is the hobgoblin of little minds." And, finally, the "power which resides in him is new in nature, and none but he knows that is which he can do, nor does he, until he has tried."

Thank you, Ralph Waldo Emerson, for the education of a lifetime, which I'd need to remember and review, to have and to hold, as I embraced life. It has brought me enormous comfort and relief. I guess my English teacher deserved her paycheck that week for sharing Ralph's work with us. But if you ask me, she should have kept Shakespeare to herself.

Taking Loneliness Abroad

My next step after high school was a post-high-school program in Israel. It was generally accepted that an Orthodox girl would seek her post-high-school year in a seminary in New York, England, or Israel. This year was accredited as part of our undergraduate program with a regionally accredited university. Aside from encouraging a healthy independence, its main purpose was to solidify the components of the Jewish female personality and character. Without the distraction of secular studies, we'd be immersed in a year of full-day, in-depth *Torah* studies, ranging from the practical—like the laws of *Shabbat* observance and the laws of keeping kosher— to esoteric, scholarly studies. Both would sharpen our minds and hearts in a quest to build the healthy, well-functioning, inspired female who could begin to take her place in the Jewish world and beyond, and to prepare our intellectual and emotional compasses for life in both the personal and professional realms.

I had applied, and was accepted, to the academic seminary that was dubbed the Harvard of seminaries. Its renown as an academy of intensive higher learning excited me, while inducing an overwhelming anxiety as to how I'd fare academically and socially, too. Going on the plane with a group of eighty other American girls seemed way beyond my social capacity. And then to lodge in a dorm; how was I—the girl who still could not easily leave her home years after that fourth-grade snowstorm caught her in its headwinds—going to do *that*?

Our plane descended into the astonishingly beautiful palm-laden ground in the middle of a heat wave. A *chamsin*, as it is called, referring to an uncomfortably hot, dry, dusty wind, did not make the transition any easier. I suppose things would have been a bit easier if I had not been wearing three-inch heels, although I did have an Evian water spray to spritz across my face, making sure that my freshly-applied makeup wouldn't melt away.

Fortunately for me, Brenna had married the year before, and was now settled in Israel, right across the street from my dorm, actually having birthed my parents' first grandchild a few months earlier. Once again, Brenna would be there to tend to my well-being. While I no longer lingered at my locker in daily crying spells, there were plenty of times I borrowed her compassion to ease me through the long days of classes, many of which were given in Hebrew, and late nights spent writing reports and studying feverishly for unending tests.

Upon arriving at the dorm, our first order of business was to wait in line for our bed linen. One of my former Baltimorean classmates, now in seminary with me, waited in line to get hers—and mine. How did she know I didn't know how to wait patiently in line for linen? I think she knew I never went to camp, where one learned things like that. Speaking of which, one loud girl from New York made it her business to tell me her theory of why I was so homesick: "Because you never went to sleepover camp, did you?" She had a point, but I made it a point all the same not to say another word to her the whole year. (Did I mention that my roommates were two of the campiest girls in the whole school, making for one of the most "happening" rooms? Yes, I suppose an anti-socialite like me deserved that. We actually liked each other, all keeping similarly late hours— me to study, and them to party.)

With no car to travel to school, we were expected to endure a fifteen-minute mountainous climb from our dorm to the school building where all our classes were held. Exercising my usual good judgment when it came to physical exertion, I set that issue quite straight during my first few days. It was not long before I discovered that the bus stop across the street from our dorm could take me in comfort to the school, while also allowing me a precious extra few minutes of sleep for which those who had to walk didn't have time. I did not realize that students were not exactly encouraged to take the easy route, i.e., the bus, until one day I walked onto the bus and sat next to my principal. Mrs. Yonaty was not the kind of principal you could talk to and expect her to smile back. Looking up at me, she questioned, "Shifra, Good Morning. What are you doing here?" With a chipper smile too big for the early morning, I casually replied, "The same thing I guess you are . . . going to school." She was reported to have been a smart lady, and I would confirm that, since she never said another word to me again about my mode of transportation.

Deeper into the year, something similar happened. We seminary girls went on a trip to the north. Brenna had bought for me a canteen to hold the water one was urged to drink while on such trips. The conditions felt a bit punishing for my sense of comfort, but when I saw the bathroom situation that would have us using the most primitive ways, what some called "earthy"—the way I once had no choice but to relieve myself at the roadside when I couldn't wait for the next rest stop on a family road trip—I decided I was not going anywhere but home to the dorm. I bid farewell, to the protests of my teachers and friends, who were so eager to tell me what a great time I'd be missing. "Oh, you don't worry 'bout me. Enjoy the nature. Give the earth a hug from me." And I walked until I found some bus willing to take me back to the dorm, where the bathroom looked almost American, and I promptly felt human again. I was also, surprisingly, quite content to be alone in the still energy of the dorm that I now had all to myself.

Cracking the Code

Throughout this year, I hung around an old friend—actually, a mutual acquaintance of Simon and Garfunkel, (as referenced in their award-winning song, "Hello Darkness My Old Friend"). It was with this pressing personal darkness that I'd frequent the *Kotel*, the Wailing Wall, where I really began to sense a special relief while facing its ancient stones—the last remnant of the second Holy Temple—that held all that was good and holy in Jewish life. Many probably know that the second Temple, the *Bait HaMikdash* (literally, House of Holiness) stood for more than four centuries before Rome exiled the Jewish people—an exile that has lasted more than two millennia. Not many know that as much of the Wall you can see above the ground, is how deep it extends beneath the ground. Reminds me of the character of a well-developed person: As much as you see, there is at least that much that is hidden.

I took every opportunity to immerse myself in the spiritual side of life during this year. I had been taught that the very air in Israel makes one wise and that Israel is the special earthly abode of G-d. Whereas G-d resides everywhere in His world, Israel and especially Jerusalem are particularly G-dly places. That meant that standards of living were higher, not in the material sense (although housing *is* very expensive here), but in the non-material sense. How people conduct themselves on a daily basis in the most mundane aspects of their lives were among the most powerful lessons I'd learn that year. I witnessed how people with meager financial resources could be so generous-hearted, inviting guests to dine on a small *Shabbat* meal, replete with great joy and gratitude for being able to share. Their trust in a Providential force guiding and presiding over the small and big pieces of their lives was uncommonly lofty. For the average person here, there was a definite sense of mattering that had little to do with their economic advancement. It was overwhelmingly focused on a different set of questions of net worth. Small pockets, big lives.

I was particularly fond of watching the women serve as "movers and shakers" of the lives of their family and friends. Theirs was a soft-powered diplomacy that moved along the worlds of their families, day to day, with the finely-honed execution and multi-tasking skills of highly-paid professionals. How they moved between the demands of their personal and professional lives left me in a song of praise for women, these Jewish women in particular whom I regarded as heroic amongst us. Often, the families were large in size, and although I was not aware of any of my own personal inclinations to mother more than a handful or so—if that many—it made me think hard about the unused years ahead of me and what would make them worthwhile living.

Taking Stock of Food

In this year, I took stock of my eating in a way I had not yet done. After a brief try at Weight Watchers conducted in Hebrew, I decided the language of feeding myself was hard enough without adding a language comprehension problem. Brenna tried to guide me, but we were two sides of the same coin. We agreed that if we'd ever kill ourselves, she'd resort to starving herself, while I'd overeat myself to death. It was no use for a naturally organized, small-boned, disciplined under-eater to think that she could actually help me. For the first time, I devised my own plan that worked—mostly abstaining from the school menu. I never told my parents that technically they could have asked for a partial tuition refund for my uneaten food. Here's how it worked. My lunches, the main meal of the Middle Eastern day, consisted of running ahead of the lunch crowd in the dorm where we ate our meals, and walking into the humongous commercial freezer to take my fruits and vegetables, yogurt and cottage cheese for the day. Free groceries in hand, I trudged up the three flights to my room while it was still empty of my roommates, who were lunching on oil-laden soup and fried chicken downstairs.

My nightly exercise was skipping a big supper. I made sure to consume whole wheat crackers along with some protein, and low calorie drinks, not allowing myself to starve. This self-made eating plan may not have been the best nutrition, but I dropped the weight I wanted to, even beginning to fit into some of the dresses of my thinner friends. I am not sure how this bodily pursuit fit into the spiritual scheme of things, though working toward balance in any area of life surely translates into better service of G-d, certainly a happier one.

As a matter of fact, our assistant principal wearily remarked to me at the end of the year that she wished some of the other girls had taken a cue from me about how to eat less—but indeed to eat—instead of resorting to the toilets. Until that point, I had not known that I was living with girls suffering from bulimia. I had not seen it up close, though I had heard that such a thing existed. All I knew was that there were times in my life I wished I could have used similar ways to help my weight situation, desperate as I was to reverse the weight gain and inhabit a smaller body. "*Abba*," I remember once telling my father, "I wish I could have anorexia so people would stop making fun of me for being fat." I didn't seem to have the discipline to do it any other way. Anorexia seemed the easy way out, if not actually virtuous, to foist that control over this desperate situation I had no other way to win. He quickly beat down that idea, "G-d forbid, don't say that." I knew I might be hurting myself, but I was so hurt by being fat. Either way, I was suffering shame; at least being thin would release me from others' harsh judgments which were unpalatable. Better to be too thin than too fat; every American knows that.

But thankfully, I didn't have that ability to starve myself. I just didn't know how or, more accurately, I wasn't willing to hurt myself so overtly, to punish myself for filling a human appetite. And I reasoned that if I could summon the discipline to eat nothing, forcing myself to go against my inner core of sane health, I could surely find the power to eat healthfully in accord with my healthy impulse to survive.

I would employ this lesson of compassionate self-care many times over, knowing that despite the persistent struggle with our appetites on any level, appetite as the desire for something is a healthy sign of being alive. That didn't always make it simple to feed myself well. Because how we feed our needs and desires, and especially how we "do pleasure," takes considerable choice-making. To state the obvious, making wise choices is paramount to shaping our lives. And to admit the painful, it is not always easy to make and execute those choices, especially when they take us beyond our comfort zone.

Being away from home, I knew, opened up wells of loneliness that were new for many of us, even those who went to summer camp. I assumed that most were just homesick, having been away from home for longer than the typical eight-week summer stint. They sought comfort in newfound friendships, which many seemed to easily make. And food now loomed larger for many, maybe because it helped smooth out the difficulties inherent in being on one's own. Now, perhaps for the first time in their lives, I saw many of my seminary mates reckon with their appetites on a daily basis, the way I had done for most of my life. I heard their constant discussion focused on weight, the way I was accustomed to doing with myself for so many years. Deliberating every food choice based on calories was a new concept. "My mother will kill me if I come home with all this extra weight" was a line I overheard a lot that year. It was obvious that for many, this was their first time facing the real threat of gaining weight for which seminary girls were notorious. The different environment served up many new daily routines, particularly with food choices that challenged even the thinnest, most nonchalant eaters for whom eating may have previously been an afterthought. They had to settle for the more processed foods and snacks readily available in their dorm rooms, with no adults monitoring their intake. Additionally, the stresses of being away from the familiar surely found release in eating more than their bodies needed.

Freedom, yes, but was this the kind of fullness that leaves one content? I had already experienced so much pain around that question, and yet I felt that I could not share the depth of my experience with others. They were new to this challenge, and to the search for quick fixes found in crash diets that I had unsuccessfully tried. I already knew that, at least for me, the fix was deeper and an ongoing process. A hard sell for a friendly conversation.

As for me, this environment turned out to be a welcome change. I had the freedom to eat privately and *not* be under the scrutiny of my family while doing so. While almost all my friends schlepped home bigger bodies at year's end, I alighted on the plane more fit than I had been in years. That is, after I actually got on the plane. Because somehow I missed it and I had to be rerouted through England, much to the misfortune of the man sitting next to an anxious eighteen-year-old, hyper-alert for any sign of turbulence.

When Loneliness Becomes Solitude

When we are on empty, we are prone to feeling that uncomfortable feeling of loneliness. To re-quote May Sarton, "loneliness yields the richness of solitude" when we face it and utilize it well. The first step is to understand that loneliness is not about how many people are around you. Loneliness can surround you in a crowd of a thousand people, while just the opposite is true—you can feel completely un-lonely when you are alone without another soul in sight.

What comprises the feeling of loneliness? It is a powerful mix of shifting amounts of sadness, fear, emptiness, isolation, hopelessness, and powerlessness. And it leaves us feeling remote and disconnected. Not being connected in deep, meaningful ways with oneself—and with others—leaves a space that is achingly null and void, desperate to be filled.

"I have worked hard, Brenna," I recall crying during a particularly rough patch of life, after doing some heavy inner work. "I feel empty, infertile. So vacant inside. I need G-d to fill me up *now*."

Whatever exactly loneliness is, I know it can galvanize us to live more largely if we work our way through it. Noticing it and naming it are important steps. When we can bear its discomfort long enough without distracting ourselves, we often can discover valuable material for growing ourselves.

Both loneliness and emptiness may not always be driving us, but they are often in the back seat, waiting to have a word with us. They can potentially help us to slow down and refuel—if they don't urge us to abandon the journey when the ride gets bumpy. We learn to read our roadmap so we can negotiate our way forward. We can locate exit ramps, or at least, ways to detour so we don't get more lost than necessary. Incredible as it sounds, there is a lot of large living to be done in maneuvering our empty and lonely spaces.

There will be times when you are on the highway, happily free of the stop and go of the usual city traffic, and other times be at a standstill in bumper-to-bumper local traffic, unable to see the road ahead. When I envision the heart as a road to be traveled, sometimes the road ahead is full of scenic rapture, while other times, there are roadblocks, leaving us no choice but to detour. That detour forces us to travel the deeper emotions that we much prefer not to have to take. But they are the signposts along the way that direct us on our journey. And as we make our way through and around, we often realize that those challenges are not in the way. *They are designed to lead the way.*

Even though loneliness was my ready companion, I now had enough solitude to begin thinking about choosing a mate. I had wrestled with myself. A lot. In the eating arena, I was finally on the thinner end again. And I had used the loneliness in Israel to propel me toward a deeper self-understanding as I was forced to fend for myself more independently. To live in a room for a year with two girls I had never met before in my life, and to learn how to be available for others, and for myself, too. How to share a bathroom with a handful of other humans; what better preparation for marriage could I get? I also invested in a closer connection with my Creator through prayer. I began to ask for, and find, more trust that G-d would lead me always and protect me, though I'd continue to feel scared and anxious sometimes about how everything would play out.

And though those struggles would rebound—in full force—I felt that for now, I had enough inner fortitude to enter the deeper waters of dating for marriage.

Marriage, a detour; in fact, a tour de force.

CHAPTER ELEVEN

Stress Rehearsal: Choosing a Mate

A soulmate is the one person whose love is powerful enough to motivate you to meet your soul, to do the emotional work of self-discovery, of awakening.
—Kenny Loggins, singer

WHEN IT CAME TO THE TEN-WEEK MARK of our courtship, I knew we were at the finish line, one way or another. That may seem like an unreasonably short time to date, but this was longer than most in my Orthodox circle of dating friends for whom the process was quite vetted before the prospective couple even met. Being the inquisitive type (no surprise here that I later worked as a radio interviewer), I was always full of questions, and had little trouble asking them. But this one was for Zack to ask.

I had decided before our next date that one of two things would be happening . . . I'd either say "yes" to his marriage proposal, or I was moving on without him if there was none forthcoming. There is nothing in life that I am happier about than not having to move on without him. Because on that Saturday night, as we sat in the Vista Hotel on the lower level of what was then Manhattan's World Trade Center, I watched as his right leg, neatly draped over the other, was shaking back and forth. I knew he did this when he was restless or excited. As my hands curled around the hotel's royal purple, velvet-cushioned seat underneath me, I knew he was getting ready to ask. Within moments, it would be my turn in life to be asked. *When it is your turn in life, you take it.*

But not quite yet.

I decided I needed to reapply my make-up first. Excusing myself, I said, "I'll be right back. And can you just do me a favor and hold this?" I deposited into his hands my heart-shaped necklace engraved with the Hebrew words, "If I forget thee Jerusalem," a souvenir from my seminary year designed to keep Jerusalem close to me at all times, and one that I do not bring into the bathroom because of its holy nature.

With a newly drawn teal line beneath my green eyes, and lips made fuller by a touch of soft, shiny peach gloss, the timing was perfect. Carefully seating myself, he returned my jewelry as I thanked him "for holding my heart in your hands." I noticed that his feet steadied. He was looking at my forearms below the open lacy cuffs of my pale peach blouse. *Maybe he is envisioning how the engagement ring he will soon be giving me will look,* I wondered. Although he didn't say anything, his sweet smile slowly spread across his smooth red lips, showcasing that childish dimple on his upper left cheek that has come to bracket my life in miraculous ways. He would later tell me that he was thinking about the constellation of "charming" birthmarks on my arms. Certain that they were not random, he wondered what story they would tell if he helped me connect the dots. Zack, it was well-known by his friends, was the consummate connector, perfect for coaxing out a disjointed story. His non-judgmental, loving nature afforded him the luxury of peacefully embracing diverse people, ideas, and situations. That was fortuitous for a quirky girl with a challenging nature.

It Was All a Setup

There is hardly a place that our sense of mattering weighs in heavier than in the process of choosing a mate. Everything you thought about yourself will now come into focus as you articulate to yourself what you are seeking in a mate, and why. *That someone will matter to you, and—even harder to understand—that you will matter to someone else.*

(And that, parenthetically, even with a mate you continue to adore, you will sometimes still face inner emptiness and loneliness—as I'd come to painfully learn in the married years to come.)

I was eighteen upon my return from my study abroad. If until then my life had been filled with rigors of any sort, it had just been a stress rehearsal. Now, the main show was starting: the dating process. Remember, until this point in life, Orthodox boys and girls did not officially meet for social relationships. We attended separate schools and social events. Seating in many places such as the synagogue and weddings was kept separate, ensuring appropriate conduct and focus. But now, at this post-seminary age and stage, our family-centered culture encouraged us to begin thinking about dating for the sake of marriage, and this was top priority for most of us, even while continuing our college education. Dating for the sake of socializing, minus the immediate goal of marriage, is not a standard practice, as its focus can often shift to impulse-driven behaviors that can badly damage men and women, leaving them with compromised morals and emotional scars.

A quick primer on dating in my world: While it is true that customs and practices vary across the spectrum of Orthodoxy, one thing is universal—now was the time for a girl to get her wardrobe in order if she hadn't yet managed to do so. This was the chapter of *shidduchim*, literally meaning matchmaking, but it was no dating game. It was also a far shout from the days of Yentl the Matchmaker of *Fiddler on the Roof* fame, who made it her business to cater to the marriage-minded singles in her community. Interestingly, the linguistic root of the Aramaic word *shidduchim* translates as *calm*, implying that this was the time in life to remain calm and trusting in G-d's ability to bring about each person's mate, sometimes with obvious miracles.

Often, one of the biggest miracles, if not readily obvious, is that moving through this process could teach us much about ourselves that we might not yet know, such as which traits we really value in ourselves and in others, as well as what we cannot ever tolerate in either. It would also demand us to grow our faith in the Creator, for who else could put together two vastly divergent entities and call it "love?" In fact, there is an actual story recorded in the Talmud that tells the account of a Roman empress who asked, "What does G-d do all day?" When told, "G-d spends His days making matches between man and woman," the lady doth protest, "I can do that. What's the big deal?" She proceeded to mix and match her male and female servants, happy with her intuitive touch. The next morning, her complaint department was pressed into service overtime, busy as she was hearing one complaint after another while tending to the bruised faces and spirits of couples who were not as mixable and matchable as she thought. She discovered that, indeed, maybe this work belongs to the Heavenly spheres after all.

For me, suggestions for prospective mates came by way of friends, former teachers, active community members, and professional matchmakers known as *shadchanim*. It was fairly straightforward: People would call my parents or me with suggestions they thought suitable on the basis of any number of factors, some intrinsic to the individual and some external. Intelligence, personality, outer appearance, professional goals, spiritual ambitions, level of religious observance, and character traits were all micro-scoped; nothing would go unevaluated in this search for one's life partner. We spent many suppertime hours on the phone, grilling the prospective match's friends and teachers for information about him, all in a respectable and confidential manner. It is one of the highest credits to the Jewish people that this particular kindness, to help someone seeking to establish a Jewish home amongst the Jewish nation, is practiced by people across the world—often complete strangers—who will make themselves accessible by phone to assist with the exchange of information. An inside joke says it all: The FBI, in this world, refers to the covert activity associated with locating one's **F**uture **B**rother **I**n-law.

Two Columns: Needs and Wants

I was still a teenager when I had this conversation with myself. I tore a piece of college-lined paper from my notebook and made two columns: Needs and Wants. My mate would *need* to be kind, easy-going, and musical—as in likes to sing. My home *needed* to have all of those in abundance if I was to have a chance of living happily in it. The other column was *wanting* more earthly things, such as six feet tall and light eyes. (I got ~~most~~ almost all of the six feet, and two blue eyes.)

As I filled in the columns, a strange, almost forgotten ache stretched across my watch hand. Yes, I remembered now my dilemma in the watch store when I was twelve. The timeless lesson of choice-making was now ticking: Choose wisely, choose what is right for you, not others, and when it fits, let the rest of the choices fall away. And there was one other piece of guidance that one of my seminary teachers gave me when I asked her how I'd know when I was facing the right one for me. She told me, "You will know with your heart." How do hearts know, and how will I know that it knows? I was about to find out.

Something Called Feelings

It was called feelings. It seems that some decisions in life you make with your head, others with your heart. While mine would be made using both head and heart, it would come down to the heart at the end of the night. For someone whose motto has always been "facts first, feelings second," this was a test of my faith in myself. Could I give over this decision to my heart powers, to that feeling part of myself that I had been trained to mistrust, to override, because it was deemed by others as too reactive or overactive? It is a lonely place, because no one else can stand in this question and answer it for you. And no one lives the answer as intimately as you will. As an incessant fact-finder who gathers information and thinks about it, maybe even overthinks, I understood that facts would have to yield at some point in the process to the power of feeling that ultimately arbitrates the decision to move forward. That this demands courage is undeniable; how could a decision of this magnitude not?

I would now learn my truth. I could rely on my feelings if I was responsible with my thinking. The Shidduch system was built on the idea that if you did the process with due diligence, then you could relax your mind and let your heart do the feeling it is designed to do. Of course, mistakes in judgment sometimes were made, and not everyone stayed married happily ever after, or even at all, but it was expected that the overwhelming majority made it down the aisle and across the threshold of some modicum of satisfying married life.

Turning a Date into a Mate

My first date was a family affair. The boy approached the front door, while my two little sisters' beady eyes peeped out from behind their bedroom window curtain. (They had been cheated out of the fun of a dating sibling because Brenna had done all her dating in Israel, coming home engaged at the spring break. She didn't mean to, but she did break Mrs. Yonaty's seminary rules: no dating and no engagement while there.) Now that my date had entered the house, my parents offered him a seat on our red velvet couch (what a loyal couch to still be holding us up all these years) and made small talk before calling me in. By the night's end, I knew he was too simple for the girl clutching her posh snakeskin pocketbook; it'd be overkill.

On to the second guy. I drove myself into New York to meet him at the home of family friends who had set us up. This was also a "one and done," with no second date to follow. (As I had learned earlier in my days with Leo, I had to hand it to the Torah on this one thing: with no physical touching to confuse the senses, reliable feelings could surface and be trusted as we were left face to face with the essence of the person.)

I spent a lot of time with the third guy. By this time, I was renting an apartment in New York while going to college and teaching middle school. While I conveniently choose not to remember if I quit or was fired from that teaching job, I have not forgotten this guy's orange vest. I like the color orange and I adore vests, but the combination was not right on him, or for me. He was warm-hearted and actually a semi-professional singer. Poetic, too. Brenna's husband, Nate, had suggested him, having known him for several years from his days in *Yeshiva*, an academy of Torah learning. He was eight years my senior, and ultimately, I thought he'd make a good marriage partner—just not mine. I knew this was so because I found myself sad and confused after each date. My feelings were stubbornly telling me something, that he was not for me, and they had my ear. Not surprisingly, he told me that he was ready to marry me, but that he couldn't ride my roller coaster. He invited me to "please give me a call when you are ready to continue with me." My roller coaster wasn't meant to amuse, it is just that sometimes I am a rough ride. So he never did hear from me again. He did intimate that I had some growing up to do; amazing, though, how fast one seems grown up when the right person comes into focus.

There was the sophisticated lawyer and the noble doctor, and then there was the personable, brilliant guy who came awfully close to hearing me say "yes." He was witty, with a clever thought always at the ready. It was his cool, nonchalant edge that had me wondering about our suitability. Cool edges on their own can be quite charming; the problem is what happens when they get provoked a bit too much, overheating and melting down. And as much as I genuinely looked forward to being with him, it was when I asked him what he'd do with me in a moment of anger (my track record proved that I could count on that happening) that I knew I deeply feared his well-guarded temper agitating beneath the surface. Enchanted smiles could quickly disintegrate into sharp, impatient frowns and follies in all but the most refined natures, a rare find indeed.

I had seen faces of anger bordering on verbal, and even physical, backlash in my life, and his was well-masked by clever, cheerful repartee, but not out of my (in)sight sharpened by past experiences. Not sure I can call those past experiences abuse; not sure I can't, either. It's all about *my* perception, and *their* intention. Although I choose not to speak in absolutes about others' intentions, I can detail my perception. I can still feel the sting when I unwittingly ruffled my mother's considerable emotional composure, leaving her the constant struggle with how to manage my limitations for conventional thinking and straight common sense, which she was sure would secure my earthly success. Nor do I forget the smack across my chubby ten-year old left cheek, courtesy of a carpool driver whose fuse was shorted by my refusal to sit in the middle back seat on one rushed school morning. And the crack of the hairbrush across my face, delivered by my mother's short-tempered morning hire, Sandy, echoes as a senseless act directed towards a vulnerable child with no voice to say "STOP." There was driving teacher Mr. Wyman who took liberties early on to berate my atypical perspective in matters of the road, not allowing me the necessary learning curve I needed, albeith a steeper one than his other students. And, yes, even my forgiving father could be provoked to put his usually gentle hand to my skin when I would not follow his repeated direction to get into my bed for the night. This was all part of my dating process, discerning whom I could absolutely trust to understand that feelings are a valuable part of a person, that limitations are often not of our choosing, and that neither feelings nor limitations necessarily have a final, hopeless claim on one's destiny.

And so on and so out, I went with a total of nine guys until Zack was suggested. Zack was the second suggestion by Nate who, incidentally, I greatly admired, actually using him as one of several bases of comparison for my decision-making on guys. Zack came forty-five minutes late to our first meeting. My parents escorted him to our ever-loyal red velvet couch while I readied myself in the kitchen. "It is very nice to meet you," I heard Zack's pleasant, upbeat voice saying to my parents, "and please excuse my late arrival. Not that I am always prompt, but I would have been more timely had a flock of birds not dirtied the car I borrowed. I stopped by the gas station to wash it off."

He promptly stood to greet me upon my entrance, accompanied by my mother who had come to retrieve me from the kitchen. With a welcoming right hand held high, he flashed a smile on cheeks that blushed easily and deeply. Later in the night, I would again see his down to earth, gracious interactions with others as he ordered and paid for our drinks at the hotel lobby. I noticed the requisite but sincere way he looked into the staff's eyes when he thanked them. Patiently holding open the lobby door for me, and for others behind me, too, was a gesture of respect I discerned was not for show. I also noticed that, once again, he was not bound by time. In the car, leaving the hotel lobby where we walked and talked over several sips of water and Diet Coke for a few hours, we endlessly circled downtown, trying to find our way back to the highway. This was pre-Waze days; he took it in even strides, dismissing any possible frustrations into light and happy air. There was little tension, only humor about how fun it was to get lost because, "How else would we get to see these lovely Baltimore sights?" All those years I had been worried about needing just the right watch, but who needed a watch when Zack was around? He was in a zone all his own, this Leo-born star. And so, when the *shadchan* called to ask if I'd see him again, I knew deep down in that promised land, my heart of hearts, there would be many more such meetings, not to mention many more times of getting lost—together.

Fully Engaged

Believe it or not, our two and a half months of dating was longer than most couples. And engagements were kept brief.

My own parents had dated twice, with my introverted father trying to propose over the phone. My then eighteen-year-old mother somehow let him know that a phone proposal was too static-y, that she'd need a live connection, to hear him ask in person. They were married six weeks later. Even Zack's sister, whose fate was to date for ten years—an unusually long time to find a mate—was engaged within several weeks, and married within two months, of meeting boy #201.

But for us, it would still take weeks. Because even if it was clear from date one that we loved each other, we still needed time to get to like each other. We call that "like-making," and we think it might be the secret for fueling two vastly different bodies living day-to-day routines while trying to figure out how on earth to keep their heavenly friendship growing. We're also fairly sure there are two other small ingredients for a thriving marriage: a good babysitter and a great restaurant. I might add one more thing: If you should marry a non-jeweler like Zack who presented his first gift by saying, "Shifra, I hope you like this bracelet"—which I have thoroughly enjoyed wearing around my neck—I'd suggest that you select your own jewelry. Have it wrapped, put it in his drawer with a note when he should gift it, along with the card he should enclose with it. That's just a suggestion if you care to have some strings and stones that you will actually wear.

We were almost ready. To be accurate, I had been ready for a few weeks to hear him ask me. We had survived the roller coaster ride, which was no less bumpy than with Mr. Orange Vest, but having the right seatmate made it fun. There were times along the way when things were stuck up in the air, and I did have to second-guess my early-on read of this relationship. On our fifth date—a trip to Columbia thirty minutes south of Baltimore—we hardly exchanged a word, leaving us both confused and unsure how to proceed. *What does it mean when you have nothing to say to each other,* we silently wondered. After both checking in with Nate, the *shadchan* whose matchmaking role was broadening to that of a dating coach, we decided it just meant to keep going out, that indeed maybe we were meant to be a couple, because this happens to real-life couples.

Then there was the night two months into our relationship when the date got started really late, after 11 p.m. Now, at about 2 a.m., we had been discussing a particular matter, and the conversation was growing difficult. It had what to do with Zack's career plans, which I thought were business-based, but it now sounded like he was expressing an interest in pursuing a teaching career. As teachers were generally not my most inspiring people, and the pay was not decent, that ambition was hard for me to entertain. When Zack abruptly got up from his seat, I was not sure if he was done for the night, perhaps even finished with me. I decided the time had come to tell him something I had not yet told him.

"I know it's late, and you have a long way to drive back home. I guess you need to leave. Not sure how we got this far—and yet still have this misunderstanding about your professional plans. I didn't know you wanted to teach. Do you, really?"

"What if, as a teacher, I could meaningfully contribute to society, although I admit that I may not understand individual differences well enough?" he innocently asked.

"There are many ways to make a difference in this world, aren't there? And by the way, many teachers don't make that much of a difference . . . and come to think of it, they don't make that much money, either." And in that feeling heart of mine, I knew it was more about the fear of too little money, not too little influence. "Do you really think a teacher can make a difference? Did you ever have a teacher who did that for you?" I countered.

"You're worried about the money, aren't you? I know; you need your dresses. You will have them; I promise. And don't worry, I would never try to teach *you* anything. You are not the teachable type, that much I know. Although by the way, I do think you are *reachable* well beyond what you imagine. You can go further than you think you can."

And with that, I decided two things: He would be my "reacher," and that he wasn't going anywhere if I had a say in the matter, which I was about to.

"I hope you will reconsider this whole teaching thing. But I think you should know that I realize you understand me remarkably well." And then I told him straight out that I really liked him, and I hoped he wouldn't go quite yet.

All that strenuous disclosure for nothing, because he had really gotten up just to stretch his overly patient legs and he let me know he had no intention of leaving—without me.

A "Belle" Curve

We did a few more outings and phone calls until that final May date in the Vista when there was nowhere to go but forward into it . . . into the heart of the commitment with each other. It was a magnificent moment, because we had worked hard to reach it, sweating the process quite a bit, but the knowing and the feeling was right enough for both of us. A miracle, if you consider that I could actually trust someone enough to say *yes*.

But not surprisingly, my habit of second-guessing did not comfortably stop at the engagement. In my twelve-week engagement, I turned to Brenna more than once, distressed about our seemingly skewed relationship. Zack was completing a stats course for his business degree while I was home calculating the probability of whether I had made the wrong choice. He hardly had time to speak, leaving me with a sampling of lonely, insecure variables about our pending partnership. Things got a lot better when his mentor thought to prompt him, a young dating boy new to relationships with women, to say three simple words over dinner at the restaurant. "I love you" can be powerful words. That was the first time I had heard them—and they fit just right. A learning curve for us both.

Kind, easy-going, great voice; yes, he satisfied the *needs* column. Especially the most important one: *I need a mate from whom I wouldn't have to hide my food.* I had seen enough of him to trust that would be the case. And it was a trust he'd come to hold and honor.

CHAPTER TWELVE

Sizing up Our Lives

Men and women are not limited by the place of their birth, or color of their skin, but by the size of their hope.
— JOHN JOHNSON, entrepreneur

HIDING MY FOOD . . . You know what I'm talking about? Not eating at my own engagement party until everyone left, and then cleaning up—and I mean perfectly—every last morsel of sugar and chocolate and cream. Sprinkles and crumbs, too. It was part of a long-sitting pattern to allow nothing edible to escape my recurring hunger for balance. Keeping pleasure under my bed for my private consumption became my specialty. And sneak-nibbling at pans of freshly cooked food while no one was in the kitchen, leaving my mother to wonder how she could have so miscalculated her recipe.

All those years hiding any form of pleasure that could be unwrapped and orally popped shaped one resolve now: This talent for hiding my food was staying behind. Nope, it would not come into my marriage. And the only way I could make good on that was to find a partner I intuitively trusted. Even though I didn't yet have years of concrete evidence on him, I had spent enough time listening, being heard, and observing Zack, to process somewhere in my subliminal being that he'd live up to this assessment. All of our interactions had been consistently honest, warm, and respectful. And the winning proof: by openly professing to me his love—for chocolate—and by showing me that he wouldn't take mine without permission, he passed the high bar I had set for earning my trust. The day he brought a chocolate candy bar from a company named SHUFRA and changed the "U" to an "I" on its wrapper, essentially renaming this bar to be mine, I knew he'd let me have my chocolate and eat it, too. By the way, he hid his food too, when you consider that his ultra-slim figure belied the junk he ate.

In keeping with the feminine capacity for changing one's mind, I thought you'd want to know that Zack actually hides food *at my invitation*. I have asked him to hide it *for* me, not *from* me. It is a loving, kind, trusting tactic I use to support myself in pursuit of disciplined pleasure.

Self-trust: The Weigh to Freedom

It is exceptionally painful to recount how many times I have signed up for—and out of, and back into again—Diet Workshop, Weight Watchers, Overeaters Anonymous, gyms, trainers, and nutritionists. With every failure came a fresh trail of hopelessness and distrust in myself and others. One of the most disappointing, but instructive, experiences happened with an Overeaters Anonymous group in Manhattan. I would travel once a month from Baltimore to New York to join a special group led by one of the OA gurus who had authored a best-selling work on eating and losing weight. We did some really weird practices, like eating our lunch together, an exercise called, "Dine with Dignity." In theory, it was designed to assist us with slowing down our eating and tasting our food. In reality, it was a very conforming exercise that did not produce a good outcome for me. I was very uncomfortable eating in a group; always have been. During the third or fourth meeting, Stephanie suddenly challenged me: "Shifra, why are you here?

You don't participate, and it is obvious by looking at you that you are not dropping weight . . . I think you should leave the group." I was not sure what to do, because I did not understand what she was really saying or why.

I put my confused self on the Amtrak, returning to the safety of my home, where I began to process this deeply over the next few days. As I was hanging up my children's school uniform shirts to dry, clarity registered. I knew what had happened, and I now had language for it. Somehow, I had unintentionally threatened Stephanie because I couldn't do the group thing. While it is true that I have a pattern of not conforming well to group dynamics that usually infringe carelessly on my individuality, it was even more distressing than that. I couldn't do what she was asking of me . . . *to mistrust myself with food.* And for the first time in my then twenty-eight years, I now knew that *the pathway for me is to restore the trust between me and food.* And from that incident, which I considered to have been a violation of personal and professional ethics (for which she later apologized), I was beginning the long trek toward freedom from compulsive eating.

Breaking Free
This was when I sought out the work of author Geneen Roth. Prompted by her permission, I began to sit still while eating my favorite chocolate chip cookie or two, or ten, as I began to understand that the relationship was between Shifra and me. Food was neither friend nor foe; it was about me in relationship with food that determined its role in my life.

Years later, when I had the privileged opportunity to interview Geneen for my radio program, we began with discussing the nature of dieting. As previously mentioned, she posited that diets don't work. In what she calls the "Fourth Law of the Universe," she explained that for every diet, there is an equal and opposite binge. Every action has a reaction, and like gravity, every diet leads to a binge. And what really drew her attention was that none of the diets touched the reasons that we turn to food to begin with; they don't even acknowledge the fact that there are reasons.

Diets were built on the belief that if I trusted myself, I would destroy myself. That if I let myself eat what my body wanted, I'd start at one end of the kitchen and just chomp my way clear across the United States. That my hunger was bottomless. That I was crazy and self-destructive. It was the belief—the false belief—that I was out of control, that my hunger was bottomless, and that I wasn't capable of working through this in a sane or self-trusting and kind way."

Our Bodies, Our Lives

Geneen says it became apparent to her that most women equate the size of their lives with the size of their bodies. They believe that the thinner their bodies, the larger their lives. That somehow, the form their body takes determines the inner substance they're allowed to feel or have in their lives. That the thinner they are, the more happiness they're allowed to have.

"I can't tell you how many women I've worked with who were utterly convinced that when they lost twenty pounds, thirty, fifty pounds, they would at last be happy. One woman attended my workshop after losing one hundred pounds. 'I feel betrayed,' she said. 'I feel like my entire life people said to me that when I lost this weight, I was actually going to have a dream life. In fact, the only thing I have is a thinner body. Because when I lost the weight, I didn't lose the problems. I didn't lose the feelings I have. I didn't lose how I feel about myself in the morning.' Those things don't change. Superficially maybe, and for a very brief amount of time; but not deeply."

The Process *Is* the Goal

Then what is the point of all this? Why try to eat well and drop extra weight? According to Geneen, *the process is the goal.* She explains that when people start paying attention to themselves and their eating, when they start trusting themselves, when they start actually eating when they're hungry, eating what their body wants, nourishing their body, sitting in a calm environment, stopping when they've had enough . . . this is what happens. The feelings they thought they needed to be thin in order to feel—such as calming down, being kind to themselves, being compassionate with themselves, taking care of themselves, and eating nourishing food—they can feel at whatever size they are. In fact, when they start living as if they deserve those things, they start finding that they really do. So, yes, the process is the goal in some way. And we learn that food is not our enemy.

She reminds us that the whole point of eating, besides for the obvious delight and pleasure of it, is to sustain our life force. "To give us energy so that we can do and be who we are. So, for instance, the point of eating a hot meal at least once a day, or eating when you're hungry and stopping when you've had enough, is that you can live a rich, gorgeous life. Not so that you can be thin as a model and be miserable. If you're dieting to deprive yourself because you're shaming yourself because you don't believe you deserve delight, abundance, good taste, and good things in your life, then it's really not going to work. Being thin will not make you happy, because you still have that place of self-loathing inside."

"Just as a teacup has a certain shelf life until somebody shatters it, we're all going to die at some point. Instead of trying to protect ourselves from this fact, luxuriate in the life you've got, in the fleeting moments of infinity that we've got every single day, instead of just trying to protect ourselves from just getting hurt."

Language of Love

As told in one of her books, Geneen says, "My cat, Blanche—or Mr. Blanche because he was a twenty-pound male cat—taught there was life that gave the appearance of things. Blanche didn't care whether I was having a thin day or a fat day. He just walked right into the essence of things. I saw there was an essence of things that I wasn't responding to, that I was judging my life on the appearance of things. And it's terrible to judge life on the appearance of things because those things fall away very quickly. And the other thing Mr. Blanche taught me was that all that love and happiness that existed when Blanche walked into the room was always inside me. It wasn't a function of Blanche. He evoked it. He catalyzed it. But in order for something to be catalyzed, it has to be there. Otherwise, there could be a million catalysts and it wouldn't trigger anything."

In addition to the languages of non-mattering I had learned while growing up, I was now learning a new one. Marrying Zack showed me it is possible to be loved for who you are, not for the appearance of who you are. The size of my body did not ever dictate the size of his love for me. I recall Tory Johnson, author of *The Shift*, expressing a similar thought: Her husband did not care about the size of her body because he loved *her*. When she dropped significant weight, she did it for herself, because it was in her best interests. A love conditioned on the unseen essence of something is a love that will grow, endure, and satisfy. Much more powerful than what can be seen is what *cannot* be seen. The depth of a meaningful connection that has grown around shared joy and pain will interpret how our eyes physically see each other. We all know people whose features take on a charm by virtue of their inner appeal. And those whose pleasing appearance cannot hide for too long their less-than-lovely inner being.

And that is why our society's preoccupation with the external has intensely hurt us all. With the inundation of visuals via social media, we have allowed ourselves to accept a widespread superficiality of what matters. This superficiality is so deeply imbedded in many of us, as we are taken in by picture-based assessments of our lives endlessly compared to the picture of others. It robs from each of us, and from all of us, our dignity and worth. It devalues us and deprives us of the beauty in our lives, and yes, of our mattering. Never has it been so hard to connect with the inner essence of life wherein enduring, authentic beauty lies.

In particular, the infatuation with thinness has taken hold of our collective senses and become one of our emotional idols. But I wonder if this irrational force, to take up as little space as possible so that we can be better seen and considered more beautiful, was really intended with a higher, less apparent purpose: to finally prompt us, a hedonistic society, to pay attention to eating in accord with our needs, with sanity and self-respect. A little holiness here, as in searching for and honoring healthy limits in our pleasure-seeking appetites. *To take joy in caring for our bodies, because they are vehicles for our spirit.* Perhaps G-d introduced this external prize to tempt us into the hard work of actually having an honest, respectable relationship with food, and with ourselves.

Feeding my body, fueling my soul . . . this is love. This is harmony—body and soul learning to live with each other so they can both be strong and purposeful. I refer to the merging of body and soul as the first marriage for all humans. Why one soul is put into a particular body is on my list of top five questions whose answers I'd love to know. Someday. For now, I know without a doubt that my body and soul were given to each other to shape, just like Zack and me.

It is this relationship with food that has been one of the greatest influences on my life—on my body, soul, and soulmate, Zack. Watching us together—food and me—has taught me nearly everything I need to know about myself and about others. Because what we do with food, we do with life.

Honor Your Appetite

I saw how our culture asks of us two contradictory things: to be large and small at the same time. It has definite expectations for us and spares no effort in enticing us to share them. *The assault we mount as we peel away the layers of confusion shapes us into people who can tolerate complexity and paradoxes, but not at the expense of half-truths and hypocrisy.*

In the Hebrew language, the word for bread is *lechem*, which shares a linguistic root with the word that means fight or struggle.

The Torah teaches that as a result of Adam and Eve's sin with eating from the Tree of Knowledge, food that heretofore was purely beneficial to mankind would hereafter carry both good and bad energy. The resulting consequence is that food would not be a straightforward pleasure anymore. We'd have to learn how to use food to our benefit, not to abuse it. When we say a blessing before eating anything, explains the Torah, we draw forth its good energy. The connection between bread/food and struggle is abundantly clear to those of us who have been on the inside of this confrontation. What essentially is a pleasurable and necessary part of life has become entangled with mixed messages that suck from food its inherent joy, leaving us only with empty calories.

Isn't it pleasant to know that your appetite is a sign of a healthy life force? There have been extended times in my life when I had no appetite. So I can tell you, no matter what, an appetite is a gift of enormous value—even when we struggle with it mightily on any number of levels.

Choose to live on your terms. Discerning what is healthy, what is nourishing—we are called to do this over and over again. Managing ourselves, our physical and emotional wardrobes—this is the process we call life. Learning the tools to hear our hungers and to manage our appetites is an incredibly worthwhile process.

Eatitude: Where Is Enough?

How we define our pleasures, how we seek them, and how we use them, tell us a lot about who we are. When it comes to food, I call this *eatitude*.

Figuring out what brings us pleasure, and how much is enough, are self-guided lessons. Pleasure is always a ratio. Just as we can only enjoy our food to the extent that we can taste it, *our capacity to enjoy something—to take pleasure in it—depends on our capacity to experience it.*

Enoughness is not in the having; it is in the experiencing. It is in the tasting. It is an exquisite balance, *and can only be found in the understanding of pleasure*, which often curiously requires our conscious efforts to receive it. Also interesting to note is that most pleasure, maybe even all, can only be experienced in small amounts at any given moment; it can be too intense, otherwise.

(Sometimes, we even need to prepare to receive the pleasure. While some pleasures are naturally pleasant, exciting, and delicious—and we need no cueing in how to *want* them—we may still have to work to maximize their enjoyment. Then there are other pleasures that we'd totally miss out on if we didn't prepare ourselves to receive them. For example, taking a well-deserved vacation can be a highlight in our lives. But don't we need to pack the outfits we like to wear? Don't we need to plan our itinerary, boring and painstaking as that may be?)

It is entirely possible to eat an ice cream and completely miss out on its taste, texture, and delight. To be so un-present that we don't even know we've eaten it (although our bodies *do* let us know). The consequence? You will not experience the pleasure of that ice cream. You have consumed it, *but you haven't tasted it*. The enjoyment has melted away and you are left with only the calories. *Calories make you fat, pleasure makes you full.* Can it go without saying that fullness is the opposite of emptiness?

Simply put: *food feeds, pleasure fulfills*.

Fulfillment: Largeness Is on the Inside

I have noticed something about mattering and people. For some people, their mattering is wrapped around a fierce sense of independence that insists on doing everything for themselves. If they can't cook and clean for themselves, for example, they suffer the terrible angst of feeling that they don't matter. And then there are some whose mattering depends on opting out of that very process by having others do it for them, usually by paying. While this attitude might be labeled by some as entitlement, this group of people excuses themselves from doing the mundane things in life because it makes them feel small, provoking a profound sense of not-mattering. While I cannot know for sure how someone becomes this kind of person or the other, I can posit that it is connected to how they have been conditioned, formally or casually, consciously or sub-consciously, to regard themselves and their purpose in this world. My royal birthstone grandmother was the eldest sister to three brothers. The word responsibility could be spelled "Grandma." Her entire MO was to assume the most mundane actions with independence and pride. Aunt Rosalie, on the other hand, was most herself when she was being catered to, taken care of. Having to do anything for herself was occasion for griping.

Here's another small illustration I saw in real time. There were two women who were asked to volunteer to arrange a room for an affair. The first woman, who carried many personal and professional responsibilities, joyfully accepted, while the second woman scoffed at the request, almost angry that she had been asked. Even though this second woman's days had many empty stretches of time that could have easily accommodated the request, she took it as a slight to her mattering, albeit unintended. She felt the sting of shame indicting her that she should do this because she had nothing better to do with herself. Yet, the first woman's mattering was triggered by accepting the very same request, knowing that it drew the admiration of others wowed by her sacrifice.

To be clear, there is nothing inherently noble in doing things you are not good at or really don't like. I'm the first to ask for help and to accept it with gratitude. I recall a brief memory of my sixth-grade class hiking trip to West Virginia's Harper's Ferry. We had to walk, a lot, on an unbearably hot day. I was straggling behind the group with my heavy, overheating body and a dehydrated spirit that was not at all interested in this hiking nonsense everyone had played up as a wonderful trip. I could not understand how a group of eleven-year-olds could have fallen for that stunt. In truth, I didn't—not without complaining loudly for our chaperoning principal, who was with me in the rear, to hear. Give him a little sweat, too.

The two of us were not alone. There was one other girl at the end of the line, miles behind the rest of the class. She was the girl who was always picked last in gym class because she *could* not catch the ball. I was the next to the last one chosen, because I *would* not catch the ball. I was too scared that I'd miss the catch or that I'd get hurt in succeeding. It was the two of us, the *could-nots* and the *would-nots*, lagging behind. When we heard the sound of four tires coming behind us, my principal asked us if we should hitch a ride. Praising him for his good judgment, I nodded with the firmest conviction that yes, of course, we should take that divinely-sent help. Into the car I plopped myself, hugging every burst of its cold air that circulated my way. In my mind, taking that ride was no shortcut; it was spirit-saving. Nothing small about that. My mattering depended on hitching that ride, getting myself out of discomfort that was serving no real purpose.

However, there are times in life that *bypassing that discomfort short-circuits our potential to matter.* If we are called into something that requires us to stay in it for a while, even if we don't understand the reason, *then there's everything big about staying there.* The largeness of that action is *on the inside . . .* even if it does not lead to an outer display of importance that can be recognized by others. And I'd come to wrestle greatly with this as my life unfolded into a home of my own.

By the way, there are many things that *look* large and important on the outside that are indeed very small on the inside. We humans often confuse prominence and importance. Celebrities often have to pay the price for that confusion, for having their mattering be on the outside, in the fickle hearts of their fans. Hired publicists determine the viability of their staged lives. How empty that must feel, and dangerous to their well-being, too, because much of this is out of their control.

It is difficult, maybe impossible, to ever fill the outside with enough.

Wealth: Saying Yes to Enough

For me, the fight against overeating is the fight against self-mistrust and hopelessness. Traveling from the group of *would-nots* and *could-nots* to "I will and I can" was a long hike. To stop saying what I couldn't do and showing myself what I could do. To believe that the needle on the scale would go from right to left, from heavier to lighter, from "no" to "yes." To convincingly demonstrate that yes, I can satisfy myself with food without overeating and gaining weight. By saying yes when it is right for me, and no when it is not . . . and to recognize the difference. And to trust that taking up less physical space does not mean that I am downsizing my spirit.

And that in any case, the size of my body is not a referendum on the size of my life.

And in this journey, I would come to define true wealth as the capacity to know enoughness. "Who is wealthy? He who is satisfied with his portion." (Ethics of the Fathers 4:1) Satisfaction is in the capacity to extract pleasure from what you have. *If you cannot experience pleasure, it does not matter how much you have. And if you can, it is surprising how little you need.*

(And more, on the most subtle of notes . . . if you can receive well by appreciating it, you have expanded your capacity to receive more, actually creating the space for more to come your way when you are ready.)

In the Belly of Love

As for me, it all comes down to the cheesecake.
One small piece of cheesecake . . . one huge slice of life.

Once a year, on my birthday, I make an elaborate ordeal of visiting a local café that sells individual slices of the most decadent chocolate-laced cheesecake, costing $10.75 a slice. That one piece sits atop a small china plate like a prized jewel. It attracts my total adoration. Like a diamond, I evaluate it for the 4 C's: cost, creaminess, calories, and cut. Yes, it has all in abundance.

With Zack sitting across from me, I take my knife and cut it into pieces, a few of which I lovingly give him. After all, part of my pleasure will come from giving him pleasure, too. I lift the fork delicately to my coral-painted lips and begin to taste the deliciousness of life. In these moments of bliss, I stretch out pleasure well beyond a mere 2,500 calories. I am grateful that I have prepared myself to maximize, to taste fully and in exquisite balance, the pleasure of this moment . . . because eating quickly, mindlessly, and a *moment more than enough* would undermine the totality of one of my most special earthly pleasures.

Yes, staying in the moment takes a certain form of discipline, but it is the wise, loving kind that pays back manifold. Patience is not my virtue. Yet I have taught myself this patience because it yields a pleasure that I cannot otherwise obtain. *This is the cost of pleasure.*

And if you tell me that being fixated on the particulars of a piece of cheesecake renders me the most physical, hedonistic persona, *I will argue it does just the opposite.* Staying in a loving relationship with food and with myself, is one of the most spiritual pursuits I know. Being fully present, in the moment, and knowing how to experience the joy of the physical, to be grateful for it, and to be gently but deeply uplifted by it so that I can move on . . . that is enoughness.

Enoughness is making the choice to let life and its outer veneer of mundaneness matter.

And that is the perfect size for living large.

PART TWO
Recovering Self

Gifts and skills are not the same thing. We're all skilled at things we don't love. But what you love, you are gifted at. And if you love something and you go as far as you can go, you are by definition great, because nobody else can do what you do. You are unique. No two painters have ever painted like each other if they loved what they were doing and they were doing their best work. It's impossible.

It takes a lot of courage to do it (follow what is calling to you) but the price of not doing it is despair. You can stay distracted as long as you want, but in the dark of the night, you feel a sense of "what am I here for?" This is a very profound kind of despair.

And don't tell me that you're not good enough to contribute. Did you really think you were supposed to be G-d? . . . And why don't you leave the question of whether you're great or not, to history? You're not supposed to be perfect. You're a human.

—BARBARA SHER, author, *Wishcraft*

Recovering Self is about the journey we take after discovering we have a self to create. We learn to recognize the core of our deepest hopes and dreams and to trust that they will come within our grasp, if we but reach for them.

If my relationship with food was one reliable portal that fed me my earliest ideas about mattering, then the other was my connection with birthing—creating, bringing something new, or newly found, into being. In searching for our purpose and passion for a life lived large, we recover the mattering self. Just as with food, we learn how to inhabit and satisfy our inner spaces, the home of our mattering.

CHAPTER THIRTEEN

Panes of Life

Look and you will find it—what is unsought will go undetected.

—Sophocles, playwright

A s you know, my life is about my slice of cheesecake. And if life indeed bakes down to a cheesecake, then I need to tell you one more thing: You need a cup of good tea with it. But it turned out that finding *my* cup of tea was not as simple as putting water in a cup and sipping it with my right pinky in the air.

Deep-seated Fears

"Zack," I said, "They are not welcome in our home."

Unsure who I was saying couldn't come, he stayed very quiet.

"We cannot keep those chairs." At first, I thought it was a cute joke—the kind that newly-marrieds play on each other—when he came running into our unfurnished rented apartment with the contagious excitement of a little boy finding his lost toy. "Look what I found. Aren't they great? Totally free, too."

This was no joke. I remained wordless, as I felt a mix of unpleasantness bubbling inside—affronted by his tacky find, hurt by his thinking this would be appreciated by me, and disappointed in myself that it wouldn't be. He thought I'd be delighted that he had considered me and our house needs as the sanitation workers were preparing to hoist into obscurity two mismatched chairs whose lives were clearly over.

He saw *free*, as in we don't need to pay any money. I heard *free*, as in we don't have any money to pay. So you can see where the storm was brewing.

"Please understand that I'd rather sit on the floor, than on those," I said, pointing accusingly at the pitiful offenders. "Like I did at the Japanese restaurant in Israel." So what if my hips locked as a whole paddy field of rice tumbled down my outfit, leaving the Japanese to rescue me from both.

I motioned to him to have a seat on the floor next to me, for what was the beginning of a l-o-n-g conversation about the importance of good chairs, and where one goes to get them.

Who could have known that rummaging through my feelings about some garbage furniture would be among the first serious, valuable conversations we'd have as marrieds? As a complicated child who could not always be heard, and certainly not understood, I was accustomed to swallowing, along with extra food, my thoughts about what I wanted or needed. But this was a new home, my home, with a new person, and I'd need to do this a different way. Zack could handle this, I knew. I wouldn't have married him if he couldn't. I also knew that it was my responsibility to know, or figure out, how to honor him and myself at the same time.

Making the effort to unseat the core issues, much bigger than just whether or not we had money, was the groundwork we needed to build our marriage. Though it'd be years before we bought decent kitchen chairs, we acquired that day a shared ditty, borrowed from actress Zsa Zsa Gabor of Green Acres fame, which pitted her sophisticated city sense against her husband's simple farm country leanings. By the song's end, she affirms, "Good-bye, city life. Green Acres is the place for me." Yes, we successfully got our marriage off the ground there at our first shared space, in an apartment complex known as Green Acres. Really.

From Homework to Housework

Did you think that getting married makes one whole? It only makes you as complete as you are ready to become. And it certainly does not make one suddenly interested or adept at domestic affairs.

The youthful rigors of homework now conceded to the growing pains of housework. I had to begin my "home schooling" by learning to distinguish a pot from a pan, a dust ruffle from a fitted sheet, and Rich's whip from milk creamer.

After so many years in school, I was now really on my own. With no well-rehearsed daily script to follow, I had little idea which path, professional or otherwise, to take. Setting up my apartment was unsettling for an undomesticated creature like me. I wasn't surprised. My "birthstone queen" grandmother had tipped me off with her comment when I was but sixteen: "What will you do when you need to set up house? Your head is always in the books." I sighed twice, once for her and once for me.

One advantage I had was that I did know how to arrange an inviting table. That was a good thing; amazing how good food you didn't know how to cook can look in the right dish on a colorful cloth. Set especially on the dishes I chose, a set of Royal Doulton bone china in a pattern called "Diana," the food held that extra spice of fine taste. England's Lady Diana (later "Princess Di") was the influencer of the day, and if you had dishes in her name, you were assured a touch of royalty on your table, even if it didn't come along with the royal cook.

I had already tested my culinary limitations on Zack, and he was not threatened. Before one of our dates, an outing to New York's Central Park, he nonchalantly brought up the subject of lunch at the park. "What a wonderful idea," I said as I wondered what was on *his* menu. When he suggested that *I* make some tuna sandwiches, I knew the time had come to let him know that I didn't how to do that, and that honestly, I was not terribly interested in learning how. He suggested that I phone his mom to find out, and there again, I broke the news to him that one does not ask his girl to get a recipe from his mother for the "best tuna sandwiches on this side of the Turnpike." (That is something, incidentally, about which I would repeatedly educate my one son Daniel: You will never, as in never ever, even hint to your future wife to ask me for the recipe of something of my making that you like to eat—assuming that such a thing even exists. As it turned out, my brand new daughter-in-law is an enthusiastic, gifted cook who has no need for my amateur half-baked recipes). As for Zack, I did tell him that I'd be willing to call the delicatessen at the corner near my apartment to order the tuna for pick up. I'd even ask them to throw in the pickles for good succor. My lodging has changed many times over, but one thing I always look for before settling down is the corner take-out store upon which my domestic harmony rests. After all, a woman should consider feeding her husband at the end of the day, no matter how unwilling she is—and how unspoiled she thinks *he* is.

Unscripted

By now, Zack had finished his college program, but was not yet looking for a job. As he wanted to continue his scholarly Jewish studies in the fashion of many newly married Orthodox men (not necessarily to become a Rabbi; that remained to be seen), I wanted to assist with the finances. I had not yet finished my undergraduate program, but could not take the time to do so, as I now needed to tend to the home and job-search fronts. My former high school principal tried to have me join his teaching staff, now that I had my newly-earned seminary international teacher's license in Judaic Studies. My father, in the other corner of the decision, gently reminded me that a teacher's salary wouldn't bring home those colorful dresses in the store window.

My decision was made when I conveniently remembered two things about my brief stint as a teacher earlier in the post-Israel year before Zack and I married: one, the note that I confiscated from one of my students, "her neckline is too low," confirming that teachers are critically graded on the merit of how they dress with class, and not how they address the class. And second, when I was once being observed by a faculty member, the critique I earned was, "Shifra, do you realize that you started teaching as you were entering the classroom, before you even closed the door behind you?" I didn't realize that, nor did I think I should have to worry about a small matter like that.

That left me with the other option of showing up to work at my parents' real estate office. It had been many years since their beginner's real estate office had been moved from our basement to bigger quarters in a real-life office building, ten minutes from their home. (FYI, their basement did not sit idly by. Surely, you've heard the quip, "We've tried to childproof the home, but they keep getting in." Once my parents' home succeeded in becoming a child-free zone, other needy souls somehow found their way to their door. Most remarkable was the fifteen-year-old kid from Israel who, in the grip of a major teenage episode, needed a quiet place to sleep for half a year straight. Fortunately for him, he came to the right house, as Aaron's bed was well-schooled in holding a teenage school dropout. My list of "siblings" grew, making me both excited and a bit nervous when I'd stop by to say hi.)

All that practice growing up with the office in our basement and pretending to be the secretary could now serve me well, I thought. But it didn't quite work out that way. For one thing, I learned that secretaries actually have to do more than just swivel on a chair while managing to stay upright, and kindly answering the phones. There were bills to pay and accounts to reconcile. Well I could learn, couldn't I? After all, I was an almost-valedictorian. But the day I made a mistake that could have cost the business $10K, I knew it even before my father said it, "Shif, this ain't your cup of tea."

Finding one's cup of tea, I was beginning to realize, was a lot harder than finding tuna sandwiches at the corner deli. It was becoming clear that one had to make her own cup of tea in life if she was to really savor it and be nourished by it. It was highly specific, and no two cups were alike. A cup of tea could burn you if too hot, but not at all satisfy if it was too cold. And making it just right would become more and more elusive.

Mothering and Tea-Drinking Don't Always Mix

Zack and I were blessed with a daughter within the first year of our marriage. Aviva was 112.5 ounces of pure, dark chocolate-haired, mild-flavored, chunky deliciousness—leaving me with forty-three unwanted pounds of un-metabolized Muenster cheese and cookie-dough ice cream. Despite a weird habit of getting her pacifier handle stuck around the top of her ear, she'd precociously develop into a model mother-in-training, replete with first-born suggestions for how to improve our parenting of her siblings who followed soon after. It would be only two handful years later that she'd tell us she was running away one snowy night (I could have told her a thing or two about snowstorms) and to check the mailbox for her note, which we'd best read if we wanted to find our other children in their beds at night. We weathered that storm well enough to attract her return to our warm home within an hour or two.

If I thought my ideal tea was to be found in mothering, let's just say it this way: Mothering does not always go down smoothly and warm your bones. It is not done as a feel-good measure in life, for if there is ever a place to trip you up and bring you down, it is here. Mothering can burn and freeze at the same time, like a fever that simultaneously warms and chills.

This was, not surprisingly, going to call for countless conversations. Deciding to have children was a weighty discussion for the first two decades of our marriage; and the discussions on raising them, endless. I knew that you can only parent "the person you are." That could only mean one thing: I'd have no choice but to grow myself as a person if I wanted to accommodate the needs of a child. Sharing my deep space would be a super challenge, starting with letting another human being literally live there. Even if I wanted to, I wasn't sure I could really do that.

For someone who liked to dance, this would require a deep choreographing of my values that would likely have me stretching well beyond my natural composition while trying not to injure myself in the movement. There were many reasons why I could want children, ranging from the selfish, expiring illusion that *mis*takes our children as belonging exclusively to us—in a way quite unlike anything else in this world that we might claim as our own—to the selfless, inspired desire to give all you can to soulfully build another human being, granting him/her the once-in-a-lifetime opportunity that we humans get in this world. And I do not overlook the most obvious benefit: having children so they will come visit you in the nursing home into which they eventually put you. And while I suppose it is inside of a woman's heart to want to mother, it is far from natural to actually do it well. I had seen the women in Israel, while I was studying there, mother large families, wondering how they made room in their homes and hearts for all these souls. Clearly, if the heart had space, the home would accommodate, too.

The answer is as individual as the souls born. I had heard meaningful rhetoric from the bold "I will stop having children when the six million Jews who were murdered in the Holocaust are all accounted for," to the ethereal "What greater spiritual privilege is there than to serve as a conduit for G-d's will to bring life to His Earth and to try to raise it for the next world? (Remember the two worlds discussed earlier?) Populate the world despite the overgrowth of problems in it." I was familiar with the biblical injunction to "be fruitful and multiply," and had been taught that we'd be asked in our post-life Heavenly judgement if we had tried to honor this part of G-d's will in some way.

All those considerations rang true, but the real answer I had for myself was that there is an internal barometer that registers as whole when you connect to, and bear, your destiny in good faith. For me, that would come to mean raising five children, a smaller quantity than many of the eight to fourteen my relatives and friends produced, but qualitatively unmeasurable, for souls are beyond compare.

One part of me knew that mothers power the world; that the work they do in raising souls is nothing less than building humanity itself, and is beyond the value of any dollar amount— which is why they get paid exactly *nothing*. But *nothing* did not sit well in my pocket or in my psyche. As for a mother's honor, it was generic; there were lots of mothers in the world, although only a select few brave souls would call me *their* mother.

To attract my half-hearted maternal instincts, I relied heavily on my entrepreneurial eye, which prompted me to consider children as investments in a company. Zack and I would share the stock, wouldn't expect fast returns, would invest in them mutually, while praying for them to yield dividends in due time. We were prepared to assess this market daily as necessary, and at all costs, to preserve their principal while balancing their risk for growth. Meaning: to help our children grow without destroying their natural reserves of personal value. Amateur stock-*builders* that we were.

Zack and I started a small spiral notebook named the "blue book" on account of its color, in which we recorded and reviewed our goals in various areas, during our once-a-week meetings that doubled as outings. Given my unending conflicted feelings about my ability to mother in the way I thought one had to, including park bench-sitting and cookie-baking—things I knew I would not be doing—this ritual helped me to focus on what I could do, not what I couldn't. As a creative mind, a restless soul, who was very young in her own unfolding, I pushed myself beyond considerable innate limitations to be as attentive as I could be while in the house, always being careful to also routinely leave my house without my children. This was meant as a concrete communication to myself that I would preserve my wholeness which was bigger than any one role life would give me.

I was acutely aware that this was to remain a fact between Zack and me, that our children would not feel struggled about, but rather snuggled with our love and valued for their preciousness. Still, while playing my hand at mothering my first several children, I was ever-so-conscious of "G-d, please don't let me destroy my children." I knew what dangers lurked in being a child, having survived them thus far. I don't mind telling you that with my subsequent younger children, I noticed a bit of a shift, finally understanding the pains of parenthood: "Please G-d, don't let my children destroy *me*."

But I must concede to this overall sentiment: that ultimately, children can be the embodiment of the magic of compounded interest. The more they grow, the more interested and attached we become to them as individuals. And with steady, small investments, they can grow beyond our highest calculated hopes.

I do realize that there was a Divine plan here—that had I been given my last children first, the first three would be even more angelic than they are, still floating somewhere in the sky because they would not have had a home to be born into. We would have all self-destructed. But thankfully, our Creator does not do things haphazardly, the way I am naturally inclined in the kitchen.

Actually, I thought I had the mothering all figured out by age nine. "Abba," I informed my father, "I will hire a nanny to stay home with the children," while my imagination had me heading out the door, kissing the children who did not yet exist, to do the glamorous work that still doesn't. With work bag in hand and pump heels on my feet, I wasn't sure what kind of work it would be, but it definitely would be money-making. Basically, why should I do the mothering when I could pay someone else to do it as well as I could, probably even a lot better?

Three decades into the experiment, I have come to better understand both matters—mothering and working outside of my family. And balancing my mattering story here between both the mothering and the professional unfolding is not unlike the actual real-life effort: a deliberate, hard-thinking, and often messy effort. From the perspective of personal mattering, mothering is both small and huge, and is also richly deserving, as children themselves are, of exclusive attention in a book entirely its own. And therefore, an executive decision has been made: While I will occasionally bring my smatterings of mothering to work here, my children will mostly stay out of sight by the close of the next chapter, except for when they think they can make the point better than I can.

Men Can Mother

I discovered something interesting: Men could mother. Mothering is not a gender: it is a spirit. Zack had proven it over and over. No, he couldn't bake, and could cook even less well than I. But he could extend the unconditional love of the maternal heart that I had seen in some of my friends' mothers. His nonjudgmental energy could nurse a wounded spirit, and uplift a hurt or disappointment. He had the listening ear of a present mother, always at the drop of his Orthodox black hat, to let his children know they were the most important part of his life. I believe there is one word in the thesaurus that I have seen listed as a synonym for that other worldly, heart quality we call *selfless:* **mother**. There were fewer favorite things to him than getting wet and cold on the sled with the kids while braving the hills of freshly delivered snow. Not me. I was already cold enough and could not bear going outside, even to have some supposed fun on the sled. Yes, we'd joke occasionally that had his heart been born into a woman's body, our family might have been double its size.

Men Can Even Birth

With that same selflessness, Zack had birthed me—if you agree that bringing someone to *creative* life can be called birthing. Time would tell this truth: Under his loving watch, (the watch he still doesn't own because mine has not yet been replaced), he'd help raise all of us into one joyful unit, especially when I was on yet another professional or community activist front. And very often, I looked to him for mothering cues as together we birthed and mothered our children, especially at their bed time. It had been a long time since I helped put my little sisters to bed. When Brenna was in charge, she had them on their beds, and out with the lights as scheduled. When I tried it, we ate and joked around, and then after I wore myself down, I left their rooms with the brilliant prompt to "put yourselves to sleep already, will you?"

"Zack, why do children need to have stories read to them when they can read by themselves?" I'd innocently ask as he read books on their beds. He'd also take family trips with them, especially on Sundays. Walks in the park and sit-downs by the brook across the street from our house were part of the routine. These were too strenuous for my high-heeled feet and my short-tempered, under-developed patience. All the while, he'd be imparting his fine character to them in the most joyful, nonchalant ways. They had no suspicion that they were learning right from wrong, just in case there was a rebellious bone in one of them that would have adversely reacted to that. (Rebellious, anti-authority bones ran on my side of the family, you may have noticed.)

Mothers at Work

Let's just be clear that, for me, the unceasingly demanding work of mothering began at week six of each pregnancy. I suffered from dysfunctional nausea, the kind that was popularized by Kate Middleton, who was hospitalized for it. *Hyperemesis Gravidarum* is not commonly known by its unpronounceable name, nor does it affect most pregnant women. For the woman who suffers from this debilitating nausea, the pregnancy can cost her an agonizing amount of physical and emotional travail. If you didn't know any better, you'd mistake it for astonishing laziness or depression, when in fact she is trying to keep her moment-to-moment equilibrium, probably having had to give up any paying work and all domestic chores that require more than two minutes of stamina.

From its onset, I'd be relegated to my bed, unable to tolerate the sights and smells of food, including the few Zack tried to make that my children ran away from, too. Any cooking that I routinely struggled to do came to an abrupt cease fire. Unable to keep down anything, I'd splash my face with water in the hopes that some would find its way into my body and hydrate it. This was pre-Zofran medicine, which has helped some women in recent years, leaving me with IV treatments in the hospital which I refused. Acupuncture, ear patches, nausea bands, and comedy shows were all pressed into service to alleviate the extreme lack of appetite that left me miserable in my bed day after day for months. Growing a baby's toes and hands while lying down . . . how hard could that be? Ever had a stomach virus? Multiply that by ten.

Children are a blessing; so are appetites, by the way, even though we struggle greatly with both at times. And I admit that I did introspect whether all that emotional ambivalence about mothering had settled itself right down into my belly, playing a part in nauseating me to the core. Just a thought.

After all that work of carrying and birthing a child into this world, people would curiously wonder out loud. "So, what do you do?" they'd constantly ask me, in the most casual tones they could simulate. What they really wanted to know is: How do you use your brain, and how do you make money? *You do make money, don't you?*

It's hard to value the home front when most others don't. I crafted a response early on this game: "I have a home business," never daring to elaborate that I considered my children to be a home business, and mothering to be my profession. Yes, despite the recurring nag that none of it mattered, I considered myself a professional mother—a mother who worked very hard at her craft, although I had little idea how to do it, absolutely no idea how to measure it, and made no money at it. It was all process, with no immediate prize—excruciating for an externally-driven, money-needing, human being like me. Unfortunately, the same could be said about my professional path; I had little idea what to do, and therefore, unsurprisingly, made no money doing it.

Sure seemed like Aunt Rosalie. She didn't work and didn't make money; she had to be supported by my parents. We knew that when her birthday cards, accompanied by checks, would arrive in the mail, they were backed with her warm heart, but no cold cash. It was likely that check would bounce, with the empty promise of a full-looking but leaking ball.

"Zack, I have to find work to call my own. Children are valuable, but they are not money-making propositions. And . . ." I drew a deep hesitation here, ". . . I need something more." I know women weren't supposed to admit that. But I was not in the habit of hiding an important truth like that from myself, and not from Zack, either. And while I had a hard time accepting that truth, he didn't. As my non-teacher "reacher," he knew quite well this was on its way, which was why he agreed that we should enroll Aviva in a playgroup at the age of one, even though I was still jobless. "It's cheaper than a room at Shepherd Pratt," he said, referring to the local place one went to recharge their mental health. We reconsidered only for a moment when the playgroup leader called to say, "Please send enough lunch along for your child; she ate the crayons today." We beefed up her lunches, agreeing that protein was a healthier food choice for a growing baby.

Finding life outside the home was not fake or foreign to me. It was most definitely a gift, not a crime, to have work to call your own. Although most of my childhood friends' mothers had not worked outside the home as they were raising us, I had seen that "working" mommy model in my childhood home. My mother worked out of necessity, but there was no mistaking her fulfillment along the way after having turned down her four-year scholarship to NYU in order to marry at eighteen and begin mothering at the age of nineteen. Parental support for my outside-the-home stirrings was wholeheartedly encouraged. "What keeps you busy all day?" was the refrain I could hear, even if it was not audibly expressed. My parents were driven and hard-working people, with lots of talent to give their business, their community, and their children. The talent might not have been hereditary, but their drive sure was. And I had not forgotten my childhood nighttime conversations with Brenna reminding me that I'd need to help pay bills, which were starting to come as regularly as my angst about my non-mattering.

There may have been a time when it was termed a luxury for a man, and certainly a woman, to try to find and train for a profession they actually liked. And even now, it is not always possible to do just that, certainly at the beginning of one's working life, which can be a most painful reality, though no less honorable. It is consistent with Torah approach to incline our professional search with our interests and G-d given talents. I recalled learning that the love for the ocean that captivated Zebulun, one of the twelve sons of the Patriarch Jacob, was his cue that "his ship had come in," i.e., his service of G-d would dock around his commercial merchant shipping business, which would in turn enrich him to support those whose callings were in esoteric, unpaid pursuits. Indeed, our particular inherent gifts are meant to direct us towards achieving our purpose, at least in part. In my mind, what differentiated a job from a career was just that: One was to exclusively earn income, while the other was to realize a bigger outcome. If this is also an American-made concept, I bought into it.

A job or, dare I say it, a career, was worlds apart from the domesticated front, which typically offers less spoken gratitude and even less immediate reward than the paying job . . . while demanding more than you have to give in patience, endurance, and enthusiasm. But I wasn't prepared to completely abandon my children while professionally finding myself. Why not? I considered mothering to be a major part of building myself. Characters get built on hard choices; sacrifice, you might say. Ideally, these are smart sacrifices you could choose, though the choice isn't always up to us and our liking. And that is why I made accommodations that only I could, disregarding the many voices of disapproval: I would limit my time in the kitchen, and absolutely no baking, not even chocolate chip cookies. That would push me over my personal limit into a world of smallness, and that is not a good place to mother from. Mothers are at their best when they can hold expansive hope and vision until their children grow into their better selves, which, I should tell you, takes forever—and shall always remain a work in progress.

And as I pondered how to further prepare myself for the paying market, I continued building the home front. I birthed a few children while taking on positions that accommodated my limited time, energy, and under-trained skills, i.e., community volunteer work that afforded me great opportunity to sharpen my people and executive skills while discovering my talents and interests. A free education, you might say. Said otherwise, a job minus the paycheck.

With three children on the home front, Zack had left his studies now to work in the real estate industry. While I manned the home front, casting about which career direction to take, I prepared the space like a couple who wants a child prepares a room in their home, hoping that energy would soon manifest itself in material form. Now in our first home (bought on the cheap at an auction by my real estate father), we were beginning to fill up the three-bedroom house with children. And that was when I called our contractor, the really-could-do everything master Joe, who also became our close friend, faithfully extending the most flexible terms of payment—pay what you can, when you can.

Calling in Joe this time would prove to be a parenting oversight or crime—depending on whose side you are on—that our third daughter Zeeva has leveled against us, with judgment still pending. For this kid, whose first word was "more," I had assigned a little motto: "Zeeva can never have enough fun, food, or friends." She had all three in abundance, this amply-sized package of enthusiasm who just wanted to be cuddled in my hip pocket all day. It was when she was in ninth grade, she has since clarified, that her fashionably teenaged panic attacks started. And she is virtually certain that we caused them.

Specifically, she came home one day and found a hole above the head of her bed. That hole was actually put there by Joe, who was acting on executive orders to knock down that wall so this room would now connect with the master bedroom. Parental plans called for the room to be renamed; it was now *Mommy's office*. Not sure how we forgot to first apprise Zeeva of this friendly corporate takeover, but we invited her to relocate to the newly-renovated bedroom downstairs, which was originally supposed to be my new office. But then I realized that the new basement room was too far away from the rest of the house for it to be functional for me. It wasn't because I was scared being all the way in the basement: no that wasn't it at all. I just needed my office, the command center, to be more centrally located. And besides, didn't she want a nice quiet teenage space all to herself? We helped her pack and carry her bags to her new quarters, soon to be appointed with new linen and carpet of her choosing. She remains flooded with anxious memories, especially when she recalls her school notes being washed away during Hurricane Isabel—that storm in 2003 that alerted us to the fact that our sump pump in her room needed a little repair. Ultimately, this disturbance in her sleeping patterns was nothing a little chat with our other close family friend, psychologist Dr. Norma, couldn't solve. Now Zeeva is a magnificent person, her strength having been forged in the stormy waters of youth. If nothing else, seems like very fine parenting to me.

And while most females I knew wanted an expanded gourmet kitchen, I wanted something useful. I was thrilled because I now had an office to call my own. No "baby" yet, but a real chair and desk to nurse my ambition for doing work that weighed heavily on my mattering scale.

As I labored under the burden of professional mothering, cerebrally knowing its importance though seldom feeling it, I continued my search for professional mattering. This process would never end, just as parenting does not. But I knew I had to start somewhere.

"Oh G-d, please direct me," I'd beg, knowing that passion, as children, is G-d given, and I didn't seem to have any yet. And if I did, it would vanish as quickly as it had appeared. Would anything have staying power? Some of my friends were busy pursuing careers in medicine and business, while others were seriously attracted to social work, education, computer science and accounting. I could not figure out what was suitable, and at times, wondered if there would ever be anything that was. There was no one in my life who held out a vision for my pathway, certainly no one who was helping me shape it. I'd have to do this on my own, as my queen grandmother would often say, "If is to be, it is up to me. *Que sera, sera.*" I would stay the course, with the constant prayer that something would have my name on it.

Meanwhile, while mothering little souls, I learned much about myself that could be integrated into my search for a non-mothering career. Staying calm in the center of child tantrums helped me to remain steady while facing tantrums belonging to bigger babies known as tough clients and co-workers who'd later emerge in my getting-paid life. I also experienced the reality that bearing the discomfort of doing small things, the kind that go unnoticed, builds capacity to do the larger things that might be uncomfortable, but are integral to moving along the continuum of enlarged opportunity. This has been translated into a Mommy motto: "If you can do it, no big deal, do it. If you can't do it, then you *must* do it, so it really is no big deal." Because every kind of work has parts that you don't particularly like, but need to do anyway.

And with my children depending on me to innovate creative excuses for why they could not do their homework *again*, or why they must be allowed to drink during class, and most commonly, why they were too tired to come to school on time, I had no choice but to become a serious communicator.

This would soon translate into paid writing opportunities. However, I am still waiting to be hired by parents to write their children's notes for similar infractions I wrote for mine: the coming late, leaving early, and in fact won't be there at all tomorrow. Free tip: Nice stationery is a huge advantage when crafting these notes, helping the words sound a bit different each time—like putting the same lettuce tomato pickle salad in yet another dish, making a sorry excuse for a salad seem a little more palatable this time.

Gazing Through the Panes

If we want a looking glass through which we can see ourselves, and to begin to grow our abilities—sensibility, responsibility, capability, flexibility, and yes culpability—it seems to me that parenting is as clear as it gets. The Torah refers to children with a Hebrew word that connotes both "your children" and "your builders." Each child hooked into a different piece of my persona, some sticking more painfully than others, but taking me in baby steps along the path of promise to building a multi-faceted personal wholeness.

If we allow ourselves to pull up the blinds and look through the window panes of our home, we notice that panes are a two-way glass. You can see outside, and you can be seen inside. This brings into focus a thought by Carl Jung: "He who looks outside, dreams. He who looks inside, awakens." It is easy to see outside when the sun is shining brightly, but hard to be seen inside because of the shadows. Yet in the darker moments, when it may be hard to see clearly outside, one can be seen inside, a lot more easily—especially if *you* are doing the looking. Raising children would have me in a constant state of seeing, serving, and observing, sometimes towards the sunny outside, and sometimes towards the darker inner sides. Assessing, advocating, communicating, searching, researching, crying and laughing—with myself and with my children—were all part of my being a professional mother with a personal touch.

CHAPTER FOURTEEN

Right Life, Wrong Turns

Most of the shadows of this life are caused by our standing in our own sunshine.
—Ralph Waldo Emerson, philosopher

"I'm here," I told Dr. Norma, "because I want to drop this extra weight from the birth of three daughters. And if you can do something about the fact that I can't get out of bed on Sundays when the girls are home from school, I'm sure my family will thank you." Yes, in that order. To me, carrying the extra weight was by far the heavier burden. That was the dangling carrot; always had been.

Married, mothering . . . and unable to get up in the morning with any kind of purposeful energy, if I got up at all. Filling a young child's fantasy from hour to hour was hard work, prompting me to say, "The years may fly by, but the days go by so slowly." Sundays were the worst because the kids were home from school. I'd fumble out of bed to give some form of cereal breakfast to three food-enthusiastic mouths attached to heads with messy hair begging to be brushed and bodies needing to be dressed for the outing I would not be going on. Zack would be the entertainment director; I'd stay behind as usual.

Was there a larger problem going on here? I didn't even think beyond the weight issue until Brenna told me that watching me was "like watching someone trying to run with their hands tied behind their back. Shif, you need professional help." I turned to her so many times for guidance. "Maybe, as usual, she's onto something before I am," I said to Zack.

I asked G-d to help me find a therapist "who wouldn't be unduly challenged by my complicated nature. You know, someone who'd be sharp enough, and humble enough, not to be tempted to think that my ready resistance was a conscious power struggle." And someone patient, "who understands that some people are slower to understand all those terrible things they need to fix about themselves, and how to do it." I was given two names of professionals by a trusted source and left phone messages for both. Dr. Norma returned the phone call first. First come, first to serve.

And that is how G-d presented this great gift into my life, a compassionate and skilled therapist who'd help me sort myself out. It was time to fix the cracks at the foundation, just enough to let the light in—and out. Brenna often reminded me, "What we don't fix gets passed down to the next generation." If there was one huge gift I could give to my children, it was to do this work in front of me. Someone else could bake the chocolate chip cookies for them; but no one could mix my ingredients for a more cohesive, better-rising me. I know you believe me that I would have paid someone to do this inner work for me, if that was possible. Just like I'd have paid someone to exercise my body for me if that was feasible. Alas, that someone was me.

If not now, when? If not me, then who? I was ready. "When the student is ready, the teacher appears."

And the first lesson I was to learn was that there was a lot more weighing on me than the extra pounds that found me during *and after* each pregnancy. It turned out that the extra physical baggage that once again clung to me as a child to its parent, was the last to be put down. Emotional baggage comes first. Always.

My Next Cup of Tee

Sipping from this next cup of tea, or *tee* in this case, as Dr. Norma was a golf aficionado, we'd work to find the holes so that we could take a swing at filling them

"Dr. Norma," I said, "I know this isn't about Zack." By now, he had earned the highest level of trust I'd ever given anyone. He was uncommonly devoted.

"Wise of you to know that, and honest of you to admit it. Brave, too."

"You know I have three young daughters I adore. But this stay-at-home mommy business is not agreeing with me." No surprises here. I never had the illusion that children would fill my heart with all the joy I'd ever need. They can do a good job, and they can do it in a way that perhaps nothing else can. But they cannot do it all. The heart and mind are big places, requiring nourishment from a variety of pursuits.

"It's that inner emptiness that I have felt so much in my growing up years. It is here again, knocking on the door." Actually, it was banging and setting off alarms to alert me that an unwelcome intruder was on its way in. My bed would call me back to its embrace, to its nonjudgmental and undemanding nature—allowing me to linger there in my nightgown while wondering what to do with my life.

Dr. Norma agreed that contemplating our purpose on this Earth is a worthwhile endeavor. "It's just that for most people, Shifra, Sundays are not the best days to do it, as they are typically well-suited for some family time." But I was busy being dysfunctional, which took about six or seven hours of every Sunday. I'd then attempt to scale the mountain of growing despair with a hot bath, hoping it would ease my way into some outfit that would make me feel human so that I could mount a counter-assault on the helpless frustration of being lost in my own life.

And even though Zack was an expert in early rising and a great whistler-while-at-work person, he understood *my* inner world. Even more, he admired it and encouraged me to do everything I could to heal and grow it, with that "motherly" spirit he so ably displayed.

There were times I'd protest, "Zack, I'm not going to Dr. Norma today. Costs too much money, not enough progress. Look at me, still overweight and overwhelmed by the needs of helpless children, including myself." He gently let me know that he was not excusing me from this class with Dr. Norma; he'd drive me if he had to. This was one course I wasn't allowed to drop. "Final." When he said final, I'd drop the conversation. Because it happened so rarely, it had shock value.

Dr. Norma offered me a lot of clarity and compassion, along with healthy doses of discipline in the form of cognitive behavioral therapy, the same medicine she administered to her students at the special school she started for children with learning differences.

"This is not a clinical post-partum depression. Nor is it laziness." She discerned that while the active stages of an inner struggle can mimic both—depression and laziness—in reality, epic battles of hope and hopelessness are being fought, *one thought at a time.* I was so grateful that she appreciated the scope of the struggle, without having to judge or incriminate me like so many others made it their job to do over the years, essentially asking me to "stop being you, will you *please?*" Thanks, I would if I could.

Neither Zack nor Dr. Norma saw this as selfishness, and they wouldn't allow me to, either. They applauded my efforts to help myself, a human being struggling to raise herself toward higher ground, above the inertia of a strong, long-existing downward pull. Dr. Norma herself knew this very well from the inside, having pursued her psychology degree while raising her five children, then leaving a marriage of twenty-five years. She knew human beings struggle and make hard choices that they hope will pay off in the long run. And that efforts yield fruit along the way, too, like the positive energy generated when on the right track. This engenders a spirit of newfound courage and enthusiasm in our lives, allowing hope to have its way with our downcast souls. And one needs healthy thinking to do it, starting with the belief that working hard is healthy, even if uncomfortable at times, and "you won't crack." If only she knew how often I felt that I was close to doing just that.

"There are significant blocks in your way, bigger than your weight. You do realize that, Shifra, don't you?" *Stinking thinking* is what she called it. "Yes, you are complicated, and yes, we will need to do some serious "re-parenting," as many people do. You will need to reach in and redirect a lot of old patterns in thought and action. I will help you, but you need to do the work. And it is *hard* work."

She made it clear that while she was exquisitely sensitive to the power that parents have in shaping us, there would be very little blaming our shortcomings on them. *That must be the hard work she is talking about,* I reasoned to myself. I'd have to get real and understand the deal: parents are human beings who were once parented, too, and really do suffer human limitations. "You mean I can't complain and insist that others are to be faulted for my misery?" All work, no fun.

"Yes, of course we will name real people and real issues, but we won't get stuck there. We move past them by making the choice that they will not stand in your way, *they will lead your way.* Anger, resentment, hurt, pain, they are all real. But they need not block your progress when you learn how to let them power it." I'd learn to get on the right side of the fight, and a fight it was.

I'd need to do the inner work to heal. Reverting to a pesky pattern of needing to know in advance the outcome and timeline, I'd inquire, "Dr. Norma, how will I know when I am 'healed,' and how long do2es this all take?" I'd learn that it was a continuum, like virtually everything in life, and that it could not necessarily be linear-plotted and neatly controlled like a dog on a leash, or more personally, like a toddler in a harness.

"I cannot give a definite answer, but here's a hint: although something might not actually become easier, you will become stronger so that it will feel easier," like lifting the heavy weights she insisted she needed in order to maintain her slim shape.

Soon enough, Norma realized I didn't play the life game the way she did. Actually, it sometimes seemed I didn't play any game the way others did. She asked me to write down things between sessions, to note on paper my thoughts. A non-journaler, I just couldn't do this with any regularity. "Never mind, we will do it your way. If you keep it all in your head, just bring your head to each session." Dr. Norma lovingly deferred to my stance, which was awkward at times, prodding me along with small adjustments that were beginning to make for a smoother stride.

"You suffer from low frustration tolerance, meaning you give up—and in—quickly and easily. Like your Aunt Rosalie." She knew all about Aunt Rosalie, and she knew when to draw her into the conversation in a way that would help, not hurt, my growing process. That must have taken a lot of skill, and restraint, on her part. And yes, of course I knew what she meant about getting frustrated easily; how many times had I told Zack I was not going back, that I was giving up. "I am not a process person, I am a results person. Forget this healing stuff."

But the weight was still there. And I had three children to raise, meaning I needed to grow myself so that I could do the best job I could, as their professional mother. Growing patience and courage and endurance, they were the names of this game.

And the one underlying lesson she constantly reviewed with me: *entitlement* is a spoiled word. Our human value is not the result of the talents you've been given, that's just good fortune that you did nothing to deserve. And nobody owes you anything for having them. You are responsible for using them wisely in the service of others—and that is where your worth is to be found and praised. She absolutely hated the sense of entitlement with which many people crowned themselves, thinking they were special because of an endowment that they had not even earned of their own accord.

In time, I'd actually have a powerful exercise to teach myself:

Take your most vexing child—probably the one most similar to you—and speak to her or him the way you would want to be spoken to. There will never be a more powerful piece of parenting than that, for it will do double duty: It will help your child, while healing you.

Sweeping Inner Corners

All topics were on the table when it came to the home front.

"I can't sweep the floor," I told Norma. "It's not that it's beneath me; it's *beyond* me."

I just didn't know how to do mundane things without thinking I'd go crazy. Making a bed was a "for crying out loud" experience. Yes, routine can set you free—if and when you are ready. Until then, it is a tear-inducing, crazy-making, conforming bit of misery that made getting up in the morning arduous and almost excruciating. All the sadness of my nine-year-old self not being able to play happily on the stark, too black and white keys of Mrs. Goodman's piano returned.

And now the demands of having to sort the laundry into categories of colors and white were not only time-consuming; *they were meaningless bangs on my mattering.* In time, I'd come to create my own system whereby any laundry that passed beneath my fingers would bathe with other clothing wanting similar temperatures and textures, and not be needlessly bothered by a uniform system. Even with a little help in the house to do things that I will never do as skillfully, I labored under starched ideas of what made a mother a good one or a bad one, and of how much I mattered, if at all. The laundry was contentedly clean, but I remained with one huge wrinkle to iron out: Where to hang my mattering?

Week after week, Norma and I would approach this inner work with the aim of aligning realities and ideals, while figuring out the best approaches to keep me on par with my stated goals which she helped me articulate. Perhaps mothering was worthy of my efforts—even if it didn't accord with my more fanciful definition of meaningful work, and certainly went unpaid. As I cast about for balance, she allowed me my individual pace, with a loosened grip that made its intended impact on my forward trajectory and eventual recovery.

My slow-to-get-it comprehension, never mistaken by her as stubbornness or indolence, began to yield to the wisdom of dozens of conversations with her. Both the force of her logic and the warmth of her heart found its mark in the holes of a spirit worn down by not appreciating its inherent human value.

Then came an important moment, the day I realized something while driving on the Baltimore Beltway, past the elegant banquet hall that showcased a colossal crystal chandelier in its three-story window, practically lighting up the road alongside.

"Dr. Norma, you know that chandelier you see while driving on Baltimore's Route 695? I find myself wondering if I see it when traveling in both directions, how do I know if I am coming or going? How can I tell in which direction I am heading?"

While she was waiting patiently for me to drive home my thought, I said, "When I am driving in one direction, that light is to my right, very close to me. When I am returning in the opposite direction, it is to my left, at a distance well across the highway."

"Yes, that's right," she said, waiting to see if my point actually had one.

"That is how healing from the past is, isn't it? As I travel, I still see it. But it is at a distance, because I am traveling away from it."

Norma, to this day, remains a dear friend, one I call upon when I need to refresh my parenting skills or press further when in uncharted fears. My parting gift to her was a coffee mug, a tea-cup, if you will, with an attached spoon in the shape of a golf tee. And hers to me was an inscription she wrote in her book *Growin' up Good*: "You are a very, very special friend. And a good mother, too."

Thanks Dr. Norma for the friendship; it is so mutual. As for the mothering, the jury's still out, TBD by some maturing individuals, some of whom now have children of their own. That, in and of itself, should give me the benefit of the clout, though I might have to wait to read their books.

As a final note on filling the holes, at which I was slowly growing more adept: I did better in real life than on the golf course. A few years back, I took our son Daniel for his foray at filling his own holes. With him sitting beside me in the golf cart I was driving, he held the club in his hand, looking like the pro he envisioned himself to be. Somehow, I rode us up on a small hill, whereupon the cart tilted downwards, leaving me hanging half-out, close to the ground. Daniel climbed out, letting me know, "You are about to fall out. I am not going down with you."

Luckily, the office staff sent someone to help me out. "We had a feeling you'd need a bit of help steering clear of small mountains. We've been keeping an eye on you from our office camera." With that, the staff member extended a helping hand to extricate me from my wrong turn. And Daniel got back in the cart and putted away as if he had been swinging at man made holes all his life.

Recovering the self that is waiting for us as part of our destiny is a demanding, relentless, and uncompromising process.

Necessary, and rewarding too—if you want to live big, and to matter.

CHAPTER FIFTEEN

Subject to Change

It is our choices that show who we truly are, far more than our abilities.

—J.K. ROWLING

IF SUNDAYS WERE THE HARDEST, this Sunday was impossible. And while I cannot recall exactly what transpired on *that* Sunday, I found myself with keys in hand. "Zack, I'm running away. I don't know where I need to go. I just know that I must." Must or bust situations were not usual, but were always unpleasant for my family, so I knew it was best for me to just leave. "Mommy's in time-out," I heard my children whisper to each other, as they graciously accepted that I would not be going on their Sunday outing once again.

I should have caught this sooner, the inside-mounting pressure begging for my attention, but I ignored it for lack of knowing what to do. I was stuck in my life, beyond a reasonable number of times a human should get stuck. Where to turn now? Was I running from, or to—I could not tell. Technically, it wasn't running; it was limping along, with a lot of low back pain frequenting my life.

With that, I plopped myself into the family van to focus my eyes, burning with despair, on the road ahead. Where *am* I going? My car drove me in the familiar direction of my children's school, habituated as it was to do the countless carpools that accounted for an inordinate amount of my motherly business. And I landed at the local Barnes and Nobles. B&N, I should add, was profiting from my kind of life, the one that was hard to figure out. But they deserved my cash that day, because a book fell into my near-desperate hands that would be my next teacher.

Welcome, Barbara Sher, best-selling author of books on creativity and overcoming resistance towards actualizing it. After several years of Dr. Norma's guidance with discovering the self that had been overwhelmed by my youth, this student was ready again. Barbara would be helping me with the next piece of work—to listen carefully and respectfully to what I needed to create, because creativity is a holy healer. It was time to recover myself: the parts that were both known and not yet known to me. Like the extra rooms I'd keep finding in the home of my dreams, I'd be swept up into a maze of wonder that there was yet more and more inside of me that I never knew existed.

Under Barbara's influence, I'd come to understand her assertion that we all have genius, a word I'd personally define as *unblocked consciousness*. That is, if you could clear away the resistant clutter, you could gain access to closets full of creative genius waiting to be fashioned. Or as author Julia Cameron[10] presents in her work, everyone has a vein of gold in which they can brilliantly perform. But as usual, I could not find mine without taking the circuitous path. I was consigned to rummaging through my closet full of unworn genius, waiting for the right match to take out and wear.

In the "No"

Just as so many of my dieting attempts left me with a trail of confusion, the elusive search for how to practically build and employ my skills and interests often left me in a collapsed state of despair. Why was it so hard to figure this out? Why, G-d, couldn't I have been given the technological brain that would fixate itself brilliantly on how to make money in the hi-tech

10 *Vein of Gold*, Julia Cameron, Penguin 1997.

world? If you are born to this young century, do try to come outfitted with that kind of brain. Forget being high-minded, drop simple logic; techno-logic is the buzz-word. It will serve you well because this is how our world is wired . . . wirelessly.

With resources competing for my limited time, energy, and money, I had decided after Aviva's birth to take a basic training as a makeup artist and color consultant. Thus was born a business selling my private line of cosmetics along with make-up application services and color consulting. I wasn't sure it would be satisfying, but I relied heavily on a good friend who came to work with me, and whose love for all things beauty would carry many a client to classy content. I was mostly able to satisfy my clients, except for when trying to indulge knotty requests— teaching me that making a client's face glow is quite a different art than the hair-blow. One day, my client asked me to style her hair. I tried to tell her that I hadn't trained in hair, but she said she trusted me. When the blow dryer unceremoniously sucked up one third of her hair, which I had to slowly unwind and return back to her head, she realized she should have believed me—that I don't do hair. After a few years, my trustworthy friend and employee relocated, leaving me with the decision to sell out and continue toward a different professional palette.

But nothing was black and white. My destiny, it seemed, wanted to call out to me in bits and pieces, in a few pages at a time, not whole chapters. Everything always seemed to be a misfit, or uninteresting, or too hard. Forever and always the contrarian, I naturally said no to most things. My family came to profile this challenge as, "Mommy is always in the *no*."

I thought deeply about a colorful comment I once made to a cosmetic colleague of mine, "I like helping people look more vibrant, but what I *really* want to do is help them to *be* more vibrant." And that's what made psychology become a thought to be considered. Other subjects on the drawing board—nutrition, social science, communications, midwifery, and commerce— were also calling my name, until something would come to dissuade me from their pursuit. "You won't like psychology as a profession," said an occasional mentor of ours. "You will feel too boxed in." Without the benefit of search engines and online programs, I really didn't understand what that meant, so I settled for my preliminary "no"-jerk reaction when hearing the words *box* and *in*, as *in the box*, something I knew I couldn't practice and thus quickly dropped the idea.

Brenna weighed in on the communications front: "Forget about a degree in communications, Shif. No degree can teach you what you already know about how to communicate with people. Waste of money and time." And more opinions, some unsolicited, were sent my way, further diminishing my choice-making to chaos.

Fight to the Finish

With so many false starts and frustrating ends along the way, Zack and I decided that with three small children who were old enough to walk and talk, but still young enough to think school was a fun place to go, now would be a better time than any to return to college to finish my undergraduate degree. Maybe finishing something concrete would help a creative type like me concretize the creativity, the genius Barbara promised was there. I would start small with one or two courses which I could work on while the children were in school. Educational psychology was a subject I needed, and so it became the first course I'd crash. Always late to the game, I called the local university that was offering the fall course. "Can I still register for this course?"

"It starts tonight, actually in about an hour," said the woman who answered my call. "It might not be too late. Call the professor yourself and ask her if she will allow you to join."

"I'll see you in an hour," invited Professor Ellen, the best kind of professor you could hope for when returning to college after a break of so many years. Seeing me engage in my usual habit of second and third-guessing whether or not I should do this, Zack said he would drive me and that he'd put the kids to bed, which he usually did anyway—two offers I did not refuse.

In this very first class, I found myself with twenty-year-olds. When the fifty-something professor with an unruly bosom and clear, twinkly light-green eyes asked each of us why we had come to her class, I did not expect to trigger the burst of laughter that erupted when I said, "I ran away from my children." And during the break on that first night, when my newfound friend, Professor Ellen, overhead me on the phone asking Zack to pick me up, she said she'd bring me home if I didn't mind her run-down pick-up truck. (It was miles better than the food-delivery driver in Israel who agreed to let me sit in the back of his truck with the groceries and deliver me home on his route, because I hadn't managed to hail a cab.)

This course led to the next professor, from whom I managed to hitch a piece of important parenting advice. It was during a Psychology of Personality class discussion about shaping a healthy psyche that I had the chance to raise a question that had been on my mind for a decade. I suppose there were cheaper ways to find out the answer, but I just couldn't resist. Is it better to err on the side of leniency when parenting or better to be harsh and strict? In a nearly unanimous show of support, almost all of those young hands voted in favor of the more benign approach, officially vindicating my free-spirited, if limited, brand of mothering.

In the last stretch of my degree program, to earn a degree that I could not imagine putting to good use but was never-theless on the "must get it done" list, I had to travel to another city for a mandatory educational weekend as part of my "final project," an actual course I had to design. I had not yet met this group of administrators or students. As I came late, I had to guess which of the two doors at opposite sides of the hall would put me at the back of the room where I could slip in unnoticed. Spotting a table with only three men around it, while the other tables were fully occupied, I reasoned they must have come late, too, and would be only too understanding and happy to have me sit with them. Pleased with my straightforward thinking, I happily settled in at that table and began to follow the flow of things. In less time than it takes to eat a half of a Skor candy bar, I realized I might have been better off staying at home trying to raise my kids. As the man to my immediate right spoke, it became uncomfortably clear that I was sitting at the administration table. Directions were never my strength; the only thing left for me to do was to inch up a bit straighter and enjoy pretending that I was on staff, and therefore mattered as much as them.

Of Eatitude and Creatitude

So now I had the degree, but again, no direction. What does one do with a degree in social science that one got because one had no other idea what to pursue? Just as Geneen Roth had helped shape my attitudes about food, resulting in my *eatitude,* Barbara was impactful in crafting my thoughts about creativity—my *creatitude.* She was the first person I encountered who understood something about working around creative resistance. In one of our conversations that I had been blessed to share with her, she asked me, "What do you want to be?"

"I think I want to be great. Don't all people?" I asked Barbara.

"No, they don't. Many say they want to be happy."

"They sound similar to me. Maybe people figure it's easier to be happy than great, so they will settle for happy. But either way, both—great and happy—are just impractical adjectives. How do I find the grounded nouns that lead to a real answer? How do I figure out my next steps?" People with whom I had volunteered in the community were beginning to throw me some direction by complimenting me with generalities, such as, *you are creative, talented, whatever*; definitely a step in the right direction. But one step does not a whole path make. Our human story, isn't it? So much potential, so little direction.

"Let me explain to you the difference between gifts and skills," Barbara began. "We're all skilled at things we don't love. We may like them, or we may not like them. You know, I used to know how to squeeze a dollar 'til the eagle screamed. To have a kid on one hip, to clean toilets and to cook and take care of the dog—I know how to do that. I was good at it, too. I don't ever want to do that. Was I gifted at it? I don't think so, but I was good enough. A skill is something you attain. But when I talk about a gift, I mean something you're in love with. I think that gifts are biological. And I think you don't love something unless you are gifted at it. If you pick something you love to do, you have the biological equipment to become great at it. Then you have to figure out how to get the training and skills you need, because it's worth investing in that."

"Okay then," I said. "We have a problem. I don't know what I want. Or maybe I want a lot of things and I can't seem to narrow it down to just one."

Barbara was ready for that. "We have inner blocks that try to stop us from knowing what we want or believing that we can get it, especially when it comes to our creative selves."

"Are you saying I am somehow blocking myself?". . . not understanding why I'd do that to myself. How does one get blocked, and dear G-d, how do you get unblocked?

"The block that brings me the most letters from my readers," she told me, "is 'I want too many things; I am all over the place.' They say that they don't know what they want, that they have no idea how to have a goal or where to go. Like what you just told me."

Good to know that others were struggling to grow, that not everyone had it worked out so straight and easy, and that there was hope to figure it out.

"Shifra, everyone does know what they want. All I have to do is talk to them for five minutes until their eyes light up. I ask them certain questions, and I can tell what they want. For example, I tell them, 'Let's just pretend you were born rich enough and you don't have to make money—what would you love to do?' Then I watch their faces very carefully. I just keep coaxing them until their eyes light up. Sooner or later, usually it takes but a few minutes, their eyes get all soft like they're talking about their own newborn baby or something. And then I start listening really carefully." In her own distinct creative process,

Barbara then leads them to a clearer path for developing themselves in ways that will matter to them.

Rolling all over this like a pool noodle in deep water, I splashed this next one, "What happens if I can't be good, great, at what I do? I am not willing to do something and not be good at it."

"I knew that was coming," she smiled. "Many people stop themselves by saying they don't matter enough or even at all. This is arrogance. Yes, arrogance. By saying that you are unworthy, that you don't have to contribute because you're not good enough, you are being stingy and cocky. Yes, arrogance is when someone says, 'I am not good enough to share my gifts with the world.'"

"Arrogance is also perfectionism. You think, 'I have to be perfect or I can't do anything. I'm not good enough.' I feel like saying: You're not G-d. Did you really think you were supposed to be G-d? Where did you get the nerve to think that? Why don't you just do your best? Stay close to what you love so you don't lose your way. Do your best, and why don't you leave the question of whether you're great or not to history? You're not supposed to be perfect. You're human."

These words were surmounting the resistance she saw was there, though I had been unable to see it. She was not finished, just in case I might be thinking to give up this challenge of overcoming resistance as a fruitless, impossible dream.

"Realize this, Shifra. There is a high cost for not having this understanding about ourselves. It is despair. People can say what they want. They can stay distracted for as long they want. But in the dark of the night, you feel a sense of 'what am I here for?' This is a very profound sense of despair. On a more superficial basis, you'll end up getting a divorce from your husband because your husband won't fulfill this gnawing ache inside you, when really what you needed to do was to take up singing. There was nothing wrong with your husband—and you knew it. You just didn't know what else was wrong. There are some people who redecorate their house every six months.

They'll never be able to satisfy themselves because they're really artists. Substitutes don't work. A friend of mine quoted a very wise lady, 'you can never get enough of what you don't really want.'"

And then, in a preemptive strike, I contended, "Barbara, have you any idea how many times I keep failing to figure this out? How do I know this time it will be different, that I can trust myself?"

"*It* won't be different. *You* will be. You build trust in yourself, by doing actions, little by little."

And then a final thought from her, one that would stay in my mind for years to come. "Don't come back without your book."

Did she say a book? Why would she say that? I am not writing a book. How she knew that decades later I'd be doing just that, I really don't know.

Movement Makes Things Happen

Barbara wanted me to understand something about taking the small steps, those petty, partial efforts that move us along in the direction of greatness, or happiness, depending on what you'd settle for.

"Talk is talk. Talk is cheap. It's hard to persuade people to actually do things and not just talk about them. Even little things. But action gets you out of your chair and into a world where happy accidents or unusual things can happen. You can bump into people who know things you never knew. So I say to people, if you don't know what you want and you feel stuck, say 'yes' to everything that is not dangerous or expensive. As an example, if you say you'd love to make a movie someday, but it costs a fortune to go to film school, I always say to pick up anybody's camera and go out to make a one-minute film this afternoon. Take action. If you do that and you find you're entranced by looking through the eye of the camera, by editing this one-minute film, you've changed your life."

Soul Shifts, Creative Lifts

Barbara was so right with this movement thing. It was something I knew, though I hated the truth of it . . . just keep moving and taking the opportunities, even though they are not the big ones. But they move you along, like Daniel's first pair of shoes on his little feet that he picked up in giant strides, way bigger than this stage called for; but he didn't know that because he thought big, even when he was small. Small steps move us along, *bigly*. Mediocre, maybe. But vital, very.

Saying yes to something, or to part of something, can open up doors that were heretofore closed. Just as my saying that first yes to attending Professor Ellen's class culminated in my finished degree. And in something else, too—another experience that would not have happened had it not been for that completed degree.

As mentioned, the last requirement for my degree was a final project, that scary, credit-heavy monstrosity whose topic I had to choose, then prepare an actual course that could be marketed and taught. What a joke for a non-teacher. After uttering a prayer for help in choosing something I was actually interested in, I chose to prepare a workshop on prayer. *Prayer: The Art of the Heart* was created and designed to demonstrate that Jewish prayer invites a person to not just go through the *motions*, but through the *emotions*. I spent several months following the instructor's prompts for researching the material and fashioning it into a binder to be read and graded on several criteria, including its relevance to the intended audience and originality of presentation. The course was divided into six one-hour interactive modules consisting of principles of prayer, and multiple creative exercises that I designed for the learner to concretize this spiritual, heart-based practice. I put the finishing touches on it with the firmest, prayerful intention not to ever present it. Remember, I wasn't ever going to be a teacher.

I finally finished my schooling, but I had another lesson coming that left me otherwise instructed.

It was in the early morning of a weather-perfect Tuesday, soon to be eternally known in world history as 9-11, when a couple of minutes in time would forever redefine our sense of personal and national security. A new era had erupted, melting down our American lives of liberty to a mix of twisted fear, rage, and disbelief over the wicked fires still burning in the hearts of humans.

On this morning when the New York skyline was falling in, I was at my son's school, bringing special drinks I had previously committed to bring that day for the boys. When I saw Daniel's class lining up at the door of the classroom, I asked, "Oh, they are going to gym class now?"

"No, we are taking the boys to the auditorium for security reasons," I was told. And with that, I told Daniel he was coming home with me.

As Daniel and I were walking the spacious, glossy-white corridor towards the front door, I experienced a sudden, over-whelming desire to see the beauty in others. And it happened right away.

A woman passed us, a woman who on any routine day would have caught the attention of my professionally-trained cosmetologist's eye for her distinctly displeasing made-up appearance. Cobalt blue eyeshadow was carelessly applied to her upper brow where lighter colors usually sit, along with an orange foundation all wrong for her ruddy complexion. But on this day, and at this moment, I effortlessly located a beauty I had never seen in her before, and not ever again. It was the loveliness of a face, human and alive. It was the inside of her eyes, the shared vision of our collective world gone ugly, that showcased a deep primal longing for survival. *Survival*—so basic and so beautiful. *So spirit. Much easier to see spirit when life is tenuous.*

This personal inner tilt was subtle and growing, finding its way into a prayer more slowly said or more deeply felt, or perhaps an act of kindness done with ever slightly more graciousness. From my side of the conflict, I can only tell you that those collective explosions unleashed a force that landed in my inner space, forcing me to launch a counter-initiative of my own. It started with a prayer: *Please let me help reconstruct a world that has been so undone,* destructed by some hidden force. A veil of contemporary evil has been uncovered—informing us that hatred still exists in the deepest regions of our world's heart. With no idea how to collectively banish it, and with human impulses run so awry, *please G-d help me harness mine.*

Looking under my car to ensure no bomb was there as the day's terror contagiously migrated to personal paranoia, Daniel and I arrived home. Before I could stop myself, which usually happens with alarming zeal as the instant second, and third, guesser I am, I ran to one of my desks (we are a multi-desk family), rummaging through the unopened pile of mail and bills and pretty stationery, to find and finger the written form of my course *Prayer: the Art of the Heart.* It would wait just two days until I picked it up and carried it, my workshop, escorting it like a reluctant child to school, into the office of Rabbi Sherman, the director of the local adult Jewish studies program. I set it down on his desk with the offer: "If you'd like, I will teach this course."

Yes, Osama bin Laden, I said I will teach, I thought as I looked Heavenward. To my thinking, all that humanity had remaining was a prayer. And we needed to start there, because it is the foundation of a relationship with G-d—the kind that gave, forgave, and preserved life for all, regardless of race, religion, or region. If our world needed anything, it certainly was that.

And with that, I had returned to the classroom as the presenter of a six-week workshop for adult learners, which I then presented again at a local women's retreat. And then again, at the invitation of a personal professor friend, for the Health Science department . . . at the state university I had returned to just a few years earlier when I took Professor Ellen's class.

Yes, Barbara was right. Movement changes us.

By my behavior—mostly my actions—I knew I had been shifted.

CHAPTER SIXTEEN

BirthRight

Freedom is the alone, unoriginated birthright of man,
and belonging to him by force of his humanity.
—IMMANUEL KANT, philosopher

"NO VALIUM; go home and try to sleep."
Ah, sleep. Why hadn't I thought of that? I was in labor with my first child. Zack and I had been at Brenna's house for a few hours (she moved back from Israel to Baltimore just in time to help me) so that she could "*doula*" me, that is, offer me physical and emotional support to help me through this, my first labor. We had called the doctor at 10 p.m. from Brenna's house to see if he'd consider dispensing some kindness, medically known as Valium. I was now in the second night of trying to convince this little insider to please come out of hiding. If you were our first, you might have also hesitated to make an appearance to a pair of un-grownups, the two young "watchless" people you'd now be calling parents.

Deciding to go home and rest, Zack and I drove to our Green Acres apartment and, through sleep-deprived eyes, I could see it had started to drizzle on this humid August night in Baltimore. Emerging from our car, I suddenly began to gastronomically unload, something I hadn't done since those beginning months of the HG pregnancy heretofore described. I ordered Zack to get back into the car and turn on its "front eyes" because, "Honey,

I just threw up the baby" and we had to find it. Zack tried to have me understand that it was just the grapes that I had eaten a few hours earlier, but I wasn't having any of his deliriously silly jokes now. Finally, after a futile search, I decided we'd go upstairs and consult the book on how babies get born. It said something about getting into bed, being sure to be relaxed, well-rested, even using a bit of music and wine to relax the woman. Without a moment's hesitation, Zack threw off his clothes, with the delicious expectation of a few quiet moments. He had hardly put head to pillow when I turned to him. "Zack, I think it's time to tell you three words I've been wanting to tell you for a long time, but have never said to you before." As he turned his awakened, blue-eyed interest to me, I whispered, "Our baby's coming."

Upon reaching the hospital with a half-centimeter left to this labor, the admitting nurse asked if I could do them a small favor: The doctor was speeding on his way, could I just contain the baby until he arrived to join the party? I told them that I didn't think it was going to work out well from my end, but if this caused him undue distress, perhaps a valium would be of help?

Training for Life

I had come to know well the rigors of labor and delivery, having personally endured them several times. I knew that as dependable as a woman usually is, not to depend on a woman's rationality on *this* day of her life; the laboring woman wasn't at her most rational. And now, after birthing four children of my own, I was being given the chance to professionally handle all this irrational charm of the laboring woman. To become a doula.

With my formal college education and my paid workshop-teaching done, I was now looking for my next professional pay. The opportunity to train as a doula traveled my way, tempting me greatly because my life-long love for the newborn human had not abandoned me. I had personally engaged the services of a doula for the birth of my fourth child, which planted the desire to do similar work one day (reigniting the thought to perhaps even train to be a midwife, an ambition I ultimately chose not to pursue.) With three girls in elementary school and three-year-old Daniel in a playgroup, I saw an ad for a doula training to be held in Baltimore by DONA, Doulas of North America. It was a full three-day training workshop that conferred certification after I'd participate in a certain amount of required births and submit detailed documentation about the birth, to be signed by an attending doctor.

Before committing, I consulted with our Rabbi—a spiritual mentor whose keen mind I respected and warm heart I trusted on account of his kind, ongoing validation for developing myself outside of my family role—who encouraged me to help others birth their babies. Maybe I could not always stay home happily to care for my own, but this option would be good for many reasons, not the least of which was that it might help me develop a small sense of mattering, purpose, and of pay. More purpose than pay, for the compensation wasn't always commensurate with the required time and effort needed for this job. In any case, I'd need to be available for others in need, on their time—even on Sundays.

As a doula who worked privately and for a hospital, I wore a beeper (pre-cell phone) because I had to be on call to fly out of my house in the space of a few well-timed contractions to support a laboring woman in her time of pressing purpose. Being on the labor and delivery floor at 3 a.m. never made me wonder what I was doing there, so natural was this to me despite the fact that I am a "born sleeper" who adores her bed. The closer to the experience of birth I could be, the happier I was. As a child, I had busied myself with one hobby besides schoolwork—cutting out magazine pictures of babies and tucking them to sleep cozily in the album's pages which blanketed them. This current mission would satisfy that personal piece that held my unfulfilled desire to become a baby nurse, long nurtured by my subliminal gratitude to Nanny Fanny who saved my four-day old life. That vulnerable newborn's spirit of sacred survival spoke of life as good and beautiful—a royal reminder that we can make it, after all. Being in the presence of a blameless baby just born cannot be experienced as anything but the show of G-d at His kindest.

Pain: The Most Eloquent Speaker

Witnessing up-close the exquisite combination of pain and purpose, resulting in the magnificence of a life newly born, was extraordinary—very often bringing all in its proximity to reach for the tissues. We were touched by a force—way, way beyond our own (and it is here that one either laughs or cries). And although I cannot bring stats to bear down on this conversation, I had begun to take notice that my birthing mothers were usually in their innermost aloneness in the night's darkest hours before the dawn, whose light would give way to this new pulse. It seemed unfair to ask her to embrace the joys of this calling, as the pain was digging into her bones, even while bringing into being that which she yearned for so deeply. The best I could do was to remind her that the pain is productive, it is not forever, and it will gift her with a remarkable joy. Many laboring moms did ask me to say some prayers with them; they held these as sacred moments, even if incredibly difficult. Ultimately, if you are carrying inside yourself something to be born, you are now its parent. You are its creator, you are its channel through which it comes into life. How awesome. (Even G-d thinks so, because He has given us a prayer of gratitude to say upon the birth of a baby.)

Even though I knew that the better part of my role was to help the birthing mother fight fear, not pain, a doula's work could be physically exhausting while trying various maneuvers to alleviate some of the discomfort and pain of one being emerging from inside another. Hip squeezes to release the pressure on the back and hot showers to assuage the mother's contracting spirit were part of my job. Sometimes, just allowing the mother to peacefully labor at home for as long as possible was the most appreciated of all, outmaneuvering the doctor on call who'd have to quickly prepare to deliver a very ready mother. This would often prompt the doctor's request to me, "Next time, do bring them in sooner, will you?" to which I'd outwardly nod while thinking, *No sir. We aim to stay away from all this tumult as long as we safely can.* Above all, while watching a life work its way into our world, I could only lavish huge doses of compassion onto the vulnerable being as it uncurled and grabbed onto the first hand that would extend to it the human's G-dly touch.

Birth Is Hard Work for Men, Too

Labor sometimes was harder on the man than on his laboring wife. At one birth, there was a guy who was tattooed from his upper bicep, bared beneath his biker's shirt, probably to his toes, which were hidden underneath a pair of clunky, night-black motorcycle boots. With a bandana tied around his head, he was wiping sweat from his brow and, was that a tear I saw? Yes, his tears began to fall as he turned to me and said, "I cannot bear to see her in pain." With all the authority I could aim in the face of a would-be gangster, I ordered him to pull himself together or to leave the room. I placed my lavender scent, usually reserved to refresh the mothers, beneath his nostrils to sniff in his fears and be more available to his wife. She looked at me with a grateful eye, "Thanks for taking care of my big baby."

At times, I had witnessed that labor could be hard on the doctor. I was standing alongside a well-reputed, experienced doctor, sensitive in manner, but clearly distracted. This was not his usual practice. I had worked with him before, and watched him at the foot of the birthing bed, fully attentive to a woman just trying to do her job. On this day, a healthy baby was born, and while baby and mom were meeting for the first time, he was supposed to make the second smaller delivery—that of the placenta, at this point called the afterbirth. Averaging nine inches in length, one inch thick, and typically weighing just over one pound, the placenta is a crimson-colored, nutrient-dense organ that attaches itself to the uterine wall, growing with the baby. Inside this membrane sac, the baby lazies around, connected to its mother by the 12–24″ umbilical cord through which it enjoys its mother's ice cream and pickles. (This has been documented as the start of the lifelong pattern of kids stealing your food, or as they would claim, *sharing* it.) When the baby vacates the premises, its former home—the placenta—also has to be totally discarded, relinquishing its lease in the mother's belly. (Mothers usually appreciate having their bodies back to themselves. I do not forget how spooked I felt at times when I watched a growing entity inside of me kicking around, moving my belly like a bed-sheet across its body.) Expelling the placenta typically takes up to a half-hour, after which time it is closely examined to ensure that it is complete, leaving nothing behind to cause hemorrhaging and—probably more important to some women—that might leave the woman still looking pregnant. Problem was, Dr. Distracted thought he had taken care of that, but he couldn't find it. "Shifra, where is the placenta?" I knew he wasn't accusing me of stealing it away in my pocketbook; he was just asking for help. I pointed to the garbage can to my side. With his gloved hands, he reached in to retrieve the red-jellied sac. Without an exchange of words, I cast him my concern, which may have been what prompted him to confide, "I am going through a divorce."

In another delivery, I had the double delight of watching twins be born. As standard procedure, the delivery of twins was set up in the OR. The team was excitedly assembled, waiting on the arrival of number one. As soon as number one emerged, the doctor delivered a little surprise of his own; he'd be leaving to fulfill his promise to attend his grandson's tonsillectomy in a different hospital. In walked the second doctor, who promptly grabbed a stool to stand on, the first time I ever saw an unusually small person in this capacity. He caught this second one, who appeared with nary a push or a peep. Doubly delightful, indeed.

Saying Yes to Being Born

But if I have to say for whom this process is hardest, it is the baby being born. "Against his will man is born," says the Torah, "And against his will he dies." Baby is forced out of a no-cost living situation—replete with free food, no rent, and a deluxe, indoor-heated swimming pool—into a new space where it will immediately have to lean on its own two lungs for air. Worst of all, baby has no nice clothing for the occasion. And while we humans do give it an unconditional hero's welcome for making the long journey, the baby is essentially alone. He now joins the ranks of humanity who travel through life together—alone.

There is one thing, though, that personally brought me comfort as I contemplated that the journey ahead of this new life would be infinitely more complex and laborious than the one he had just completed. I knew that G-d equipped this soul with a battery pack called *Teshuva*, inexactly translated as repentance. Before G-d created this world, He realized that this world of people would self-destruct if not given the opportunity to correct the mistakes it was bound to make. Putting a piece of Himself inside a body would seem like an impossible, not to mention daring, feat; how do you combine the pure with the impure and call it whole? But in placing this Divine piece called the *neshama* (literally, soul) into a body, He breathes the kiss of great mattering into man. Armed with G-dliness, man now has the incredible power to distinguish himself from animal by overriding his base, bodily impulses. Pure instinct no longer rules the day and night; his thinking mind does.

Yet because man is designed with both heavenly soul and earthly body, he will make mistakes. He will sin, meaning he will miss the mark. G-d knew this, and therefore gave man the ability to get back on track, to return to his soul nature, which allows his body to purposefully move around in the world. He'd need to make adjustments, to restore his humanity. He would have to assess where he went wrong, and to determine how to move past it. *Teshuva* is actually one of the Torah's 613 *mitzvos,* Divine commandments. With this incredible kindness to man, G-d installed a delete button of sorts—allowing man to undo the bad and to remake himself. As with birth itself, *Teshuva* is a supernatural phenomenon.

And now at birth, although the baby is given a volunteer-sewn hat to cover his cold head and cozied in a freshly-heated blanket, he'll be battling the natural elements soon enough. Testing his mettle, this friction will cause a reaction; it must.

Teshuva is the gift that directs the reaction to be transformative. It is, in fact, the highest form of creativity.

Dearth, Be Proud

There is a prayer that I was taught to say after eating certain foods, known as the *Boray Nefashos*. Its twenty-two words speak of how *G-d creates souls, and their lack, in order to sustain them.* It tells me that a lack is actually a creation that G-d designed. Why on G-d's Earth would He design lack? Clearly, so that we humans have something to do here.

In providing us with lack, He has given us purpose: To grow whole. Sometimes that means reversing the lack; sometimes it means building around it.

Growing whole is very individual. It cannot be imitated or even taught. It has to be struggled, birthed, cried, and belabored. Laughed and loved, too.

And herein lays the recovery of our wholeness. Newfound possibilities that were hidden, albeit always there, emerge for us.

You don't have to be born into a royal family to be noble. We are often (mis)taken with the outer display of what we really admire—the inner freedom to know our worth and our mattering. This is the birthright of royalty, which means it is yours because you are a child of Gd.

In the family that Zack and I were constructing, we had few rules. After all, the fewer the rules to break, the less strict discipline we'd have to administer. But there was one: *each child is beyond compare.* Simply put, we disallowed the unhealthy impulse to compare themselves with each other and with others. Competition is risky business, because while it can objectively invite the best from within us, it can just as easily stifle it.

The day we stop competing to be someone else is the day that the opportunity to matter knocks on our door. We will never be able to compete with being someone else. Only we can pull our self, body and soul, across the finish line the way all humans must. That is what awesome journeys are all about . . . until our last moment when they quite literally take our breath away.

CHAPTER SEVENTEEN

On Air: Lessons from the Studio and Stage

Creativity is intelligence having fun.
—ALBERT EINSTEIN, physicist

"WHICH ONE OF YOU is in labor?" the nurse asked while looking at my seven-month pregnant belly as I accompanied a laboring mother into the hospital.

Maybe it is time for the doula to bid adieu, I silently mused.

I had been working as a doula for several years when Ayala, my fifth child, was born. The joy in the sublime work was still there, but the unpredictable schedule of erratic hours was becoming too cumbersome to manage. It was when I was "out on a birth call" that I answered Zack's.

I could hear a hungry Ayala in the background. "Shifra, I think she is hungry." Good call, Zack. Understanding that I could not leave a laboring woman whose birth was taking longer than all of us predicted, Zack offered to bring Ayala to the hospital for her Mommy-made meal. Youngest children, I have since learned, can be very particular in their tastes. This one refused to take the bottle I had left behind. There was little choice but to excuse myself for a few short minutes to nurse her in our van's backseat, leaving my soon-to-be mother to the colder care of others monitoring her process in the middle of this late night. It was hard enough to nurse a child altogether—sometimes I imagined that the child would eat me all up, sucking me into oblivion. I knew; it was time to retire my lavender doula handbag with its soothing scents and smells, along with my official doula badge.

While G-d is not an equal *job* employer who gives the same tasks and tools to humans, He is an equal *opportunity* employer. True, He does not give the same external opportunities to each person, but He most definitely grants each with opportunities for inner wholeness, though it may look very different from person to person. I was on the lookout, always.

BirthWrite

And now I would transition yet again. What could possibly take the place of helping birth babies? Something professionally significant for me emerged, quite naturally. It was called live radio.

How was that opportunity fertilized? The time between helping babies to be born wasn't lifeless. I kept Barbara's ideas about movement close to my thinking, remembering to take small opportunities in areas that I was beginning to understand I was gifted at, and held my interest. There were many community organizations that needed the time, attention, and energy of women who were willing to offer it. Unpaid, of course. But eventually, these volunteer efforts creating press releases, brochures, bios, and whole events for non-profit organizations moved me into a paying profession known as writing. They also put me in the "cross-airs" of being media-interviewed, eventually landing me a seat delivering live radio.

Can I be honest about the business of writing? As a member of a family whose finances were grounded in the real estate business, writing danced on the edges of artsy, as in not money-making enough. I was not one of those people who considered having a byline to be an exciting accomplishment; fame was an impractical commodity. The bottom line, financial compensation, was much more compelling. And also *writer* as a title, if I may say, did not hold my esteem. Most everyone fancies themselves a writer, but there is nothing fancy about much of what is written. And worst of all, please forgive me for saying so, I could not shake the notion that writers were people who were desperate to be heard. I had long promised myself that I would never write if I suffered that condition. That is what therapy is for, and it is done behind closed doors. Remember, I was not accustomed to being heard, to even thinking that I should be heard. Writing for the public might be therapeutic in its process, but that's a fringe by-product, not its point. There are people who insist that this is therapeutic for writers. I resist their insistence. While healing is never-ending, as life continues to happen, writing publicly is the post-process. Just my humble opinion. So, why did I write? That's quite literally another chapter in this book.

I know. I just liberally leveled unfair umbrage against my own. Let me write it back a bit. How many books had I read that really did help me when I needed it; authors whose words were spirit savers? To repurpose a thought from Helen Keller[11]: "But a little word from the fingers of another fell into my hand that clutched at emptiness, and my heart leapt to the rapture of living."

I suppose this was all just an inelegant way of saying that given a choice, I wouldn't have ordered the writing chops from the entrée of professional services. With so many savvy subjects to study and get paid for, writing seemed to matter little. Why pay someone to write? But when I reworded it to its highest common denominator, I understood that writing is communication. I could be sold on that. Communication was a discipline that I did respect. There was value in the process of passing information and understanding from one person to another. It is the essence, the building block, of relationships—personal and professional. And writing is but a single genre of communication.

---

11 *Optimism, An Essay,* Helen Keller, T.Y. Crowell & Company, 1903.

I may not have chosen it, but it was clearly choosing me. And I had waited a long time for something to do that. As a result of my volunteer work for various organizations, writing projects began finding their way to my desk, with the imperative to understand the message and then help others do the same. Accepting that this was to be part of my path forward, I stopped fighting it and opened a writing and communications company, meaning I would now be charging for my services. I did enjoy assisting individuals and enterprises with arranging their oral and written communications. And I found out something about doing work that is a good fit: You don't watch the clock. Actually, the time passes the way it does when you are getting a great massage . . . way too quickly, the exact opposite of how it (mis)behaves when exercising.

The contracts were diverse. As part of my professional responsibilities for one client, I was tasked with coordinating an annual retreat for educators. Orchestrating both the marketing materials and the public media relations, as well as recruiting the presenters and participants, was the perfect job for the non-secretary who loves having many files open—all at once. Also gratifying were the mission statements I wrote that helped my academic clients gain acceptance into graduate programs in law and social work. Perhaps my favorite assignment was the crafting of messages for an online greeting card company, capturing both the funny and furious pieces of life between its beginning and end. Barbara was right: *You get good at what you like. And what you like, you are gifted in.*

Soon after I incorporated, my company was personally recommended by a satisfied client and subsequently contracted to produce and host the first run of a radio program that aired on a major radio station in the Mid-Atlantic states. This was work I was totally ready for; in fact, I had been waiting for this kind of opportunity that would tap my communication skillset for a project that I considered purposeful. Working each week to produce relevant programming to address the social, educational, and spiritual needs and interests of a predominantly Jewish audience, I created the content and arranged the interviews, which I conducted live for one hour every Sunday evening in the radio studio. I was joined each week in the studio by the sound engineer, a friend screening the calls, and the program director under whose auspices I was delivering this show. Attracting sponsors and creating their commercials was a big part of my job, too.

The show featured live interviews and call-ins which offered my listeners the opportunity to converse with my guests about a variety of topics, including domestic abuse, women in philanthropy, eating issues, dating and parenting, prayer, and educational initiatives by the Israel Institute of Technology. I reached out to people whose work around these issues I valued and wanted to share with others. The authors, the philanthropists, the community activists, the artists, the singers, the psychologists, the entrepreneurs . . . the people who made their lives—and mine—matter. People who wrestled with life, with themselves, and came up on the other end with something to offer me as I was trying to do the same. People who didn't give up. That was how I came to interview bestselling authors Geneen Roth and Barbara Sher, whose work is referenced in this book. When feasible, the interviewees joined me in my studio; otherwise, they joined me on the phone line.

Conducting interviews was thrilling because that is what I like to do best—asking the questions others can't or won't or don't. How did I know I was good at it? My interviewees told me. So did the listeners. It was a skill I actually learned early on in my life, having sat in on many interviews when my mother would be hiring her next secretary or housekeeper. My siblings and I were allowed to sit in quietly, afterwards eagerly registering our opinions which were heard if they were lenient on people who my mother desperately needed in the upstairs and downstairs of our home.

While I was enthused about moving forward, there were a few unwell-wishers who expressed their cutting concern: "We're waiting for you to fall on your face." Not sure what I did, or perhaps didn't do, to deserve that boost, or was it boast, of *their* cocky condescension.

But it made me ask myself one question: "Do you think you can withstand the rejection that is sure to come your way?" I understood that kindness doesn't always prevail in all hearts and that I'd likely be privy to the scorn of others for one reason and another. I knew I could handle it; I had good practice over the years, having failed with great success. I would continue to learn from it. I would use it, but it wouldn't get to stop me. I'd remember the pre-Internet, long-distance writing course that took me some time to complete. Ten years, it took. "What did you learn from that class, already, that was worth your while for staying the course?" people asked me. *I learned that I don't like to give up, especially when people are waiting for me to do just that.* With that settled, I showed up for the show.

Sampling the power of an hour each week, this was a delicious cup of tea I wanted to sip for a while.

A Grounding Experience

Those hell-wishers didn't have to wait long for my fall, though they would have been impressed, and disappointed, too, at how easy it all sounded.

If you've ever been inside a recording studio, you know two things: the clock's second hand is your master, and dead air space is your demise. Your mind had to be on your subject, but your eye always on the time. The first order of business, to choose the show's opening music, was effortless; Yanni from the skating rink would be there with me.

It was the second week of the program. It was a lighter show than the first week which featured the issue of spousal abuse. The first half of this show was to present a woman who put Jewish concepts and lyrics to Mother Goose rhymes. Because she lived in Israel, my sound engineer and I prerecorded this segment earlier in the week, which was then to be aired on the live program that Sunday night. And now, as the program's opening music gently yielded to my voice announcing our line-up for the next hour, I took a brief commercial break before playing this prerecorded guest segment.

Seconds before I was to reenter air space, the sound engineer said, "Shifra, we have a problem. I cannot get the track of your interview to work."

"Larry, what does that mean?" I asked.

"It means," he said, "you have ten seconds until you start speaking. Welcome to live radio, Shifra!"

And with that, I unexpectedly faced an audience, if you could call talking into space "facing" them. I confided that we were having trouble with the recording, and that while waiting for it to join us, I would start to tell them about what the Jewish Momma Goose had told me. Fortunately for me, I had my notes from the interview in front of me. To the point, I remember those few minutes as some of the most connected, raw, honest moments I have shared with my audience, whom I always sent out into the new week with this heartfelt closing: "May I be the first to wish you a week ahead filled with clarity, sound health, and a deep sense of purpose." My heart raced, but I rose to the rejection.

All those years of being up in the air had finally landed me a position on air, in the radio station. I was flying high.

Changing Scripts, Building Character

I was ready for that unscripted, unexpected bump in the ride, for the scariness of having to change a script last-minute. I had managed to survive something similar with an event I was producing a few years earlier. It was between the birth of child number 4 and child number 5, namely Daniel and Ayala. I was part of a volunteer team of five women tasked with keeping alive a dying entity known as the school donor luncheon. These were the olden-days luncheons that my mother and her female associates worked so hard to produce month after month. But women were no longer penciling luncheons on their monthly social activity calendars, unless it was a business lunch. After some success in changing it to an annual affair, even that was too demanding on the new millennium's woman who was now at full-time work outside of the home. Thus was innovated the annual Donor Dinner Theater, which showcased a buffet dinner, an upscale auction awarding prizes to the lucky ticket holders whose tickets had been selected from the box next to each prize package, and a show of talent such as a singer, dancer, or some other entertaining figure to delight the women for a few hours on a Sunday evening in November.

It was one of these dinners that had prepared me well for live radio. For one thing, I learned the art of being media-interviewed as I was the spokeswoman for the event sharing the details on someone else's live radio program. But much more instructional would be what to do when you have no script prepared.

I had contracted with an internationally-celebrated motivational speaker to address a beyond-sold-out crowd of five-hundred women. It was two o'clock on Sunday afternoon, four hours before the start of the evening. I was walking the auditorium floor with one of the crew, collaborating on the layout of the hall. As an unprecedented format, this was to be a crowd that was very promising for our school's much depleted bank account. My cell phone rang.

"Shifra, this is Esther Javits."

"Yes, Mrs. Javits, we are looking forward to seeing you soon."

"Shifra? Shifra, I am so sorry. As I am stepping onto the plane, I was just notified that my mother passed away. I cannot come tonight."

I understood, of course, that she would not be flying the Delta to Baltimore and that *I was up a creek without a paddle,* as my Aunt Rosalie used to say. I turned to my colleagues, who wore my same disbelieving expression. Although we desperately phoned around for a suitable substitute, even offering to fly someone in on a private plane, we were without a stage presence that night—on this eagerly anticipated, second most-profitable night of the school's fiscal year. And worse for me, someone had to stand in front of the mic on the big stage flanked by majestic thick gold curtains to tell the people to enjoy the magnificent cuisine and fabulous auction, but that one little detail would not be as scheduled. And that someone was me. No matter how much I begged each of my committee members, they said it would fall to me, since she was basically my hire. "Your hire . . . your fire."

Where was my mother now, when I could have used her speechwriting talents? What had she tried to write in my ninth-grade valedictory address? "I stand here in deep humility." Standing on the stage, next to the flag that my friend Sarena carried as the class valedictorian nearly two decades earlier, I would now say those words and mean them, adding: "Dear Ladies, when we scheduled this event five months ago, we did not know that this date would come to pass in a most unexpected way. Mrs. Javits called me today at two o'clock and said, 'Shifra, I am so sorry. Please will you send my warm wishes and greatest apologies.'" I then uttered the traditional wish that is expressed upon comforting the bereaved, "I know you join me in extending our heartfelt sympathy. *May G-d comfort her among the mourners of Zion and Jerusalem.*" There was a compassionate silence in the room, and for someone who was used to having the final word, I walked off the stage without it.

A Lesson in Nourishment
I enjoyed live radio, delivering a mixture of entertainment, inspiration, and information on a weekly basis. This weekly tête-à-tête nourished my creativity—my human (im)pulse throbbing with purpose and joy. Having extended the contract three months past its original agreement, this cup of tea was now finished and I'd have to put it down, very satisfied.

Another thing I'd learn to discontinue, incidentally, was my weekly post-show, sit-down dinner at the local Dunkin Donuts: one extra-large Coolatta with enough whipped cream to float me home, twinned with a full-size muffin or chocolate Boston Crème donut, making Boston my favorite city for that whole minute.

It was at this time that I had invited a nutritionist named Marie into my life; and I do mean my life, because our conversations centered around my life, always hitting my actual food choices only towards the end of our biweekly hour. Since it was clear to me that I related to food the way I did to my life, I knew enough to understand it was time to solicit additional guidance with making the healthier choices that would also translate well to my food. And even though I had learned many years earlier how to distinguish a fat protein from a lean one, hint: usually by its taste, I heard myself telling the man behind the ice cream counter that food was grouped into two: steak and ice cream. He was totally agreeable, though he kept his leanness by perpetually cycling on a stepper he kept behind the counter so that he could take my money while keeping his shape.

Over the years, I'd learn the number one lesson in nutrition: Never let yourself get too hungry, as it is too difficult to feed yourself well in that position. Actually, I would have understood that from the Torah itself had I been mature enough to digest it when I first heard it years earlier: A righteous person eats to satisfy his soul (Proverbs 13:25), the implication being that attending wisely to one's physical needs in a timely manner is virtuous. And the harder lesson: Feeding yourself well is a choice, and although some of us may want others to arrange our meals and feed us, it is huge to take care of ourselves until we can arrange for that. The most satisfying lesson I'd sample: DD has better choices on their menu that could leave me satisfied and healthier—both at the same time. Yes, I now usually opt to leave the whipped cream for others, along with the extra pounds they can carry better than I.

CHAPTER EIGHTTEEN

Securing Your Identity

Before I can live with other folk, I've got to live with myself. The one thing that doesn't abide by majority rule is a person's conscience.

—Harper Lee, author, *To Kill a Mockingbird*

"SHIFRA, YOU'D MAKE A GOOD funeral parlor director," dead-panned the career counselor whom I consulted to take inventory of my growing post-radio skills and interests. Writing projects were now entering and exiting my home office, with the mainstays being resumes and cover letters, company mission statements, brochures, business letters, and press releases for businesses needing to communicate a clear, compelling message. It was time again to assess how to expand my writing enterprise. The comedian counselor continued, "You are compassionate, with one ear always inclined to the ground," her expression for listening out for the deeper, bigger things in life. "You could offer the comfort and direction that makes a difference to people in their lives at this time." She was advising me to forget about my pen that purposefully writes for businesses and instead undertake the business of last rites, where I could bestow meaning, power, and purpose to this final chapter of a person's earthly existence.

Please believe me that I have nothing against funeral home directors. I even wrote a few eulogies that were read at funerals. But, I wasn't dying to become one. I was better suited for bringing souls into the world rather than escorting them out, into the next. I knew this from the time when my grandmother passed on, and I helped to coordinate the special tradition for family members to guard the coffin-encased body of the deceased until the burial. In this case, we had set up a rotation amongst her many grandchildren and great-grandchildren to ensure the loving vigil at the funeral home from 5 p.m. Sunday night until the funeral at 9 a.m. the next morning, with Zack, Zeeva and Daniel agreeing to do the graveyard shift, from 2:00-5:00. Fifteen-year old Daniel was also with me on my 11:00 p.m. shift a few hours earlier. As Daniel was not one for a big show of sad emotion, I asked him for permission to do a little mourning, to which he said, "I am walking out for a few minutes. Just don't lose it, Ma."

I passed on this career suggestion, and once again, I was searching for next steps. *Time for more movement,* Barbara would say. I was actively living the question of how to employ myself in the work of life.

No One Is You-er Than You

Have you heard the quote, "I do not worry about identity theft . . . no one wants to be me." As a line, it might be pithy and get some laughs; but if it is our motto, it is a pity and far from funny.

As America's favorite childhood doctor, Dr. Seuss, wrote: "Only you can be you." No other choice. How are you going to put YOU into service? When a drop of water falls into a river, it has no identity. But when it falls on the leaf of a lotus, it shines like a pearl. Author Leo Tolstoy had this simplicity to record: "It is within my power to serve G-d or not to serve him. Serving him, I add to my own good and the good of the whole world; not serving him, I forfeit my own good and deprive the world of that good, which was in my power to create."

Early Creative Encounters

I was steadily growing into a creative life that could be measured. Even had something to show for my work aside from yet another new writing desk—a few writing awards which tempted me to take myself proudly, flimsy etchings on my fragile ego.

I remember my first simple creative encounter that did not serve my young ego well. I still hear my fit of funny as I enthusiastically decorated the head of my then three-year-old younger sister Sima with talcum powder on the day we moved to a new house. "Who is cleaning this up?" my mother unproudly remarked, completely missing my creative cuteness that whizzed right over her head. I remember thinking, *Why can't Sima's head stay this way; why must it be cleaned up?*

Many years later, at the close of my school career, I tried a smarty stunt in a desperate, but failed, attempt to pass a final English test. We had to memorize two of Shakespeare's speeches for the test, but would be asked randomly to write just one. Busy playing Pac-Man the night before, I could only commit one to memory. Slight problem: I was given the test asking for the other speech, the one that I did not memorize. Faced with a decision, I tried my hand at charming my English teacher into giving me at least partial credit. "To be or not to be is not the question now. Whether 'tis nobler in your mind that I write nothing or to write something, and maybe just suffer a C." But this teacher, who was never a fan of mine, gave me zero credit for the effort, and just shut down the creativity she was hired to inspire.

Fatherly Inspiration

My father should have been well paid because he gave full credit to my many efforts at mattering. And because he inspired them as well.

I had recalled a story from the Shabbat table of my youth that my father lovingly fed to us, one that I shared with my radio audience. There was a Talmudic scholar who made a celebration after authoring several classic literary masterpieces, which are still being studied worldwide in Jewish academies. This is the story the scholar told publicly at the celebration:

When I was but a young boy, I overheard my parents discussing my future. Disappointed in my lack of achievement in my studies in which they had desperately hoped I'd excel, they felt they had no choice but to apprentice me to a shoemaker who would instruct me in the art of shoemaking so I could earn a livelihood. Somehow, this dialogue deeply unsettled me and inspired me to redouble my efforts in my studies.

In time, this scholar gained renown for his scholarship and great wisdom. At this celebration, he then asked a question whose existential message potentially reverberates in the hearts of humanity: *What would have been so bad if I had become a shoemaker? In a final judgment before my Creator, I would have been able to account for my life, to tell Him sincerely that I had engaged in my craft honestly, and certainly helped many people to clothe their feet. But then He would have said to me, "If that had been your given destiny, you would have been great. But where is the book that you were supposed to write? And where is that other classic work you were able to write?"*

Concluded the scholar, *"I would have had to face the intense pain of untapped opportunity, of a missed mission, of an un-actualized life purpose. And for this, today, I give thanks to my Creator."*

Bound by Mattering

Opportunity has many faces. Not all missions in life are famous and easy to celebrate, and maybe that makes their mattering all the more remarkable. While speaking about forward movement and securing our identities, I'd like you to meet an extraordinary woman named Rachel. On her behalf, I had involved myself with one of the hardest, least understood advocacies in the Jewish world—that of freeing a woman whose recalcitrant husband refuses to issue a *Get*, a Jewish divorce. Rachel has the status of an *agunah*, a chained woman. Without the Get, she is bound to her marriage with no happy possibility of remarrying and rebuilding her life with another partner.

Her call for help dialed into my life after I had applied as a volunteer to visit women prisoners in a prison thirty minutes away from my home. Maybe this sounds intense, though surely not shocking, that I often felt locked into myself, unable to access my life. And that unleashed a deep sense of empathy for others closed behind man-made bars—the final, outer manifestation of an inner disarray that had gotten way beyond their control. I could painfully imagine how they must yearn for the chance for release, to move beyond this current life to one of their higher choices. "We don't currently need your empathy," stated the director of volunteers, thanking me anyway.

G-d favors good intentions, apparently, and brought me a similar opportunity to serve Rachel, a most deserving person who was so unfree, through little fault of her own.

Zack and I had known Isadore before he became Rachel's husband, from the time we lived near him during our five-year stay in New York. He was complex, but that didn't scare us. He became increasingly difficult once he got married, and that *did* scare us. Shortly after he entered the security-lock business, he became engaged to a girl from Baltimore, having us as his happy guests at his Baltimore wedding. Zack even accompanied him on the day of his wedding to serve his every need. It didn't take long for the couple, who subsequently moved to Seattle, to set their marriage woes on our dining room table during their occasional visit back on the East Coast. They confided their growing misery. Helping people marry was my calling; mediating their unhappiness was not my cup of tea. But as matters escalated, I was drawn into their burning hot conflict.

It was a refreshingly plain September day when my phone rang with a call from Seattle. "Shifra, I need your help. He will not allow me to play my piano and he has cut off incoming phone calls." It was Rachel.

As an English teacher, Rachel was all smarts when it came to books. But in the study of men, she had not yet learned how to separate the exclamation points from the question marks.

She, an unguarded, pure-spirited, generous-hearted soul, had little inkling that a dark side burned in some people which, if left unchecked, would cast sadistic shadows over everything in their paths. Isadore was one of the walking wounded—a hurt, twisted character in desperate need of healing his pathetic dysfunction for not being able to take responsibility for his own well-being, never mind that of his family. Blindsided by his own pain from having been constantly abused in his youth—harshly hit by his volatile father, conditionally loved by his un-empowering mother, and taunted for his strong-willed nature by his four siblings—he could not begin to admit, or even to see, how his actions devastated others. *Toxic* is the word for a person who cannot contain himself healthfully in his own boundaries, sure that everyone is invading his. Nothing was ever his fault. He could take no ownership of his actions and reactions, while effortlessly robbing that which belonged to others, including the engagement ring he gave to Rachel. Once the marriage was clinically deemed irreconcilable, leaving Rachel and her children on their own, Rachel's ring suddenly disappeared from her apartment. He denied our suspicions when confronted, counter claiming that he had no way to access her home—an excuse with a hollow ring, considering he was a master of the lock, adept at trespassing on others' spaces with, and without, their permission. He'd repeatedly try to steal his children's love from their mother by constantly assailing her character as unloving, selfish, and harmful to them, totally displacing his faults onto her. It left them with years of therapy to undo those doubts he wickedly dumped onto them.

He hadn't always been so unhealthy. Like all of us, his character developed along a continuum, a sliding one in his case. I don't know what causes some to eventually fall into their worst selves, while others rise to their highest. His earliest family interactions no doubt set him up for an overwhelmingly lonely struggle to find and feed his personal well-being. The fact that he was stubborn had mostly translated well for him, as he found strength to do hard things, including leaving his Israeli home at a young age to build a life in America for himself. This was a tough, principled man who had an uncommon resilience, having weathered his stormy youth. He still got up every morning, smiled, and took up his academic studies in good faith. While still in his pre-wedding days, he was a pleasant presence in our growing family, joining us for meals, trips, and once even fixing our fridge door, which had been left unhinged by a bored child. Isadore often demonstrated an agile ability to spin the truth, while still preserving it. When he saw a traffic stop sign, he considered it to be an *invitation* to stop, not an order—similar to the "Drink Coca Cola" ad, which couldn't actually mandate one to do so. Yes, maybe that thinking was a red flag of a flagrantly disobedient nature; but if pressed into healthy purpose, couldn't that mark someone as the kind of person who makes life brilliantly funny, flexible, and forgiving for others?

But in his case, he disintegrated into a sullied strategist, turned against his own best interests. He got caught in his own extraordinary strengths—his stubbornness, his resilience, his principle-driven ideals—that he could not fully master, refusing to accept the psychological treatment that could have stopped him from losing his decency and dignity to their deceptive grip. Like ocean waves, strengths turned wrong are deadly. A riptide of revenge that he could not outride pulled him under, threatening to take others under with him. Nothing was as important to him as winning, defined as controlling his wife and his children, all of whom he desperately tried to suck back into his life. When he could not do that, thanks to a court-ordered restraining order, he was left with the most empty, but dangerous, of fights, that of the "principle of the matter." He'd now fight to the finish, even if it would cost him his liberty and life. His victory would be in holding hostage the happiness of his wife and children, as well as avenging the legal treatment he was made to suffer—outrageously unfair by his faultless reckoning. Being denied custody of his children while having to open his stingy pocket to feed them was an undeserved judgement he wouldn't overlook, inviting his wrath of rage. He would give them not a penny, while raising generous sums of sympathy from kind hearted people who didn't know better than to believe his story. Replete with details that he rearranged to interlock fully, but falsely, to indict Rachel of all the world's wrong-doing—how she turned their children against him and against religion, which he himself so badly misconstrued (the most obvious of which is his refusal to grant the *Get* which the Rabbis ordered him to do), Isadore cleverly cleared himself, leaving him the victim—a role he played with great virtue.

"Illegitimate hatred never disappears. It may switch scapegoats, but it will remain ever-present and undiluted. It cannot be appeased: It poisons and blinds the soul, devours the memory and the mind, and kills the capacity for compassion and insight. Its destructive power stems from a history of horror that has been repressed and stored in the body but that, without effective therapy, has no direct access to the conscious mind. Hating and offending an innocent person, using him as a scapegoat, can only strengthen the walls of our inner prison of confusion, isolation, fear, and loneliness; it cannot free us. A house built out of self-betrayal will sooner or later fall down and mercilessly destroy human life—if not that of the builder, then that of his children, who will sense the lie without being aware of it and who will end up paying the full price for the hidden arrangement." [12]

Dealing with an unevolved person drowning in his own chaos is both painful and exhausting. And dangerous. Shortly after Rachel's September call to me, Isadore called me. "If you dare help her, I will hurt you and your family." He carried a gun; I knew he meant it. Sampling his viciousness put me on guard, but the only kickback was to reload my resolve to help my friend. We knew her safety was in question, which is why I begged her to immediately hang up on a phone call she made

---

[12] *The Drama of the Gifted Child,* Alice Miller, pp. 115-116, Basic Books, 1979.

to me from the supposed privacy of her bathroom. If Isadore had heard, and to be clear it was every bit in character for him to eavesdrop, he'd have dealt harshly with her, sparing no verbal or physical beating. Without trying hard, I could imagine that I heard the cock of his pistol in the background.

Rachel had not known any of this before her marriage. She had not used her teacher's red marker to put an X on this guy as a husband. All she knew was he had served in the Israeli army, and was now a locksmith in the business of securing people's lives and their homes. But tragically for her, he had ransacked her interior, and made her world a very unsafe place to be. To condense their ten years of marriage into one word: prison. They were now cellmates, not soulmates.

Soon enough, she became schooled in the harsh lessons of ground combat, having to fight for her very mattering. As a gifted musician, Rachel was denied her voice. Isadore had thrown away the basic keys to her human dignity and security. The many daily and nightly interactions that soulmates take for granted and so depend on each other to have and to hold, were denied her. Birthing her first child was made unbearably more painful when she was forced to go to the hospital unaccompanied by her husband. For the second birth, he managed to show up just a minute or two before the baby did. When the mounting injustices overpowered her spirit, she knew it had come—the time to escape. Under the cover of the night, no blacker than her days had become, and with the help of a few friends, Rachel packed up her children and was ushered onto the airplane. This move would be the start of rebuilding her collapsed inner space.

And in the intervening years, fourteen in all, Rachel has managed to thrive and to tend to her human garden of four children, blossoming despite the lack of oxygen-rich paternal influence. Her melodious voice has become even more resonant—with the passion and purpose of a faithful woman who set herself free, knowing that her formal freedom is just a matter of Divine time. I think Helen Keller would agree that

Rachel has defined optimism and taught others how to hope. "A man must understand evil and be acquainted with sorrow before he can write himself an optimist and expect others to believe he has reason for the faith that is in him."[13] And that she "cannot be argued into hopelessness."[14]

And now we are left at the distance to pray that his spirit, violently bobbing up and down, caught on the jagged pieces of his stormy personality, will resurface whole one day. Meanwhile, this mockery of a man—spinner of sensation and driver of drama—keeps himself ensnared in his own lies, fettered behind bars of defense that no master key has been able to yet penetrate.

As for him, in a twist of hate, he is now jailed for having continually refused to pay alimony and child support. I have been invited to see him in jail several times. Being militarily escorted through a nearly endless circuit of cold, metal bars that can only be unlocked by guarded faces of steel assaulted my senses. I was accustomed to coming and going on my own accord, the taken-for-granted privilege of basic freedom. Yet, I was surprised that inside a jail there lives a peculiar spirit of freedom—the freedom from having to build your life because you don't really have one. Or worse, to fool oneself into thinking that to die in jail in the name of a poor principle is the highest freedom one can attain. I was beginning to understand why a human being might choose to stay imprisoned. *Being free and forging your identity is hard work.* Fighting for our inner, authentic freedom, to matter, we are all in combat. But the prize is worth the fight; you get your life, not the life someone scripted for you. As Dr. Norma taught me, "Get on the right side of the fight."

While he sits in jail (and we in the loyalty of Jewish law despite its vexing complexity), we continue to have the collaboration of an advocacy team, comprised mostly of men, who extend their high trust and deep compassion to Rachel. Witnessing a man take captive a woman's right and happiness evokes our fiery impulses affronted by such cruel audacity. With great

---

13 *Optimism, An Essay*, Helen Keller.
14 Ibid.

determination to set the matter straight in a way that satisfies both Jewish and civil codes of law, we continue to support her, and will not give up the intricate fight for her freedom, which she richly deserves. Along the way, though, I don't mind sharing that I have interfaced with grown men who have allowed themselves to cry at their collective powerlessness, at the fact that one of their own could do such a thing to another human, leaving a manmade trail of misery.

Patience With the Process, Plucking the Prize

In actuality, being called into a process is generally against our conscious desire. We may not understand, fully or ever, why we have been invited, or called into, a particular process, circumstance, or relationship. I had been called into a heavy childhood, with all its accompanying anxious, shamed, and lonely non-mattering. As far as I know, I had never asked for a complicated and weighty childhood, exacerbated by a complex thought process. I was given it. And it has taken me to prized places and purposes that I may never have traveled on my own.

While hopefully we feel fortunate to have many of the spaces we inhabit, we cannot ignore the fact that we must transcend others. By transcend, I don't mean to circumvent; I mean to ride them through. That is what I call process. As Geneen Roth said, the only way past it is through it. Staying with the process, and moving through it, will yield prizes that we couldn't have named. *Always maneuvering ourselves out of the process may cut our discomfort short, but at what cost to our potential?*

While creating our identity and our mattering is an ongoing, perpetual question mark—relieved by periodic dashes and punctuated with rare exclamation points—*not living our purpose is a harsh life sentence.*

CHAPTER NINETEEN

Holiness Is a Creation

Art, like morality, consists in drawing the line somewhere.
—G. K. Chesterton, novelist

I T IS NO SECRET. I cannot draw a straight line. I cannot walk a straight line. And I cannot stand straight, or still, in one. When it comes to life, though, I have learned how to make some distinctions so that I can actually move forward. Small examples: how to be critical of a classroom policy without disrespecting the teacher, how to turn down an invitation without seeming disinterested in the happiness of another, how to know when I need to feed myself with food or to keep myself hungry. And even if I can't be straightforward—challenging for complex people—I can be upright.

"My teacher hates us," then-fourth-grader Aviva announced one early November evening at the dinner table. I excused myself to the bedroom, picked up my landline and called the principal for an appointment: "An emergency, can I come talk to you tomorrow morning?"

"Mrs. Cohen," I prevailed upon the principal, "This teacher needs to leave. She is asking, begging, to be relieved of her duties. If students can say that about a teacher, if they can think their teacher hates them, then it is clear that the teacher is telling us all she is no longer happy in the classroom. Do her, and us too, a favor and invite her to pursue work in another field."

By the turn of the week, Aviva had a new teacher. How many times do we have to discern the deeper part of a communication, listening to the signs beneath the spoken language? No judgments; only discernments.

Drawing Lines in Life

Holiness is about drawing lines, straight or otherwise, that connect us to our larger lives. Without boundaries, life is one amorphous, shapeless blob of disintegration and disorder. This deprives us of the pleasure of purpose which thrives on distinctions and differences that make life an exciting place to live.

In his view, author Herman Wouk saw art and religion as disciplines that could affect similar outcomes for larger living. "Religious symbol and ceremony aim, like art, at the shock of truth . . . religion and art both fight, on different fronts, against the dull rust that habit puts on the wonder of things." [15]

No matter where our purpose takes us, the "art of holiness" can always come along, too. Whether or not our lives mark us as prominent for others to notice, they are nevertheless important. Mostly, our core identity resonates on the inner realm, and for that, we need to discern for ourselves bad from good, good from better. Distinctions, not necessarily judgments. Distinctions allow us to steady our path without blocking someone else's. Judgments, on the other hand, divide by putting us ahead while impeding someone else and leaving them behind.

Holiness can be found in every time and space of our lives. *Without exception.*

And in recovering my identity, I would use Torah-defined holiness as the grail. In this way, I'd have some sense of what to pursue and what to discard, personally and professionally. I was

---

15 *This is My G-d*, Herman Wouk, pp. 50-51, Back Bay Books, 1992.

on the lookout for the specifics in my life. How would I create of it something that would resonate as true and worthy, and how would I measure that? For me, this question belonged to the world of spirit. And in my life, the worlds of body and spirit both belonged to the Torah.

Bed, Bath, and Beyond

"Total renunciation of sex is, in some faiths, a major discipline . . . part of spiritual ennoblement . . . for such austerity, Judaism has no match."[16] For a married Orthodox woman, the spiritual life would embrace sexuality, not disgrace it. It would be holy. Holiness, like charity, begins at home. It was in my bedroom that I first became intimately acquainted with the concept.

It started with Zack and me keeping our engagement brief. For one thing, this is encouraged by the Torah as a show of respect for the discipline it demands from the engaged couple. While Torah laws of *negiah*, restricting all direct physical contact with the opposite gender—other than very close blood relatives—regulate our interactions, it is fully understood that marriage confers its special touch on the couple. Waiting for those first moments intensified the anticipation, making a longer than necessary engagement overly taxing on the soon-to-be couple.

Once coupled, this new pair was meant to continue to nurture and always protect the relationship with what is called *shalom bayit*, domestic harmony. The home is regarded as a miniature sanctuary of G-d's earthly abode. G-d is called the Host; we are just guests in His world. Yet, He has modeled the art of being a good guest who comes when and where He is invited, and leaves when He is not. He is comfortable where you make room for Him, and that includes the kitchen or the bedroom, or somewhere even more private, like your heart. Strange as it sounds, G-d was a partner in our relationship from night one, but seldom wished to unnecessarily intrude on us.

---

16 *This is My G-d*, Herman Wouk, p. 139.

In His wise, fatherly way, He brought a few gifts for the couple's wellbeing, to help grow them as a couple and to protect their delight with each other. Technically known as *Taharat HaMishpacha*, family purity, this Divine instruction is a mainstay of the Jewish couple. In brief, it renders a moratorium on intimacy between husband and wife at certain designated times, followed by the woman's immersion into a ritual pool of water known as the *Mikvah* (literally, gathered waters). Although both husband and wife take responsibility for the abstention, it is the woman who will have the pleasure of immersing in the Mikvah. Indeed, this is considered one of the three special mitzvot of the Jewish woman.

More specifically, these laws of family purity, with the Mikvah as its crown jewel, are part of the gift package of *Shalom Bayit*, domestic harmony, which puts at the center of its observance, of all things, the woman's reproductive cycle. In this female-driven universe, the physical contact between the couple would now be governed by the woman's monthly cycle. While closeness between the couple is a month-long right, the pleasure of physical contact would be limited in most cases to two weeks of every month for the menstruating woman. Since Jewish Law dictates that the menstrual state lasts for a minimum of five days, this commandment directs the couple to maintain a physical abstinence for at least twelve days—counting at least five days from the onset of the menstruate cycle and seven days after its complete cessation, whereupon the woman takes her privileged plunge in the Mikvah.

What did this mean for me? For one thing, at least one of my beloved luxuriant baths would be in preparation for the Mikvah each month and would now be considered holy, since it was part of the preparation for immersion into the Mikvah. It also meant, without going into the details of its observance, that G-d was invited into our bedroom. We trusted Him. In this deceptively simple idea, He was protecting the marital love from being taken for granted. As the ultimate *Shadchan*, matchmaker, I trusted Him to know how to inspire the best in the couple, to keep them on the edge of satisfaction—wanting, not waning. To set them up for pleasure, by disciplining it. Had this not been Divinely mandated, it is clear no man or woman would have ever dared to devise such a system, because of its cleverness and its seemingly superhuman demands on the naturally hungry, healthy human appetite. And just as my overeating impulses were undergoing rigorous redirection, G-d gave us a way of training, restraining, and maintaining our creative energies.

Taking it from the ritual to the spiritual, that's what it was all about. I was willing to share our relationship with no one, except G-d who brought Zack into my life and was invested in keeping us happy. Because in that time of physical separation, husband and wife still share their hearts in the days and nights, just in separate beds. If nothing else, I have to confide that having a bed to oneself every so often does wonders for a good night's sleep as well as having some self-time on which I personally thrive. As for Zack who has said that "I am me when I'm with you," this is quite a G-dly accomplishment.

Once again, I'd understand the supreme value of discipline for the purpose of eventual pleasure. Saying "no" to one thing now means saying "yes" to something else. Learning how to communicate and touch each other in realms other than the physical was indeed a strenuous, but rewarding, marriage exercise. Here is where the depth and meaning of a marriage would continue to grow.

Preparing to Be Holy

In preparation for this new married life, a woman known as the *Kallah* teacher (*Kallah* is Hebrew for bride) is hired to teach the bride the special collection of laws that would from now on govern her personal monthly calendar. Remember, this was one of three special commandments for women. When seeking my Kallah teacher, it occurred to me that I had already learned a lot about marriage from my summer soaps and evening television dramas. Not meaning to be disrespectful, I confidently said to the Kallah teacher I chose, "I know a lot already. Care to add anything?" With the patience of a wise woman, she said she had just a few quick ideas to share with me. She then proceeded to teach me the laws as well as the divine concepts about the holiness of marriage from the Jewish perspective. I have to admit that those television soaps I had watched were more fresh than clean, leaving the two of us with a lot of work to tidy up my underdeveloped thinking on marriage. Even though I asked more questions that probably took her beyond her comfort level at times, she slowly and methodically helped me to feel safe and happy about this new life I was marrying into.

Fast forward a few decades to the pre-wedding conversation I had with one of my engaged daughters who asked me, "Any words of wisdom you wish to share with me, Mommy?" I make a brief study of teaching, "Take very good care of yourself. When a woman is well-cared for, her husband and family have a better chance at being happy. Second, the goodness that a man gives to his wife will get piped through to her children. Attract his goodness; it is good for you and your children." One more thing that I couldn't resist, "Holiness is not found in how many children you have; it is in who you become as a result of working to raise them." And with that, I sent her off into the warm, deep waters of marriage.

Holy Cow!

You know that food and I have a long and scarred history, only recently becoming more sacred. But I was caught off guard when I discovered that the kitchen could be a holy place. For me, the kitchen was the most dangerous place in the house. Not only because I could possibly overeat. If I was there for a minute beyond my small tolerance for all things domestic, I'd become edgy and begin to dream up concoctions for my next calling in community work. That is how I became involved with numerous community organizations, my favorite being the one dedicated to helping singles with finding their mates. Yes, kitchens can be holy places, I suppose.

Maybe wherever you can serve up love and joy can be holy.

And maybe the kitchen is the most natural place in the world to do that. In fact, when we were renovating our desperately outdated kitchen in our home bought on the cheap, we consulted with our spiritual mentor about how to redo—but not overdo—it, materially speaking. He surprised us by saying, "The kitchen must have a lot of love in it. Make it a comfortable and convenient place, without excess luxury as you define that." Through food, one could help keep a family's body and soul together. I knew it was true, even though it didn't *feel* like that to me. Wrapping all that love, sandwiched between one meal and the next, wore me down.

No (Chocolate) Chip on My Shoulder

All these cooking and baking phobias might have something to do with my friend Faygie. Faygie and I were nine when her mother left us in her kitchen to have fun with her mixer and chocolate, sugar, and eggs. I have no clue where her mother was, but when she came back, her wallpaper was dotted with a new brown and white hue that did not sit well with her taste-ful, light-green and peach flowered wall. Her choice words of rebuke found their mark, snuffing out any culinary impulse that might have been lurking beneath my pile of books.

My baking days never did get better. I do not know what circumstances brought me to try my hand at baking a Duncan Hines cake, the kind that there is "just no way to ruin." The box said to mix by hand. It struck me a bit odd to actually do it this way, but I wanted the chocolate to be just right, so I dutifully put both hands into the lava of chocolate, ordering it to unite into a cohesive unit of bliss. The entire bowl became so stubborn under my touch that it refused to pull itself together, even under the influence of the hot oven. It was an unbeatable success, all right. That is how I became a mother who has never baked a chocolate chip cookie in her life, although I know the best place in town to buy them for those who contend one cannot be a real mother without ever having served up a cookie. In all fairness to myself, I did once take a cooking class in someone's house, but when I fell asleep at the fire watching the food simmer, the cooking instructor politely suggested that I take up a different subject.

While we're on the subject of baking, it was hard to believe I was related to my daughter Basya, whose skating teacher I had recruited to help me learn to skate. Once cradling in her domestically-gifted hands a twenty-pound bag of flour—more economical to buy, she had me know—Basya dancingly said, "This is my Torah." I knew this was no leap of faith for her; she was on solid ground with her tongue-twirling. While I didn't exactly get fired up about her baking affinities, I was cool with them. For her, baking was prayerful. She had a ready love and joy in taking earthy, raw ingredients and organizing them into a life-sustaining, tasteful concoction. As long as it wasn't conta-gious, and that I could continue to use my version of a prayer book, I could live in harmony with a female who liked to bake, did it well, and—even more challenging—considered it holy. We had even worked out that her kitchen escapades would hap-pen at night, after I was asleep, and that the mess would be gone by the time I surfaced in the morning, praying that she'd bless me with a delicious sampling of her holiness.

There was one time when she still had to do some secretive tip-toeing around me. My mother happened to have an extra kitchen mixer to give away. (How does one just happen to have an extra monstrosity like that, casually sitting around? Maybe she won it; she certainly put in enough tickets at these char-ity auctions to deserve to win. Why couldn't she win some-thing practical that I could use, like a desk?) She offered it to Basya, knowing the gadget-deprived kitchen in which she was growing up. Out of the corner of my eye one day, I saw Basya sneak in something through the back door. I was almost sure it was the dog my kids were threatening if my behavior didn't improve . . . that probably would have been quieter and cleaner than the mixer. I told her as long as I didn't see it, she could keep the animal.

As a final word here, all these multi-layered differences

between mother and daughter could have made both of us feel like a failure. That is why I am glad that I had taken the time years earlier to send her a message, albeit in a bit of an unconventional way. Near the big red 'F' at the top of her fourth grade math test, I affixed my requested signature, along with an unsolicited personal comment, "Looking 'F'orward to continued success." I am not sure how I scored in her teacher's book, but I think that was the right role for me to help secure Basya's winning way.

Besides, I think that when mothering is a win-win, that might have something to do with holiness. Serving up love and joy . . . especially where fear and anger could have untastefully mixed in the batter.

Bread-making Gives Rise to Holiness

For a non-baker, I wondered about fulfilling another one of the three special mitzvot of the Jewish woman: baking bread for the Shabbat. Technically, this bread is known as Challah, which is most popularly recognized by its braided oval appearance. Although its significance is multi-faceted, this baking ritual symbolizes a woman's considerable strength in bringing blessing into her surroundings. At its core, it is comparable to baking the "Show-breads" that were baked and showcased in the Holy Temple. And although the Holy Temple is no longer standing and directing our daily lives, this task is considered as pleasing to G-d as the sacrifices that were brought when that spiritual system was in place.

So for someone who doesn't bake, how was I going to be holy? I decided that I'd do this with my head, using my hands as its emissary. Though the kneading of the flour brought me no sensory pleasure, I'd cerebrally delight in the purposefulness of the action. Through the years, I have come to observe that the braided loaves remind me of little fetuses tucked deliciously away, baking in its mother's warmth while rising higher and growing to its potential. So even though I don't like baking, I could—as a former doula—delight in helping to birth little fetuses.

Your Money, Your Life

And if we really want to discuss holiness, why not toss in the green dough known as money? The Talmud tells us if you really want to know who a person is, look at three things: his cup (his demeanor while intoxicated), his temper, and his pocket.

My parents' office, which had outgrown our basement and moved into a home of its own, was the heart of remarkable generosity to its family, employees, and to the community at large. How many loans were graciously made here? How many donations were quietly given, saving countless lives and building so many others—all with their hard-earned money? They live the belief that G-d piped money through them to help others, always allocating at the very least one-tenth of their earnings that the Torah instructs each person to give. Their demonstrated faith bespoke their conviction that money that came their way didn't belong to them; it was merely their privilege and responsibility to dispense it to those whom G-d in His infinite, unfathomable kindness did not do so directly. Even more, in a counter-intuitive but not counterfeit way, I was taught that the financially well-endowed benefit from the poor even more than they are needed by the poor. Why? *Because it gives them the chance to fulfill their earthly mission, which is, inexplicably, bound up with giving money away to others.*

Holy Art

There are many ways to make our lives matter. It is not always what we do; it is how we do it. Not so much the action, but the reaction. While on this human journey, life is not an EZ-Pass system through which we can speed; it is not prepaid. We have to pay as we go, taking the high road of holiness, steering clear of crooked lines so that we can produce an extraordinary work of art . . . our lives.

CHAPTER TWENTY

Grow for It!

To live is to be slowly born. It would be a bit too easy if we could go about borrowing ready-made souls.
—Antoine de Saint-Exupery, author

"**A**RE YOU OKAY, MA'AM?" asked the friendly, Indian-American man behind the Dunkin Donuts counter one night when he saw me emoting sadness to Zack over a cup of coffee he just prepared for me. It was 1:00 a.m. A wet, stormy, dark Sunday night it was—on the inside.

"I'll be fine, thanks. Nothing that my usual order can't glaze over." That was his cue to bag my usual: two chocolate and one white munchkins, usually throwing in a free fourth for Zack. I was long past my pattern of using super-sized sugars to disconnect me from feelings. Much less food these days, but still lots of feelings due to something that I had invited into my life that was beginning to overstay its original welcome. As it overtook my energy, driving me too often out of my house to the caffeinated sugar and cream comfort of the local Dunkin', it was time to follow my homing instinct and find inner balance.

I had been working for several years to help carry the call of a local organization dedicated to helping singles meet and marry. It was getting hard. We were constantly trying to pair good leadership and adequate funds to keep it all going, because we totally believed in the work's importance. That very Sunday afternoon, we had sponsored a community-wide event to generate funds for the organization, arranging seats for three hundred people to enjoy a ventriloquist. Owing to a slight fumble in scheduling, namely Baltimore's Ravens were in the playoffs this Sunday, most of our crowd passed on this one, with only twenty-five non-football fans cheering us on. The performer, I'd like to tell you, was on top of his game, professionally presenting his show as if he was playing to a full audience. It was a great show, but with no showing, we lost money—money we sorely needed.

Stirring around this disappointment with my straw, Zack and I both knew that this work wasn't my cup of tea or, in this case, coffee; why was I doing this arduous job? It was often frustrating, mostly thankless, and always non-paying. Although one tear brought the next, I knew that I could not abort the mission. It was a test of faith; who makes the matches anyway? "Just shush up, show up, and let G-d work through you," was my singular motto for this one.

When Purpose Comes Knocking on Your Door

Why did I even bother? It had something to do with purpose. Purpose helps strengthen our mattering. Actor Richard Grant said that the value of identity is that so often, with it comes purpose. What was my life without purpose? Isn't having an individual life purpose the birthright of all human souls? Philosopher Immanuel Kent thought so: "The human heart refuses to believe in a universe without a purpose."

And with purpose, comes passion and patience. *This three-some—purpose, passion and patience—are fundamental to recovering ourselves.* Yes, finding this threesome is an arduous journey in its own right—one that has to keep being redrawn—but they will show up at your invitation. When you open the door and welcome in purpose, it usually presents in good company—with passion and patience in tow. When I accepted this organizational work, I was eager to welcome in all three— abundant purpose and passion, with a steadily-growing patience to handle the details. But now they were all being tested.

I couldn't say no when I was first approached. The organization was just beginning and doing important work, work that was not being done by others, and I knew we had to try to help. We could not solve the whole issue, no. But neither could we absolve ourselves from doing the part that we could.

So even though my initial response years earlier when first approached by its director to help raise funds for this struggling new local organization was, "No, Dena, I will end up costing you money, not making it; trust me on that," I joined the team, coordinating its debut fundraising event. And I stayed on for years, after most others had left.

I doubt that I would have brought this organization into existence of my own accord, but once here, I could not let it die. I would purposefully "doula" it to life. As the years went by and we struggled to find capable, devoted board members to carry its mission, I labored under its mandate.

Despite this Sunday's "un-event"ful fiasco, we soon found ourselves on the cusp of new leadership and working towards another crucial fundraising event, a final push to keep it going. Daniel and Ayala had long been insisting that I stop giving away their private time with me, to the community. They had made it very clear that they did not enjoy this sport of mine, even though it did often leave them with delicious take-out food, which in any case was better-tasting than anything I could have made. Ayala's bedtime rituals (which I had finally grown into) were usually interrupted by an incoming, pressing call related to the organization, as she was still serving up the details of her day. They had extracted a promise from me that I'd step back from the game after one more big effort. I believed if I could just keep it going a bit more, our efforts for new faces and funds would be rewarded. "Can you do that? Can you just help keep the ball in the air a little longer?" I asked myself, with them shaking their heads in the background, wondering if I'd ever really step away from it.

I wasn't keeping score, but technically, it was G-d's turn to serve. And G-d stepped up His serve, shadowing our resolve. Within short order, new life began to kick around from inside the organization. A reconstituted board created new initiatives. And all this renewed purpose, patience, and passion energized us to arrange a parlor meeting for potential high-level supporters. I worked alongside a prominent multimedia company to write, film, and produce a video about the work our organization was doing to help our singles. While this tender video opened eyes and hearts to the plight of the marriage-minded singles amongst us, pockets still stayed relatively closed. Counting the money after our guests left didn't take very long—there wasn't very much. Returning to my home late that night, drained and dispirited, I joined Daniel and Ayala outside on the lawn swing. When they saw my disappointment at the amount of the expected money we didn't raise, Daniel stood up and said, "I feel so bad for you. I should hug you." Ayala joined in the show. The weather suddenly turned misty, as I was touched by their first-ever show of empathy.

And G-d showed His empathy, too. Because the expanded leadership and massive funds needed to continue our work indeed reached us in a way we couldn't have anticipated—the exact amount, in full, that we had projected to net at the parlor meeting. My volunteer colleagues and I were stunned into a sacred, breath-taking space of seeing G-d's hand. To us, it seemed an overt miracle. For G-d, just another infinite way of helping humans who have maxed their best efforts in trying to help one another.

With the organization now secured, I was now ready for my purpose to relocate elsewhere. As I took the time I needed to find myself again, I wasn't walking away from such a faith-building occurrence with a casual dismiss of my heart. I would use the surge in faith to carry me upwards to the next piece of purpose, of mattering. I now officially stepped back as I had promised my children I would.

Booked Up

I think the psychiatrist Thomas Szasz got it right when he observed that people often say this or that person has not yet found himself, but that the self is not something one finds; it is something one creates. We work to create the true self in bits and pieces. It is not found as one whole entity up front in life. Rather, we discover, recover, and uncover it in phases, as we travel our experiences that map out who we really are. *You are not who you become; you become who you are.*

I was about to learn something very important about creating the self. The poet A.R. Ammons had clued me in about identity: You have it when you find out not what you can keep your mind *on*, but what you can't keep your mind *off.*

And there was something that was beginning to fit that clue.

Although I was occupied with writing for others and had no intentions of hiring myself to fashion a book of my own, I could not release the sense that the radio interviews that I had conducted could be meaningful to others. They'd be perfectly suited for a book. Zack had long believed that I'd one day write a book; maybe it was his upbeat way of keeping sane while having to hear my constant flow of thoughts. Thinking back to my school days, my reports and test papers were always the longest, once even prompting my teacher to say she needed a wheelbarrow to carry my term paper home, and that this undoubtedly portended a writing career. These ever-present whispers motivated me to consistently stay inside the writing track by attending writing workshops and boot camps and taking courses in multiple writing disciplines. So, was writing a book a lifelong desire? It was, and it wasn't; it would depend on what else I could professionally actualize. It seemed like the kind of thing you squeeze in between other pieces of your life. And it definitely didn't seem like something that would matter too greatly, either way.

As I was, once again, repositioning my professional goals with several pathways stretched in front of me, writing that book based on the radio interviews somehow seriously put itself on the ballot—but it wasn't getting my vote. For one thing, I knew the conventional wisdom that insists one has to read a lot if one ever expects to be a credible, if not incredible, writer capable of writing a book. But I, for one, do not read tons; of fiction, hardly none. A very picky reader am I. And for another, way bigger thing, I am of that sort who keeps thoughts on the inner circle, with those who have earned my trust. Why put my mind out in the world to be misunderstood, mocked, and muted? So when this book calling had tried a few years earlier to get me to write it, I had managed with great relief to tuck away my transcribed program notes and shut it down.

"Mimi," I had said to my therapist friend, herself the author of several well-known psychological works, "I feel like I could, that I should, be writing it. But I don't want to write a book." I said that, but wasn't sure what I meant by it.

"Shifra, I don't know anyone who writes a book who doesn't want to." And as she prompted me through the ambivalence I was clearly fighting, she asked, "What's the pull in it for you?"

I got still enough to hear the beginning of a tear. "My Aunt Rosalie didn't matter." Stopping to just breathe and to hear what I had just said, I talked through the tearful emotion, trying to connect it to the book I wouldn't be writing. "I just wish her life could have mattered more. And I wish, with the deepest pieces of my heart, that people, including me, could feel that their lives are large and that they matter."

I knew with certainty this hurt me to the core. But what did that have to do with a book about radio interviews? I couldn't find a connection. *I realized that even if I had the pull to write the book of interviews, I did not have the palpable push.* And so I dropped the whole idea, with Mimi's approval: You can't write a book that you don't want to, that you are not ready to write. *Relief.*

But again, a few years later, that call to write a book . . . it was getting louder and louder. Try as I might, I could not outrun it this time. Because it was growing more uncomfortable to ignore the heart's hounding. This insistence, agitating just beneath my radar, was beginning to drive my professional engine, gaining G-dspeed. Facing once again the fact that feelings can direct us, I was overrun with deeper-level thoughts (known as feelings) such as, "What happens if the thoughts that people shared with me could ennoble and heal others? Or even just delight them the way they had for me?" Did I have the drive and ability to offer it, and if I did, didn't I have the responsibility? Did I have the right to withhold that?

I could hear Barbara Sher's voice in my innermost, "Who do you think you are *not* to do this? This is not humility." And her last comment to me, years ago, re-voiced, "Do not come back to me without your book." I surveyed this inner landscape very carefully. I knew that in life it was impossible to predict in whose words one could find meaning, healing and wholeness. It could often come from the most unlikely places, from the broken and struggling, from the dispirited and disconnected pieces and people in our lives. As G. K. Chesterton wrote, "Humility is the mother of giants. One sees great things from the valley, only small things from the peaks."

And maybe it could also come from the experience of one who had to be rushed to the hospital by ambulance one Friday night, having just hemorrhaged so badly that she needed a blood transfusion. It was in the throes of this curve-ball that I found out firsthand that sometimes the smallest words of hope can deliver big doses of healing. Other women who had a similar experience offered me their stories of healing and built up my reserves of courage to care well for myself.

The crisis had begun with monthly excessive bleeding over a period of a year and a half, sponsored by a uterine fibroid, a benign tumor that can co-exist in a woman's body peacefully . . . until it cannot. Uterine fibroids have three different first names, depending on their exact location, which also determines if and how they will matter. My resident was a submucosal fibroid; its job is to make a woman bleed a lot each month by interfering with the ability of the uterus to contract and stop the cycle. It began to dictate my leaving home schedule a few days each month, as I did not know when and where I'd pass big clots that would demand my special attention. When it unleashed its full talent, putting me in an emergent situation, I knew that I would need to decide on a course of action, as we were no longer compatible.

I was appreciative of this "first home to my children" as Brenna called it, and felt it worthwhile to try to preserve it. And that was why I met with thirteen doctors in total, all of whom advised various strategies to remove it, or the uterus. If the growth is small enough, it can be removed quite easily in a non-invasive outpatient procedure. Mine did not fit into that category, making the decision much more complex. One specialist advised that he could not remove it the way I wanted, "If I remove it that way, you may not make it out." Coming upon a book he wrote, I discovered an expert in fibroid care to whose California office I over-nighted my images. His assessment: This fibroid was positioned such that it was absolutely causing this excessive bleeding and that it was worth finding a highly-skilled doctor who would try to remove it non-invasively—with the willingness and the skill to change course mid-surgery as necessary. Exercising faith and patience was a study in its own right, not the subject at hand—other than to say that you can have faith and you can have fear, but you cannot stand in both at the exact same moment. We must constantly choose faith above fear as we reach higher. In keeping with a core Torah teaching, situations like this, while not invited by us, gift us with the opportunity to build our spirits faithfully, ultimately bestowing blessings into our lives. By expanding our faith, we enlarge our capacity to receive G-dly good. Gratitude has my signature for the grace G-d bestowed on me on that day when His messenger, the talented doctor, succeeded in removing the entire fibroid with the hoped-for procedure, restoring my life to a blessed balance.

One of my greatest thoughts, as memorable as it was rare, was about my custom-made mothering designed for my two youngest children. I had some moments while lying low to actually realize that no one else would have a clue how to manage these mouth-driven minds. I decided it would be important for me to recover so that I could return to that worthwhile challenge. Finally, maybe even for the first time, all those years of maternal efforts were registering on my mattering scale, reweighing the notion that I could hire someone to mother in my stead, doing at least as good of a job, if not better. All of that "stinking thinking" bled right out of my system.

From the Depths

With that situation ameliorated, and with the community organization in good hands, I was sufficiently rebalanced. . . . just in time for a rewarding, decade-long freelancing contract (my most time-consuming and profitable) to abruptly end. With that, I began to feel that familiar pull that I'd need to step into the next professional space . . . a book. The whisper grew into a small voice that insisted I follow through with this book project featuring the radio interviews. They were all transcribed so that I could begin to organize the themes and select the interviews that fit them. And I was beginning to discern that one central underlying theme for all the interviews was inexplicably linked to how I experienced Aunt Rosalie' existence, or perhaps more accurately, her non-existence, and the collateral damage it cast on my life that was considered to be similar to hers. If I had the pull to write this book before, I now also had the push.

With the extra space in my business day, I was now ready with a growing desire to write the book, the details of which would fully present itself in due time. But its purpose, I already subconsciously knew, although it would take some more time to acknowledge, and then a whole lot more time to embrace. It was deeply connected to that whole mattering question embodied by Aunt Rosalie, though some of the radio material would also make it into the book.

If you think that writing a book would now become my sweet dream, though, I'd like to share with you something about dreams. They don't always lull us into a contented, comfortable night's sleep; sometimes they actually awaken us. Here was the dream I had when I was racing these book-writing thoughts around:

I was driving my car, approaching a construction site that was clearly marked as such. In front of me I saw an abyss, a huge empty hole. It was not blocked or roped off. No DANGER sign here. Somehow, my car continued on, perched precariously with its rear wheels firmly on the paved road while the front half teeter-tottered over the abyss. The front of my car inched too closely to the abyss. My car, with me driving it, fell into the unknown stretch.

As I went falling down, down, down, I prayed and sang. I could hear voices around me . . . I was alive.

The poem Dr. Norma had given me so many years earlier flashed brightly:

Let me fall
Let me climb
There's a moment when fear
And dreams must collide

Stepping into the unknown is sometimes *that* terrifying.
And the process often demands *that* much courage.

The quote from British public servant Charles Wilson surfaced in my mind: "A man of character in peace is a man of courage in war." I knew I would continue to battle this calling. It would take more courage than I had, and would require one more thing: Prayer.

Praying: A Weapon in the Battle of Wills

If the three P's—purpose, passion, and patience—are a three-some, there is one "P" that I call awesome. I refer to the capital "P" as Prayer. And in searching for the courage to move forward, I knew where I had to turn. As pastor Harry Emerson Fosdick wrote, "The best guarantee of a character that is not for sale is the battlefield of prayer . . . fight for the power to see and the courage to do the will of G-d." I knew that on this battlefield, tears, not blood, are shed.

As a highly personal and creative process, prayer is an unsurpassed opportunity for a human's growth and development. Even so, Torah refers to it as "service, or work, of the heart," underscoring the idea that it is not a simple endeavor. Certainly not as simple as the ad I saw for an online service: For $7.95, *Prayers Heavenbound* would beam one's message directly to G-d via advanced technological satellites. If you fall for that, you are *overpaying* and *under-praying*.

I was young, in first grade, when I first encountered an actual Hebrew prayer book, a *Siddur*. We were given it after learning how to read the Hebrew alphabet, the *Alef-Bet*, and we were allowed to pray from it every morning, saying the words out loud together. One day, we were at the part of the prayers where we were taught to stand with our feet together. Feeling more hungry than holy, I turned to my desk mate, wondering out loud what she had brought for lunch. Mrs. Weiner did not like that one bit; she took away my Siddur, and told me to sit down. All I remember is being happy that I didn't have to stand anymore, along with a sad feeling, too, that I was being denied participation in a group conversation with G-d. And then there were the many times when I found it hard to pick up the prayer book at all; too strenuous to get quiet and concentrate on words, especially while feeling uncomfortable in a human-garbed, weighed-down existence. I wonder, also, if an incident from years ago in the synagogue had left me with a residual resistance towards prayer. While I was supposed to be praying in a group with other pre-adolescent females inside the sanctuary, my group leader found me talking outside in the hall. This was a good reason for her to knock my eleven-year old head, a little too hard if you ask me, into the hallway wall, unceremoniously confiscating my siddur "that you don't deserve."

I can say that I had seen fervent prayer up close. I remember my queen birthstone maternal grandmother praying. She did not know how to formally read from the Siddur, though I once begged to teach her, but her sincere words and tears fell out of her heart all the same. I have long held the notion that her prayers sustained Grandpa for a miraculous twenty-one years beyond my fourth-grade year when he became ill. And that his end came with no warning, for she would have prayed him out of his death had she been given the opportunity.

Praying Your Way Forward

To cope with this process of unfolding, I began to utilize what I call the *Hoping Mechanism: To cope is human, to hope is Divine.* Even if I couldn't pay my way, I was learning how to pray my way. Because what I couldn't make happen, my Creator could. I had witnessed this a thousand times . . . that in every man-made plan, there was at least one small unknown, uncontrollable piece that only G-d could execute so that it would work. Read world history books, and you will see how the fate of nations hangs on this unseen, but not unrecognized, fact.

This sure was true in my family's history: Grandma Lolly's late-life fate certainly hinged on G-d's intervention. She was in her mid-nineties when she stopped her "'round the block daily drives" in her brown two-door Pontiac. Although she didn't smoke her daily two packs of Virginia Slims anymore, having exhaled that habit at the age of sixty-nine, Grandma Lolly knew how to keep herself content, if not busy. She would use the first part of her day to pray, watch television, converse with Aunt Rosalie, and walk around in her home with her walker, overseeing the growth of years of unopened mail that over-took her den. Then she would rest on her living room chair, engrossed in her trademark, trance-like thinking about her world until 3 a.m., at which time she'd check the door locks just two more times before falling asleep. She'd awake at 12 p.m., beginning her daily schedule again. Despite her admirable attempts at self-care, the day came when we needed to forcibly move her from her Richmond home to Baltimore. At the age of ninety-eight, and at a weight twenty pounds less than that, we did not know if she could survive the nearly three-hour trip, but we knew she definitely wouldn't survive long if left for even another week in her home.

I hated the thought of kidnapping someone, forcibly removing her from her home of sixty years—asking myself if this was an Arik Sharon-like maneuver of uprooting people from their homes of happiness, thinking we know better what is right for them. Or worse, doing it because it is expedient for us. Ours was a family decision with which we struggled for months, and though still riddled with indecision, we finally executed this maneuver on a fair-weather Columbus Day. I knew that this excursion may have looked similar in action to Arik Sharon's shameful schtick, but thankfully, it offered a very different result. While loyal discernment may have eluded the Israeli political powers of 2005, who left an entire human community in a deprived existence with inadequate resources to help resettle everyone, ours proved life-sustaining. Grandma Lolly lived front and center amidst her doting Baltimore family for four whole years from the exact date she came to us, passing on at the age of 102.

At the time of this unfolding mission, before my father suddenly showed up at her door, we knew we had to somehow make sure that my Aunt Rosalie would not be there, because she would have interfered with the move in a loving, but misguided, effort to protect her mother. Aunt Rosalie lived around the corner on Grace Street, but spent most of her days and part of her nights at Grandma Lolly's house. As planned, my cherished cousin Sylvia circled the block in her car, reporting that her mother Aunt Rosalie had just left Grandma's house to go to her own. But how could we possibly ensure that she'd stay there long enough to allow my father and cousin to remove Grandma Lolly from her home and safely put her and her few belongings in the car before her return?

That was the piece G-d tended to, all by Himself. Ever so naturally, He employed one of His forces of nature to erupt across the street from Aunt Rosalie, summoning forth a fire engine that blared down Grace Street, attracting everyone's concern and curiosity. My aunt became focused on the goings-on of the fire department while chatting with neighbors. By the time she had returned, Grandma Lolly was secured in the car, leaving Aunt Rosalie with the choice to come along or stay behind. For the record, Aunt Rosalie graciously accompanied Grandma Lolly, though she later returned to Grace Street to try to live on her own, which she did for a short time until she needed an assisted living facility.

I knew not to judge G-d by human limitations. That He was way larger than any of the challenges He had created. And that He created these challenges as opportunities to prod us to something bigger and better about ourselves that we couldn't or wouldn't have accessed on our own.

Astro-NOT

Along this path towards developing my understanding for writing this book, relying on G-d showed itself to be the most reliable avenue. Getting myself out of my own orbit always proved beyond me. No satellite, even one pre-loaded with prayers, was going to get my life unstuck. I was in orbit, going around in dizzying circles, with human gravity pulling me down. Only G-d could defy that and lift me up. And set me straight, or at least upright. In strengthening myself, I had partially cracked the code: I would always be complex, complicated. It was both my fate and my fortune. My task was to remain happily complicated, but not to be difficult. The last vitamin in the world I'd need to supplement is the "B-complex." Discovering how to say "yes" to something, instead of "no," would hold the key to inner movement.

And I might add that there were "concerned" people in my life who were all too happy to point out that I thought way too much, and to just stop thinking. I would certainly think about that, I assured them. But that's like telling an astronaut in space to stop floating around. One cannot elude his natural habitat. I floated weightlessly in my mind like an astronaut in his spacesuit.

And there was a prayer for this Astro-Not which Brenna sent me, aptly called "Knots Prayer:"

Please untie the knots that are in my mind, my heart and my life.
Remove the have nots, the can nots, and the do nots that I have in my mind.
Erase the will nots, may nots, might nots, that may find a home in my heart.
Release me from the could nots, would nots, and should nots that obstruct my life.

And most of all, I ask that you remove from my mind, my heart and my life all of the 'am nots' that I have allowed to hold me back, especially the thought that 'I am not' good enough.

Answering the Call

As I prayed for small signs along the way to help me understand how to move forward, I began to get them. The first was immediate: an email that came from a man who was leading a national effort to help the single community, and had been very helpful to our organizational efforts. In his subject line sat the words "Answer the Call," referring to an article he had written about this work he was doing. He could not have known that this was my first, but not final, working title for this book. I allowed this to serve as an early signal to turn the page and proceed.

And now, in my life, I was learning an amazing, if inconvenient, lesson: Even if *this* book would not be written, a different one would come calling. Callings don't let up that easily, *because G-d doesn't give up that easily on us*. It was beginning to make itself clearly known as part of my purpose.

I knew I'd need purpose, passion, and patience once again to answer this call. And while patience is a virtue, it's not naturally one of mine. But personal experience has a way of getting deep into your bones. And digging into you, uncomfortably. As essayist Anaïs Nin noticed, the day came when "the risk to remain tight in the bud was more painful than the risk it took to blossom." And so, along with purpose and passion, my patience to actually do the process caught up with me, too.

I realized that I could not write the same book that I would have years ago, just like the reader never reads the same book twice. As we change, what catches our attention changes. And now that my attention was fully engaged, I wanted to marry this new purpose which I was only beginning to understand. I decided to continue to pray.

Prayer: Purpose Unearthed

I had learned that if prayer feels like a burden, I was not experiencing its greatest benefit. At its ideal, it is the privilege of *unburdening* oneself to the One Being who can actually deliver us, and who really wants to.

If I asked you to write out the word "prayer" as an acronym, would you have written this?

P= purposefully
R= reaching
A= above
Y= your
E= existing
R= reality

If we want to reach for something that might be beyond us, that is not a reason to stop. That is a great reason to go. *And to grow.*

CHAPTER TWENTY-ONE

Scared to Matter?

*I may not have gone where I intended to go, but I think I
have ended up where I intended to be.*
                                        —Douglas Adams, author

As you know, I took up skating in the heavier moments
of my life. When I fell, I learned that I could get up. And I
observed that healthy movement of any kind would propel me
upwards.

Small leaps outside, huge reaps inside.

There was something I didn't know at that time about
skating and myself. Barbara Sher taught it to me in our radio
interview with a random example that turned personal. Here it
is, excerpted from our on-air exchange about skating:

"I love to ice skate," I told her, "but I am not particularly
gifted at it. But you said what you love, you are good at."

"Okay, so what do you love about it?" she asked.

"I love the grace and freedom of movement," I answered.

"Do you feel the grace and freedom of movement when
you're doing it?" she probed.

"No. But I enjoy it, particularly when I am skating to special
music, a piece of intense Yanni music," I added.

"What you are gifted at, Shifra, is movement to music. And the thing you like about ice skating is that it gives you a little more freedom of movement than you would have if you were just standing in your living room. If you could stand on the ice in your bare feet and do free form to the same music you love so much, you'd also feel wonderful. You just wouldn't have to learn the skill of skating."

She continued, "You like skating because it's basically dancing, movement, but with more speed and freedom in it. And it's worth developing the skill of ice skating because it might give you pleasure in a way you really enjoy it. But what you really love is movement to music, and you are gifted at it, or you wouldn't love it."

So now I knew that we humans are very particular about our likes and dislikes. We just need to understand our own language so that we can create ourselves accordingly. For me, mattering is the music in the movement; falling or rising, I was moving.

The But Stops Here

I had learned from Barbara that there are powerful blocks on our mattering. We all have resistances that obscure our path to wholeness. That knock us off course, leaving us feeling weaker for the wear. All sorts of negative emotions agitate to bring us down, especially the small feeling of jealousy, which clings to the spirit like fat to a body. *Exercising our mattering shapes flabby emotion into strength and power.*

But, which version of your life script are you holding and acting out?

I started out with a life script that directed me to *not* matter. Clearly, I was to play the non-mattering part, like Aunt Rosalie. But as I mouthed those powerless words, I felt compelled to rewrite the imbalanced script so that I could voice very different lines. They were not the right size.

As you play your role, other characters shift accordingly. When your script lines change, theirs do too. They accommodate your shift; they must, in order for the show to go on. And while some may choose to stay behind or say they have no choice but to do so, the power of mattering is that it invites others into their own larger lives, too. Mattering is magical in that way; the experience of honoring oneself gives one the wherewithal to extend it to others.

Creativi-Tea

My life's trajectory was brewing a special tea, after all. It was called *creativi-tea*.

I could well intuit by now that human beings have to create in order to matter. It is just part of the human terrain; we are born to create. Just as our Creator does, so do we. Whatever it is and wherever it is, creating brings us from hole to whole.[17] It is not just about joy or pleasure; it is about wholeness.

And I think it is our only hope against the emptiness that strains the human heart and drains it of its mattering.

Teeing off with Dr. Norma had begun my process of healing. I had repeatedly learned that it is not what we say "no" to in life, but what we say "yes" to, that allows us to realize our vitality. I began to consume nourishing food and healthy ideas about mattering, both of which helped me create meaningful movement to which I could dance.

I came to understand that while G-d gives opportunity to all, He is not an equal opportunity lender. *He lends different abilities to people so they can cash in on their life's purpose.*

Mind Your Matters

Somewhere along this circuitous life line, I have a stick drawing I scribbled when I was in an unfertile cycle of life, laboring under the heavy illusion of non-mattering. It features a long-haired little girl with hot blood-red tears falling down her face. In the speech balloon, she says, "I cannot make meaningful music." For humans who are born to sing, not being able to find harmony in life is cause for great pain. And while pain provokes us to reach higher, joy is the energy that sustains the growth.

---

17 *The Artist's Way,* Julia Cameron, Tarcher/Putnam, 1992.

Explore what matters to you. What do you laugh about, and what makes you cry? Noticing that will tell you so much about what is important to you, about what "gets to you." What makes you happy? Lucille Ball had a good point when she remarked, "It's a helluva start, being able to recognize what makes you happy." Was Mark Twain just joking when he said, "I can tell anybody how to get what they want out of life. The problem is that I can't find anyone who can tell me what they want." Is it so hard for us humans to know what we want?

And while we work to figure out what makes us happy, I have learned that much of life happens in the slower moments, in the low spaces *between* refreshing clarity and purpose. Learning how to do life *here* is what I have learned that mattering is all about. We can't always wait to feel like taking the next step; that makes *us* unreliable. We shouldn't always wait for others to validate our next step; that makes *them* unreliable, since humans cannot always come through for us the way we hope and, even sometimes, expect. And if we wait until we are sure of everything, it will be too late. *It is the small, often tentative, steps that will lay down the large, enduring path of joy.*

As a clue to what makes you happy, I'll ask you this question: If you could redecorate one room in your house, which would you choose? You and I can still be friends if you said the kitchen, but I don't think we can do tea together, because for me, it is my home office (a library, when I want to be elegant about it), or simply the room with my desk to hold my thoughts. Give me a little food and a lot of thought, and I am happy. Mr. Twain, now that I know what makes me happy, can you please order for me a new writing desk, the one that completely encircles me, that spins around me with different work stations as I sit still? If it doesn't yet exist, can you help me create it?

Your home holds a lot of clues about your mattering. What you choose to buy, to wear, and to display says much about you. What colors cover your walls, and what pictures adorn them? In my home, I do not use the color blue; the lifeless threads of a baby turning blue suppress my life force. I will live for as long as I can recover that young sense of hope that my nanny breathed into me. And even though I regret that I never had the opportunity to personally thank Fanny before she drew her own last breath, I sometimes thank her silently when I see the color orange in my home. Uplifted by its vivaciousness, I am reminded of her lifesaving breath—and that of my Creator who put her at my side. And I thank G-d for investing His breath into me, the breath of human mattering.

Power-phrasing one of my queen grandmother's favorite sayings: Be it ever so humble, there is no *space* like home. Largeness is on the inside. If I have done my work here well enough, I have demonstrated that it is not the outer places, but the inner spaces, that often hold the greatest potential for large living, for mattering. While human attention goes to that which the *eye* can see, mattering belongs to that which the *I* can behold.

Finding one's life purpose, one's cup of tea, requires us to stir up the pot, even if you, as I, don't like kitchen duty. It is not always comfortable, but what bliss it is to hear the musical hiss of the teapot ready to make you a great cup of tea.

Birthing a Book, Parenting a Purpose

And, as I mentioned before, my next cup of tea had been hissing for a while. I am not known for being the quickest learner around. But when I thought about my aforementioned dream in which I had fallen into the abyss, I got it. I knew I was in a deep space, and that I must begin to act.

To be candid, it was an intensely soul-searing space.
And, actually, you are in it with me at the moment.
Because that space, my friends, is the book you are holding.

When I was in that space, I came to understood *that* I'd write a book. And *why* I'd write it. But *what* exactly was I supposed to be writing? Was I supposed to combine the radio interviews with Aunt Rosalie's life? The working title was ever-changing, making this the first time in my life that I felt strangely entitled and unentitled at the same time. For G-d's sake, *what* was I supposed to be writing?

And G-d did not forsake me. He put into my Walgreen Pharmacy line—where I was standing neither straight nor still—a person who caught my full attention. G-d was conspiring with my August calendar that day, because I wasn't supposed to be in that line at all. I was supposed to have been at a three-day stipend-paying conference in New York . . . except I hadn't been accepted. A woman from Israel would be presenting insights from her recently authored book exploring the male and female roles in the Orthodox world. To be considered for the program, I submitted several essays, investing tens of hours into their writing. I knew that I had exceeded the intended demographic (20-45) by more than a thousand days, but was advised to submit the admission essays *just in case. Just in case* never happened, and that was how I ended up in the Walgreens line waiting to print a photo taken the day before—at Jonathan's house in North Carolina.

Jonathan is Zack's first cousin. We had stayed at his large, inviting home so we could participate in the unveiling ceremony of his mother, Zack's aunt. Because New York would not have me, I decided why not join Zack in North Carolina for this important occasion? I might have reconsidered, had I known that I'd have to dare down his dog, Turbo, who had taken a liking to me, advancing towards my new pair of smooth hose with an over-friendly, wet tongue. He didn't take it personally, later resting with permission on my forgiven lap while he eyed the late night news, and I, him. Once put in his "down boy" place, he responded well to my photo prompts the next day, when I photographed Jonathan and his two dogs—with the undisclosed dogged intention to turn it into a gift that this plastic surgeon would like. Jonathan's dogs were his prized, free-reigning residents, with the more spoiled Turbo even having his own personalized pint-sized potty. Weeks later at a family wedding, Jonathan asked Zack and me to step out into the hall where he unbuttoned his white dress shirt to show us he was wearing our gift: a tee shirt decorated with the photo of Jonathan and company. A dog-gone good choice for this master.

My apologies for veering out of that Walmart line, the one with that special person right in front of me. She was an African-American woman, with a noticeable joy on her face. Her hair, the color of salt and pepper, was wrapped in a small Sunday-Church bun. She opened wide her unguarded smile, a pleasing accessory to her proper, long-sleeved, high collared white blouse paired with a flowingly-feminine floral skirt. A summer-white shawl with thin fringes held her shoulders as she turned toward me with a soft greeting. I immediately saw the dignity of her prayerful soul; it accompanied her every move.

And this was how I knew that Charita Cole Brown had just written a book about her bipolar life, defying the verdict that she'd never get married or have children, both of which she did. And that she was in a writing competition for promising first-time authors, whose first prize she ultimately won: a book deal that would traditionally publish, and nationally market, her book.

And she'd casually tell me something one day, months later, that wowed me: "Shifra, I never go to that pharmacy, because it is not in my neighborhood." Same here, by the way. It was a one-time occurrence for each of us, courtesy of the ride her relative gave her, a favor for both of us made possible by G-d. Charita would soon become my personal friend, encouraging my fledgling book-writing efforts with her sensitive and clear guidance, her signature paper butterfly bookmark she gave me as "writing wings," and her prayerful prompts to let G-d lead the way. Her first piece of writing advice to use the first-person voice got me going, but it was her second prescription that kept me going, and that I'd need to remember, "They want you to write your story the way *they* remember it. Be true to *your* story."

And so I have been, true to my story.

Processing Pain

With Charita's successful experience, I decided to explore this writing retreat that hosted a national competition as a possible avenue to grow my understanding of this book project I had committed myself to develop. At the very least, receiving some professional support could help me move forward with shaping my book.

I took that next small step, Barbara-style, submitting a piece of my work to be reviewed by the CEO of the retreat. And that was how he came into our lives: *Mr. Steve, it is a pleasure to meet you.* After his preliminary read of a brief sampling of my skeletal work in progress, Steve had this to say: "Shifra, your work lacks structure and to be honest, is undisciplined." Well, Steve, to be honest, I'm not that big on discipline, whatever you mean by that anyway.

"But," he continued in his email, "I like something about this. What is developing here, and you as author behind the book, hold much appeal to me." With that, he invited Zack and me to come up to the retreat for a few days "to discuss how this might unfold."

On our maiden trip to Vermont, with the multi-hued brilliance of her majestic October mountainscape towering all around us, Zack and I were hardly through the front door when we heard Steve say, "By the time you leave here in a few days, you will have a clear direction for your book."

"He doesn't know who he's dealing with," I said later to Zack, writing off his promise. "There is no way that in a few days he'll be able to get me to figure that out. In fact, you know what? Let's get out of here now." I was tired from the flight and the ensuing two-hour car drive from the airport to the retreat. It was raining, and I wanted to go home. Just those usual "no"-jerk reactions when I go somewhere new.

But that would prove to be the first of several times that Steve was at least one or two steps ahead of me. Because before leaving the retreat three days later, I had unpacked a direction for the book. It was a process that involved a few steps, including standing behind a lectern in the cozy, coral-colored couch room with a fireplace to read a few pages of my work and answer questions he posed. After that, he sat us down with his assessment: "Continue with the process; you sure can tell a story. Are you ready to tell yours?"

I didn't know I had one. "Steve, I don't have a story to tell. I have a message to communicate, but that's hardly a story."

"Shifra, everyone has a story."

"But mine doesn't matter."

And that, I'd soon come to learn, was exactly my story.

I knew that continuing with Steve and his team would both direct and support my professional work with clear objectives and measurable goals in place, including the chance to win a book deal if I chose to enter the competition. After broadcasting my lingering questions, radio-host style, I told Steve I had but one remaining question for him. But before I could ask it, he answered, "And you are not alone. You have an excellent coach." Seeing that I was not sure if he was referring to Zack or himself, he pointed his finger inward.

"And one more thing, Shifra. This is your time. If you don't do it now, you won't." I knew he was right. I told myself something that I once told you: *When it's your turn in life, you take it.* And this time, as I was deciding how best to engage in the work, I didn't wait to reapply my make-up, as I had done when Zack was preparing to propose.

Instead, Zack and I took a long talk around the duck pond, right outside the nine-bedroom retreat house wherein each room bears the name and style of a celebrated author. With the subliminal influence those nights having been Mark Twain, who already existed in my life as the man who popularized the idea not to let schooling interfere with education, I was primed to consider the merits of the writing life. Adapting his thought for my purposes here, I knew I could "not let knowledge get in the way of wisdom." If I was to write this book, I'd have to trust in the wisdom of my experiences, no matter what degree I didn't have or might still get. This was not about degree or pedigree.

I gazed longingly at the raft of ducklings paddling on the water, together in their natural habitat, aware of their utter joy of being in a shared space that was right for them. And although I couldn't quite make out their conversations, I could hear some of mine. Their rightness of fit wasn't lost on me, as I was overcoming my initial brooding about being here. As my stay was completing, I sensed that I was in an appropriate place for me, for now, and that I would wade in the writing milieu. It was a right fit, it was *becoming*, like that swimsuit my grandparents had given me so many years earlier.

And with this decision now made, it began . . . the intense, unending, gaggle of inner questions that still haven't completely stopped. All this movement over so many years was coming down to this: writing this book. Why? How many words each day must I write to reach my goal? Will it be a memoir or fiction? What about that discipline I will need? What if I cannot go the distance? What about rejection? *What ifs* and *hows* would dominate my energy I needed to invest in the work. Yes, I'd have to be willing to live in the question, because I decided this: *An unanswered question is way better than an unasked one.*

At some point during the next few months of initial writing, some of which I did at the retreat, Steve and Charita (who was there, coaching the participants in the competition I ultimately joined) saw that something was not going well with my process. Collaborating on the sofas positioned by the dining room's large front window overlooking the entrance path to the retreat, Steve and Charita settled on the one sofa across from mine, with Zack on the armed chair to my right side. Steve, a huge heart of a man who cannot hide his ceaseless curiosity, disciplined drive, and unabashed, limitless love for words and those who wield them, announced in his deliberate, considered way of speaking, "I feel that something is in your way."

I stared at him, a habit of mine when I don't yet really understand what someone is saying. "Do you know what is blocking you here? You have gone inward. That, to me, means you are scared of something, Shifra. You are not owning your story. I want to help you, but I don't know how to penetrate this."

I sat uncharacteristically quiet for a few minutes. "Steve, you are right. I think I know what it is." He realized something I had not yet. While trying to keep this professional effort cerebral, i.e., it would get my best head but not my full heart, I was harboring a deep level concern that I'd hurt people in the process of doing this work, including myself. He was right; I didn't know if I could own my story.

Owning something means committing to something with all you've got, no holding back. Telling the inside truth, you are aware of the cost as you manage the opportunity with the risk. As in building anything, it is a brutal effort at times. Oh, how I envied those whose work demanded only their sharp, heartless minds. Ownership has a high price, and in this case, it would cost me privacy—a priceless, luxurious possession that I zealously guard. It could cost me valued relationships. A dear writing friend, a bestselling author no less, begged me to listen well: "You cannot talk candidly about your inner world, including your childhood and mothering. You mean well, but people will destroy you. They will rip you for anything they can misconstrue in your disfavor."

Sell out now, I told myself. *Cut your losses and move on. Maybe go back to school for that psychology or business degree, after all. Or communications; I just wouldn't tell Brenna.*

But then I recalled what one of the judges who was assigned to give a rush of confidence to the weary writers in the pre-judging stages, before crushing them in the final round, had unloaded: "I hope Shifra doesn't let Shifra stand in her own way." What did that mean, I asked him, quietly understanding that I had a long, storied history of doing just that—giving up before going the distance, creating enough drama and doubt to un-become, to undo my best efforts, and to keep my limited energy tied up in knots. Conjuring up the worst outcomes that may not even come to pass was a non-mattering position I knew well. All those powerless patterns of thinking that would destroy me if I didn't fight them. Helen Keller's mindset was helpful now: Doubt and mistrust are the mere panic of timid imagination, which the steadfast heart will conquer, and the large mind transcend.[18]

I knew what I had to do: *get the head out of my way.* Time to let those well-honed feelings do the work now. And if there ever was a time that I'd need to heed my own words, it was here, as I shared with you: "You can shortchange the process, but at what cost to your potential?" Yes, I could curtsy out now, but then what? Who would tell my story, if not me? Be it ever so humble, it is mine. Who'd become me, if not I?

I had consulted once again with my spiritual advisor with whom I discussed such life matters. Aside from Barbara Sher hinting years earlier about a book I would write, our rabbi, a world-class Torah scholar who'd encouraged me years earlier to do doula work, surprised me at one point by saying he thought I'd take up writing the book "inside me." It was only natural for me to return to his office for his thoughts on writing this kind of a book, the kind that might not put all in a great outer light, rather shedding light on the darker, inner fights of being human.

He was clear as he was concise: "As long as your family, the main characters here, are okay with this, do it. That no one comes up perfect, that's perfectly fine, because no one is. Struggling to grow, striving to reach . . . this is all important, great stuff. Sharing with people your personal narrative with the desire and intention of helping them matters. You will have nothing for which to apologize."

And I replayed in my mind what Brenna had said a few months earlier, when I was deliberating whether or not to commit myself to this professional project. Her heartfelt words penetrated this stubborn resistance: "Write to the pain. If you can do that, you have your story. Do it." And my parents echoed that, not really understanding the story I'd tell, but hopeful it

---

18 *Optimism, An Essay,* Helen Keller.

would land well for everyone. How incredibly gracious, deserving of the highest tribute I could give to these great people who were allowing themselves to be placed into a story that did not always gloriously uphold them.

Extending our Family

Dare to Matter was now being born.

Still wont to use birth phrases as a retired doula, I'd say this book had now become a child begging to be born. My family respectfully organized itself around it, leaving me space to carry it. I even asked Marie, the nutritionist, if she thought I'd gain weight during the process. She reassured me I wouldn't, as long as I remained connected to feeding myself well, especially as strong thoughts and feelings would, of course, surface. Although I wasn't nauseous, I was moody, trying to hold onto my equilibrium while birthing the book. Had I known that this labor would be like my natural births—long and tiring—I might have begged Dr. Norma for a psychological epidural to block my growing nerve needed to do this work.

And one thing I should admit: my disfavor for writers, and I daresay for teachers, was rearranging itself. Like the small characters on the eye chart that can suddenly be clearly seen with the right prescription, there was something in doing this work that reached across the cynicism, opening my eyes to the work writers and teachers do. Maybe it was less about being heard than prompting others to hear themselves.

And as the work intensified, I was now like my laboring mothers in the night's loneliness preceding the birth light. And if you must know, I turned to Zack in the dark of these moments, his compassionate hands catching my naked tears. I'd enjoin him to please let me stop this project; that I had changed my mind about writing it. I don't want to carry this anymore. But he, and I, knew there was no turning back. Not if I wanted to honor this piece of my mattering. I had to, for myself.

And for Aunt Rosalie: You might have left this life wondering about your purpose in it. I think we all do, to some extent.

But I am coming to see that G-d has a way of working it all out. I hope that your story, told through mine, furthers our human mattering, for each of us and for all of us. The world of mattering is the one I'd like to share and bequeath to my fellow life travelers. I couldn't have known how this would all come into being, and how your message got entwined with mine, but that is how a Divine-inspired humanity works. Connections are deep, unseen, often not understood until G-d sheds His light on them.

With this resolve to forge forward, this book soon enough took on a life of its own—a growing baby whose big, longing eyes I imagined were depending on me to carry the burden, to let it grow, and to allow it to be welcomed into this world. *But why are you looking to me to do this?* I would rhetorically ask this book in utero.

As its mother, I knew well that it would not be simple to parent this purpose. And once again, Zack birthed with me. With some rhyme and even less reason, I put fingers to keyboard to answer the call. As I "played" the writing keys, the blurred vision of Mrs. Goodman's piano with the too-black and white keys emerged. What was that sound I was beginning to hear? Could it be meaningful music, after all?

Beneath my fingers now lay a different instrument, but with the same goal of making music. And just as skating wasn't the dance itself, the piano wasn't the instrument I wanted to play. It was the music I had been after all along.

And now, as this story closes, I trust yours to begin to open more fully, the way you envision it. You cannot yet envision it? Keep doing the work in front of you until you can. Small steps, big strides; *guaranteed.*

There is just one more thing I really wanted to share, because I thought you'd want to know. But, I had to decide against it; it was premature. I pray it will find its way to the next book I am envisioning, and whose labor has begun.

Prepare to Fall . . . into Your Mattering

Indeed, Dr. Norma was right when she told me the meaning of that poem she gave me so many years ago. "Shifra, it means you are about to do some important, life-altering work."

Let me fall
Let me climb
I will dance so freely
So let me fall
If I must fall
There's no reason
To miss this one chance
The one I will become
Will catch me

⟜

Human, alone, and uniquely whole.

Mattering is the music we play when we move into our inner, G-d given space.

DARE.

EPILOGUE

Whereto from here?

You and I have spent many hours together. I cannot really know if and how this all resonated with you.

Many times along the way, I wanted to opt out of this work. You know that already. Obviously, I didn't act on that recurring impulse. Instead, I presented the details of my inner story with one intention: to communicate the message of mattering. I stood in this question of mattering for many years; I still do a lot of the time. With this book, I worked toward understanding the question more clearly. In exploring multiple threads in my life, I arrived at a definition of mattering. And, I offered ways for how we can create it.

Because I trust there is a far larger story here: Yours.

I wanted to give you something to have and to use as you work on your life's story. That is why I have lifted out of each chapter the objective lessons around which my story unfolded. And for some reason which seemed like it mattered, I have named them **Matterings**. They are the thoughts about hope, holiness and happiness; love, loneliness and loyalty; money, mothering and mattering; pleasure, pain and purpose; faith, feelings and falling; religion, royalty, and recovery; and shame, smallness and spirituality.

Matterings are not always simple to think about. Often, they are prompts to delve deeper, into the unseen places that lie still until they are invited into our lives. And you know by now that it is this internal landscape that has held my avid interest, and holds far more of your power than you might have imagined.

Dare it all down... As if it matters...Because you do.

For your monthly MATTERINGS e-note, email
Shifra@ShifraMalka.com or visit www.DareToMatter.org.

Chapter One   THE HEART OF NON-MATTERING

1. Traumas can be slow, steady, seemingly unremarkable assaults on something intrinsic to the healthy functioning of a breathing organism. Consistent, enduring messages of non-mattering fit this ill.

2. The language of not mattering is held together by notes of disdain and discounting. Its main sound is guttural and harsh: Do not be who you are. Worse, who do you think you are?

3. Fault lines, the shaky ground beneath all who tread, are a consuming place for all to be amply faulted and hurt.

4. The secret to a loving, peaceful, respectful marriage: Your wife or your life. One cannot negotiate his wife's well-being and status as his prized priority. This is non-negotiable.

Note: Because the MATTERINGS (in the Epilogue) are original compositions, they are proprietary and may not be used or reproduced for any purpose without the written permission of the publisher or author.

5. Being frightfully aware of dysfunction, we are helpless to know how to heal it.

6. Following scripts with misguided characters is asking for a lopsided performance.

7. Not being invited to be who you are creates an unwelcome divide in the spirit, obstructing a healthy path towards wholeness.

8. Not-mattering and loneliness are twins, sharing the same faint heartbeat of a life yet to be lived. They co-exist in a colorful and dark place, desperately agitating for the relief of a redemptive light. Very little can satisfy the growing hunger these twins endure. One can never be enough, have enough, or do enough . . . Enoughness is not within the rational and reasonable reach of this twin pair.

9. Complicated children can be difficult to raise.

10. One may be complicated, but can learn how not to be difficult.

11. Unconditional love allows everything in life its individuality, its purpose, and its power . . . to matter. With unconditional love, we can extend a potent belief in the worthiness of the complicated person, activating natural wellsprings of hope and drive and discipline . . . and, ultimately, of mattering.

12. Allowing the rightful position of each allows for the healthy boundaries of all, forming the basis for/of a well- functioning relationship.

13. One need not define oneself by another's standards and one must not measure oneself against any soul other than the one G-d breathed into one's body. Each soul has a reason for being, and all souls are precious and beloved by G-d who created them.

14. Reading your life script and practicing your lines is the beginning of mattering. Take the lines you have and say them as if your part is big and powerful. Telling the real story, no matter how few the lines, is big and powerful. It matters because you do. And it opens the door to the bigger opportunities for which you are waiting.

Chapter Two   FIRST STEP: PREPARE TO FALL

1. Do you want to live large and matter? Prepare to fall.

2. Like fat cells, shame easily multiplies and gets in the way of a good fit.

3. Others' presumptive limits for us don't get to define our path.

4. Basic rule in falling: Keep your composure, keep your hands close to you, get up quickly, continue with the move you fell on, and be prepared to fall again.

5. Dance represents forward movement that has us flowing into our spirits, showcasing our release from its weighty bonds of human limitations.

6. To live large, you don't need a sizable body that takes up ample space. Nor a thin one that doesn't. You need your spirit, yourself.

7. Small steps make large strides.

8. Be willing to fall, for that is the
pathway to rise.

Chapter Three STRUGGLING TO MATTER

1. No one is too small to live and to assert a presence.

2. We have one life to matter.

3. The capacity to opt into our lives and to inhale the
life-sustaining air of a large life requires that we find,
and act on, the hope that our lives matter, over and
over again.

4. How large we hope is how long we live.

5. Free spirits may be tied down for a while, but they manage to find ways to manifest their strong presence.

6. While food does not sing or smile,
it sure can feed the constant hum of
fear and emptiness.

7. The shame of being different can leave a scar so thick
that it can, even decades later, superimpose itself on
every fiber of life.

8. Clothes have the power to hide or
reveal what we allow them to.

9. The scars and cracks that are left behind as we grow do
not just magically disappear. They demand and deserve
our attention.

10. As with any resource that is abused, using it to plug up the holes essentially makes the crack bigger and much more dangerous.

11. There is a strong connection between the reality of an urgent appetite and increasing poundage and one's deep feelings of not mattering.

12. Mattering happens on the inside, and when it doesn't, the cracks open wider and destroy everything in its swallow.

13. There is great value in learning how not to block the light that wants so badly to come into our cracks, into our brokenness.

Chapter Four   TALES FROM INNER SPACE

1. Whole or cracked, your contribution will take root in this world, if you—and those you trust to help you—wisely prepare the ground.

2. Making, and taking, the time to do this process with oneself or with a trusted other will reveal the light between the cracks, the purpose alongside the pain.

3. As the pain subsides, we have the opportunity to glimpse the beauty that has been created in its stead.

4. Our pain is highly subjective. Keep your eye on your pain; that's where your prize is.

5. The anxious spirit dresses itself around life and cloaks even the lightest of events with an opaque struggle.

6. It is a human's nature to be scared of that which we do not understand. Yet it is a fact of living that we can unwittingly precipitate that which we fear.

7. Build, don't destroy, and trust yourself to know the difference.

8. How do we remove the blocks? By challenging them. By staring them down and rearranging the power grid that denied you the power of your being.

9. Shame is one huge block that shuts down our mattering—quickly, quietly, and unequivocally.

10. Shame is mostly propped up by fear, and violates our deepest selves. Unless we confront the shame, our sense of passion and purpose will collapse into a heap of non- mattering.

11. Confronting shame is the willingness to stage an offensive against the lie that we do not matter, then finding ways to manifest our mattering.

12. Shame cannot be seen, but is highly visible, which means it needs our attention to heal; our mattering depends on it.

Chapter Five   MONEY: A CURRENCY OF MATTERING

1. Facts first, feelings second. Both are hugely important to living life large.

2. The process of ordering numbers around is hugely different than the process for arranging human affairs.

3. The value of a currency called love has the ability to build and impact lives in similar ways as money.

4. By being invulnerable and never lacking, we can never learn how to ask and then to luxuriate in the relief of receiving, and in the subsequent bond of gratitude and closeness that would be created.

5. While physical bodies are separate entities, the healthy spirit is not limited and confined.

6. When the flow of love, of connection, is cut off, we cannot reach the inner places of wealth and enoughness.

7. A spirit that is cut off from love is cut off from mattering, and ultimately from its highest self.

8. Love can absolutely attract life's big things, such as authentic and enduring beauty, trust, and honor. These acquisitions may look different than the ones money can buy, because these cannot be bought. Indeed, they must be wrought.

9. Having everything easily in equal measure would bankrupt our spirit, while having to make choices builds it. It is in the choice that our mattering grows.

10. By bankrupting people's mattering, we create an inner emptiness that can be capitalized. The message is clear, even if it is false: You can buy your way into mattering.

11. Manipulating human prejudice and pride, money can also inspire and translate the charitable impulse of the human heart into transformative action and reaction for ourselves and others.

12. Enrich the world with your particular wealth.

13. Generosity isn't about having money; it is about being wealthy.

14. It is large to build with what we have, and not to destroy because we don't yet have what we feel is needed.

15. Taking ourselves to the limit of our existing resources with the hope that it will open up to something bigger to show for our efforts is both large and noble.

16. To matter, we must act large in the moment despite any perceived smallness of the circumstance.

17. In the Torah's definition of various currencies, including might, wisdom, wealth, and beauty, their values are plotted along an inner eternal graph rather than an external one.

Chapter Six   FINDING FRIENDS AND FAITH (& FUNDS) IN THE FALL

1. You'll see it when you can envision it. Vision is a huge asset which requires the currency of faith and the drive to live large.

2. The crypto-currency called faith is designed to work as a medium of exchange. It requires trusting in the rightness of an idea, and in G-d to make it happen. It affords one the ability to pay attention to his dreams, to opportunities that are bigger than what's possible right now, but that can be pursued until they become "possible, then probable, and finally inevitable."

3. Good friends matter, and they help us matter.

4. Music moves us from the world of perceived reality to one of possibility, from linear to lateral, from prose to poetry, from fear to faith.

5. Lonely hearts do not easily forget the smiles sent their way on the darkest days.

6. It is the profoundest of truths that our sense of trust is shaped at its core by our earliest relationships, usually with our parents, who are proxies of G-d. The way we feel about G-d is deeply shaped by how we experienced our relationship with our parents.

7. Family dynamics have huge spiritual consequences, for now, and generations to come.

8. Foster steps towards shaping faith in G-d. He can guide us through the shards of brokenness to shreds of wholeness.

9. Increasing our faith activates the Heavenly flow of abundance.

10. Faith presupposes that you will ask G-d to help, and that you believe that He not only can, but that He will.

11. As with other assets, friendships often have to be secured with material means.

12. In human form, and via the human form, the spirit agitates to express and communicate its essence in a tangible way. To matter is to concretize spirit. We must concretize spirit with whatever worldly currency we have at any given moment.

13. If something matters to you, it must come into being. It must take up space and consume emotion. It must have a way of being seen, heard, felt, touched, and smelled.

14. The choices we make tell us, and everyone else around us, what matters.

15. Our human spirit endows each of us with the inalienable right to make life large, to imbue it with the wealth of meaning that is consistent with our spirit.

16. Humans can easily become dispirited, falling for the idea of spending an earthly currency such as money, in exchange for counterfeit mattering.

17. We learn to glorify emotional idols, unless we are taught how to smash them. They will destroy us if we do not neutralize them first.

18. Here, the buck never stops; it is the language of the land.

19. Wealth is a ratio of what you have to what you need. And it is not only in the having; it is in the being and in the giving. Just like our mattering.

20. Enoughness is that exquisite balance in which body and spirit peacefully co-exist, live, and love.

21. People are far more powerful than money itself. Generating trust between people is good business.

22. Ideally, money is our servant, not our master.

23. Using one's material resources to express spirit expands our mattering. Abusing them contracts our mattering and that of the people around us.

Chapter Seven   A SMATTERING OF MATTERING

1. One's mattering is often subtle and quiet, while still gathering massive and unexpected energy as we move along the continuum of choices in our lives.

2. G-d stands by us humans, giving us not only first chances, but second chances too, when He discerns our determination and courage for things that are important to us.

3. When doing a kind deed, do so with a full heart, even if you are uncertain of its worth. Because we can never really know.

4. What is love, if not loyalty? We don't know what we love until we see what attracts our loyalty.

5. If power drives the outer world, a woman's influence drives the inner.

6. Power controls, influence compels. Power pushes, influence pulls. One is external, the other internal. And eternal.

7. What is at the core of a woman's being? Royalty.

8. Royalty is a sense of mattering that cannot be taken away from us, or compared with anyone else.

9. Show me her clothes; I will tell you who the woman is.

10. Regal grace stems from distinctive inner qualities, the force of beauty connected to strength of character—humility, modesty, and kindness, above all.

11. Showing up to inhabit our fate becomes our destiny. This is royal in the deepest sense of the word.

12. Ultimately, any default between man and his fellow man disturbs one's personal connection with G-d.

13. We cannot depend on others to know our truth.

14. Our choices can build what our circumstance didn't.

Chapter Eight   THE SOUL OF THE MATTER

1. It matters greatly to be human because our lives have a Divine purpose and, if recognized and honored, a promising future.

2. Being Jewish, or human for that matter, isn't a disposable piece of identity.

3. There are many ways for all of us to bring light into this world, because there are many acts of spirit we can do.

4. It is our decisions that show us what matter to us.

5. Often in life, small and big decisions are not made in favor of what you like best, for it is often hard to directly know that. They are made by ruling out what you don't like, until the happy moment of clarity shows what you do.

6. If you wish to glimpse your kingdom, look at your name.

7. If life hasn't yet given you big circumstances, then you make the big choices that will transform fate to destiny. Fate is small; destiny is large.

Chapter Nine   RIDING THE LONELINESS

1. Finding our mattering requires strength, strategy, and stamina to capture our individuality and to recapture the largeness of who we are.

2. To be human is to be lonely. We travel through life together, alone.

3. You cannot be touched on any level until you are ready.

4. Unbecoming is a lack of congruence, a lack of rightness, that badly wounds one's inner core that cannot grow and become. It becomes stunted, or even undone. A great loneliness finds it way inside the spirit, and has a way of inappropriately rearranging healthy boundaries.

5. Unbecoming and loneliness feed off each other, making a cycle that keeps one going in circles of despair with no exit in sight.

6. Greatness lies in facing our mistakes, leading us to higher ground.

Chapter Ten   DRIVING AWAY THE EMPTINESS

1. Experiencing failure is vital to actualizing our potential and living life well.

2. Every downswing will bring, in due time, its upswing.

3. Despite the persistent struggle with our appetites on any level, appetite as the desire for something is a healthy sign of being alive.

4. How we feed our needs and desires, and especially how we "do pleasure," takes considerable choice-making.

5. Not being connected in deep, meaningful ways with oneself and with others leaves a space that it achingly null and void, desperate to be filled.

6. There is a lot of large living to be done in maneuvering our empty and lonely spaces.

7. We often realize that challenges are not in the way; they are designed to lead the way.

Chapter Eleven   STRESS REHEARSAL: CHOOSING A MATE

1. When it is your turn in life, take it.

2. The dating process is the time in life to
remain calm and trusting in G-d's ability
to bring about each person's mate,
sometimes with obvious miracles.

3. We can rely on feelings when we are responsible with our
thinking.

4. Neither feelings nor limitations have a
final, hopeless claim on one's destiny.

5. Learning to like each other—like-making—helps fuel a
marriage.

Chapter Twelve   SIZING-UP OUR LIVES

1. Food is not our enemy. Restoring trust between ourselves
and food is the pathway to healing.

2. A love conditioned on the unseen
essence of something is a love that will
grow, endure, and satisfy.

3. Much more powerful than what can be seen is what
cannot be seen.

4. Never has it been so hard to connect
with the inner essence of life, where
enduring, authentic beauty lies.

5. Take joy in caring for our bodies because they are
vehicles for our spirit.

6. Harmony is feeding the body while fueling
the soul. It is learning to live with each
other so both can be strong and purposeful.

7. The assault we mount as we peel away layers of confusion shapes us into people who can tolerate complexity and paradoxes, but not at the expense of half-truths and hypocrisy.

8. Our capacity to enjoy something, to take pleasure in it, depends on our capacity to experience it.

9. Calories make you fat. Pleasure makes you full.

10. Food feeds, pleasure fulfills.

11. There is nothing inherently noble in doing things that you are not good at or that you really don't like. But there are times when bypassing that discomfort short-circuits our potential to matter. And then, there's everything big about staying there.

12. Humans often confuse prominence with importance.

13. It is difficult, maybe impossible, to ever fill the outside with enough.

14. The size of our body is not a referendum on the size of our life.

15. If you cannot experience pleasure, it does not matter how much you have. And if you can, it is surprising how little you need.

16. Staying in a loving relationship with food and with oneself is one of the most spiritual pursuits.

17. Enoughness is making the choice to let life and its outer veneer of mundaneness matter.

18. Enoughness is the perfect size for living large.

Chapter Thirteen   PANES OF LIFE

1. Marriage only makes you as complete as you are ready to become.

2. Mothering can burn and freeze at the same time, like a fever that simultaneously warms and chills.

3. You can only parent "the person you are."

4. There is an internal barometer that registers as whole when you connect to, and bear, your destiny in good faith.

5. Mothers power the world.

6. Mothering is not a gender; it is a spirit.

7. Children are a blessing, as are appetites, even though we struggle with both at times.

8. It is most definitely a gift, not a crime, to have work to call your own.

9. It is consistent with Torah approach to incline our professional search with our interests and G-d given talents.

10. Characters get built on hard choices; sacrifice, you might say.

11. Bearing the discomfort of doing small things, the kind that go unnoticed, builds capacity to do the larger things that might be uncomfortable, but are integral to moving along the continuum of enlarged opportunity.

12. Passion, as children, is G-d given.

13. Children can be the embodiment of the magic of compounded interest. With our steady, small investments of patient and loving attention, they can grow beyond our highest calculated hopes.

14. Mothers are at their best when they can hold expansive hope and vision for their children until their children grow into their better selves.

Chapter Fourteen   RIGHT LIFE, WRONG TURNS

1. The heart and mind are big places, requiring nourishment from a variety of pursuits.

2. The active stages of an inner struggle can mimic both depression and laziness, but, in reality, epic battles of hope and hopelessness are being fought one thought at a time.

3. Efforts yield fruit along the way, such as the positive energy generated when on the right track. This engenders a spirit of newfound courage and enthusiasm in our lives, allowing hope to have its way with our downcast souls.

4. Parents are human beings who were once parented too, and also suffer human limitations.

5. Our human value is not the result of the talents we've been given; that's just good fortune that we did nothing to deserve. Nobody owes us anything for having them. We are responsible to use them wisely in the service of others—and that is where our worth is to be found and praised.

6. Take your most vexing child and speak to her or him the way you would have wanted to be spoken to. This is powerful because it will help your child, while healing you.

7. Recovering the self that is waiting for us as part of our destiny is a demanding, relentless, and uncompromising process. Necessary and rewarding too, if you want to live big, to matter.

Chapter 15   SUBJECT TO CHANGE

1. Genius is unblocked consciousness.

2. You build trust in yourself by doing actions, little by little.

3. Small steps move us along, bigly.

4. It is much easier to see spirit when life is tenuous.

Chapter 16   BIRTHRIGHT

1. Pain is the most eloquent speaker.

2. If you are carrying inside yourself something to be born, you are now its parent. You are its creator, you are its channel through which it comes into life.

3. In placing this Divine piece called the Neshama (literally, soul) into a body, G-d breathes the kiss of great mattering into man.

4. Teshuva, inexactly translated as repentance, is the G-d given gift that allows man to return to his soul nature, which allows his body to purposefully move around in this world. He can undo the wrong and remake himself. This reactive reset is transformative. It is, in fact, the highest form of creativity.

5. In providing us with lack, G-d has given us purpose: To grow whole. Sometimes, that means reversing the lack; sometimes, it means building around it.

6. Growing whole is very individual. It cannot be imitated or even taught. It has to be struggled, birthed, cried, and belabored. Laughed and loved, too.

7. The birthright of royalty is the inner freedom to know our worth and mattering. And it is ours because we are the children of G-d.

8. Competition is risky business, because while it can objectively invite the best from within us, it can just as easily stifle it.

9. The day we stop competing to be someone else is the day that the opportunity to matter knocks on our door.

> 10. Only we can pull our self, body and soul, across the finish line the way all humans must. That is what awesome journeys are all about . . . until our last moment, when they literally take our breath away.

Chapter 17   ON AIR: LESSONS FROM THE STUDIO AND STAGE

1. G-d is not an equal job employer who gives the same tasks and tools to humans. He is an equal opportunity employer, giving each person opportunities for inner wholeness.

> 2. When doing work that is a good fit, you don't watch the clock.

3. The number one lesson in nutrition: Never let yourself get too hungry. It is too difficult to feed yourself well in that position.

Chapter 18   SECURING YOUR IDENTITY

1. Opportunity has many faces.

> 2. Like ocean waves, strengths turned wrong are deadly.

3. Dealing with an unevolved person drowning in his own chaos is both painful and exhausting; dangerous, too.

> 4. Being free and forging your own identity is hard work.

5. Being called into a process is generally against our conscious desire, but can take us to prized places and purposes that we may never have traveled on our own.

6. Staying with the process, and moving through it, will yield prizes that we couldn't have named.

7. Always maneuvering ourselves out of the process may cut our discomfort short, but at what cost to our potential?

8. While creating our identity and our mattering is an ongoing, perpetual question mark—relieved by periodic dashes and punctuated with rare exclamation points—not living our purpose is a harsh life sentence.

Chapter 19   HOLINESS IS A CREATION

1. Holiness is about drawing lines, straight or otherwise, that connect us to our larger lives.

2. Without boundaries, life is one amorphous, shapeless blob of disintegration and disorder. This deprives us of the pleasure of purpose that thrives on distinctions and differences, and that make life an exciting place to live.

3. Distinctions allow us to steady our path without blocking someone else's. Judgments, on the other hand, divide by putting us ahead while impeding someone else and leaving them behind.

4. Holiness can be found in every time and space of our lives, without exception.

5. Holiness, like charity, begins at home.

6. Taking it from the ritual to the spiritual—
that's what Judaism is all about.

7. Holiness is not found in how many children you have; it is
who you become as a result of working to raise them.

8. When a woman is well-cared for, her
husband and family have a better
chance of being happy.

9. Life is not an EZ-Pass system through which we can
speed; it is not prepaid.

10. It is counter-intuitive, but not counterfeit,
that the financially well-endowed benefit
more from giving money than those who
receive it. This is because it gives them
the chance to fulfill their earthly mission,
which is, inexplicably, bound up with
giving away money to others.

Chapter 20   GROW FOR IT!

1. The threesome — purpose, passion, and patience—are
fundamental to recovering ourselves.

2. Finding this threesome is an arduous
journey, but they will show up at your
invitation.

3. When we open the door to welcome in purpose, it usually
presents in good company—with patience and passion
in tow.

4. We discover, recover, and uncover our
identity in phases, as we travel our
experiences that map out who we really are.

5. You are not who you become; you become who you are.

6. It is impossible to predict in whose words one can find meaning, healing, and wholeness. It can often come from the most unlikely places, from the broken and struggling, from the dispirited and disconnected pieces and people in our lives.

7. As a highly personal and creative process, prayer is an unsurpassed opportunity for a human's growth and development.

8. On the battlefield of prayer, tears—not blood—are shed.

9. The Hoping Mechanism: To cope is human, to hope is divine.

10. G-d created challenges as opportunities to prod us to something bigger and better about ourselves that we couldn't or wouldn't have accessed on our own.

11. Callings don't let up easily, because G-d doesn't give up that easily on us.

12. Prayer unearths our purpose. It is not meant to burden us, but an invitation to unburden ourselves.

13. We are our souls, not our roles.

14. Reaching beyond ourselves is a great reason to go . . . and to grow.

Chapter 21   SCARED TO MATTER?

1. Negative emotions agitate to block our mattering and bring us down, especially the feeling of jealousy which clings to the spirit like fat to the body.

2. Exercising our mattering shapes flabby emotion into strength and power.

3. As you play your role and your script lines change, so do others. They accommodate your shift, as the power of mattering invites others into their larger lives, too.

4. It is not what we say no to in life, but what we say yes to, that allows us to realize our vitality.

5. While pain provokes us to reach for higher, joy is the energy that sustains the growth.

6. Noticing what you laugh about and what you cry about will tell you so much about what matters to you.

7. Much of life happens in the slower moments, in the low spaces between refreshing clarity and purpose. Learning how to do life here is what mattering is about. It is the small, often tentative , steps that lay down the large, enduring path of joy.

8. Be it ever so humble, there is no space like home. Largeness is on the inside.

9. While human attention goes to that which the eye can see, mattering belongs to that which the I can behold.

10. Do not let knowledge get in the way of wisdom.

11. An unanswered question is way better than an unasked one.

12. If we don't fight to neutralize our emotional idols, they will destroy our mattering.

13. Creating our mattering is our only hope against the emptiness that strains the human heart and drains it of its mattering.

14. Mattering is the music we play when we move into our inner, G-d given space.

ACKNOWLEDGMENTS

The COVID-19 pandemic has us in its powerful Divine orbit. Now, in addition to our inner storms, we have an outer one raging, too. Thirty-three million Americans have been told they are not essential, to stay home. That they don't matter. How are we supposed to get out of bed in the morning if we don't matter? We are standing in so many questions, not the least of which is the question of mattering which we explored in this book.

But there was another question for me as I was finishing this work. Publisher Dede Cummings had just called to discuss a rather small issue: "Where are your final edits?" And while I had quadruple-guessed this project enough times to nearly snuff the life out of it, I had one more opportunity to pull out of this commitment.

"Why don't I just opt out, right about now?" I loudly remarked to Zack. "I came this far, but it doesn't matter. I am not comfortable with this self-revelation, which I had not bargained for when I began this whole idea. Now's the time … to stop." Zack has learned well to just stay quiet, until the storm abates. And until I call Brenna, just one more time.

Somehow, you are holding this book. And while I still can't explain why it ultimately happened, I can say how.

There were people along the way whose support was so complete and their embrace so enveloping, that they invited the full measure of my courage and conviction.

No one told me that writing acknowledgments would be so much fun, and time-consuming. Here they are: my thank-you notes, sans my personal stationery and stamps.

Steven C. Eisner: For showing me what a little structure, a lot of discipline, and another's belief can do for a human being. As the talent scout and CEO of When Words Count, a writing retreat in Vermont for promising authors throughout the United States and Canada, you are the primary force behind this book. What would have happened if you had not looked past the outer disarray of my original submission to discern the inner story that was emerging? I'd rather not think about it. If I wasn't your quirkiest guest at the retreat, I apologize for shortchanging you. I do not forget the struggle over the book cover design which, to use your words, we "wrestled to the ground," along with some difficult decisions about how to reposition characters while retaining the integrity of the story. Your perceptive eye, sensitive heart, and vigorous mind have served many individuals, perhaps none more than me. And to your dear wife, **Neile**: For your inviting, welcoming ways during our retreat stay, and for becoming our family friend along the way.

Ben Tanzer: For being the one who brought this book to the finish line. As its hard-working, phenomenal story editor and publicist, your attachment to this work was remarkable and a great blessing that I do not take for granted. I also admire that you kept your word not to work on this book during *Shabbat*, and for not pushing me to go on the page beyond where I told you I could. Your professional prompts every page of the way led me to a dramatically deeper story. How you knew where there was more dialogue hiding in between the sentences and greater clarity in the words yet unwritten, I really don't know. "Show here, tell there" will stay with me as long as I write, and you have sufficiently halted my causal, inaccurate use of the words intuitive and instinctive. You brought your Ben-brand of magic to the process, guiding me back to the page, again and yet again. Authors have heavy lifting to do, including the mental part of getting out of our own way. Thank you for pulling me out of my own headwinds; that is not an easy task. You are a runner in life, on multiple tracks, and I do sometimes wonder if you ever stop to sleep.

Dede Cummings: For your ready desire to publish this work. I recall with deep gratitude how you greeted my first six chapters—with reverence and enthusiasm. Your love for life is not superficial, and that makes you a genuinely wonderful person to know. You are an example of grit, talent, and niceness, all packaged into one WOW of a woman.

Emma Irving: For your skilled, diligent, and gentle way of guiding the audiobook from its conception. You understood how connected I felt to the audiobook, which I call my firstborn because it came into the world first before the e-book and paperback. A bright future has your name on it.

Peg Moran: Your initial editing of, and generous praise for, the early work offered me that indispensable first dose of confidence designed to let me think that perhaps I could go the distance here. You let me dance on the page, and you clapped for every forward movement I took.

Cathryn Lykes: Your outstanding effort in editing the completed manuscript left me tired just thinking about it...and with almost 4,000 more edits for me to do afterwards. You also demonstrated an unequivocal understanding that the **Matterings** at the end of the book would be particularly satisfying for many readers.

Asha Hossain: Perhaps we cannot judge a book by its cover, but we definitely adore you for yours. We gave you a moving target in designing this cover, and you took great aim. Your generous, skilled collaboration produced multiple compelling concepts, ultimately uncovering the vibrant one that adorns this work.

Charita Cole Brown: Please read Chapter 21 to know that you are among my most cherished friends. You helped me to understand that I have a heart after all...and to let it do some of this work. And to trust G-d with it all.

Jamie Cerniglia: Aside from your extraordinary technical expertise in arranging all eleven hours of the audiobook in your Zero-V-U recording studio, you made it a pleasure for me to record it. You gave me plenty of water, helped me figure out how to pronounce some words that I knew how to write but had no idea how to say, and conspired with me to chance the critique from readers for inserting several words that you knew were my personal concoctions. You helped me decide if and when to chase an uncooperative phrase and to re-record it more effectively. You also understood how intense it could be to sit in the studio for hours at a time, once telling me how exhausted I looked afterwards, to go get some sleep. And I hope you did the same, after doing 30,000 edits on it.

Judith Krummeck: For serving as my first live interviewer and for validating the courage it takes to write a memoir. You would know, since you did the same thing in writing an award-winning memoir of your own.

The congruence of both your writing and speaking voices is an unusual delight.

Suzanna Davies: Your social media expertise allowed you to brave the task of building a platform around this book's message. All the bolder, considering that your four young children love your always-cheerful attention as much as I do.

Adam Robinson: You developed an exciting website, in keeping with my vision for a "home" for this book that would be uplifting. Your impressive command of website design continues to amaze me, and I look forward to our ongoing collaboration. WordPress and I have become good friends, thanks to you.

Dr. Norma Campbell: You knew that I couldn't do it your way, and so you let me find mine. That must have taken quite a bit of strength and humility, both qualities with which you are greatly endowed. You worked with me to build, not destroy, myself and my family. You have been our trusted therapist, and family friend, for over three decades— and your hair still hasn't turned grey, at the turn of ninety.

Marie DeMarco: You entered my life during my radio days. Helping me to connect those dots between my relationship with food and my life must have been a challenge, since I don't draw well, and definitely don't draw straight. Hearing the back story to this story that was being written, and then wasn't being written, and then was again—along with the details of my child-raising and community activism—you know the inner track I am balancing in all of this. You always tried hard, and with great dignity, to prompt me towards compassionate self-care so that I could carry the weight of these details, without gaining it. Let's continue the discussion about whether writing this book is, or is not, cathartic.

Rabbi Yaakov Hopfer: Yours is the singular voice of discretion that reverberates throughout this work. Your vast Torah scholarship is renowned, but it is the knowing guidance of your exquisitely-attuned heart that has made your phone number known by people around the world. I don't want to think about my life trajectory had you not been in it to guide me. My family, and I in particular, would look very different without you in our picture. Your influence has powerfully shaped the contours of my marriage and parenting. And of course, this book. When accommodating my ongoing need for particular direction with what and how to handle specific areas in the story, you never made me feel small or unequal to the challenge. It is the great who can lift up the small. How abundantly blessed our community is to have you at its helm.

Barbara Sher: When you read the early version of this book's cover copy, I knew you were not well. Nevertheless, you let me know how gratified you were by the influence your work exerted on mine. You left this world a few days before the launch of the audiobook, but your message lingers large in the lives of the many who learned it.

Rabbi Joseph Friedman: For investing your resources into my weekly radio program. You gave me a rewarding decade of working alongside of you to further many social and educational initiatives which benefitted countless people. I learned a lot from you, including the importance of a faith-abiding persistence, and that G-d gives second and even third chances to make our lives matter. Your resilience is exceptional ... and so is your wife, **Elisabeth.**

Martha Goodman: What kind of friend agrees to just read five chapters (because that is all I would allow you to read)? A friend who is unselfish, incredibly intelligent, and knows better than to ask for more than I can give. From our time together in the radio studio, you have been a trustworthy friend whose depth of character is a rare find which I greatly value. I don't quite know how to reciprocate the favor of your friendship, but I am willing to learn.

Yitta Halberstam Mandelbaum: Although circumstances limited your ongoing involvement with my developing work, you made it clear how much you believed in it. Your early comments powerfully moved me along in a way you may never really understand. Or maybe you will, if I say it this way, "Your words utterly, utterly, utterly blew me away."

Rebecca, my sister, and to my sister Hadassah's husband, **Abe:** You made yourselves available for hours to read and discuss segments of the developing work, because I needed three things which you lovingly gave: direction, confirmation of facts, and enthusiasm. What a privilege to call you my relatives.

Rabbi Moshe Rubinson: For reading the manuscript twice, and then taking even more time to offer your well-formed thoughts about the material. You had no problem saying that you laughed and cried on the pages, even helping me to understand where the story had personally exerted itself. What an incredible favor to perform for someone who you knew was still so uncomfortable with writing it. Clearly, you perceive the deeper side of life, which is why Zack and I welcome your friendship and collaboration with future works.

Signe Lauren: You recently re-entered my life after a hiatus of twenty years, our friendship rekindled over a cup of coffee and a book I gave you to read—mine. Renewed friendship is so sweet. And you have been a keen and kind reader.

A Distant Relative: Upon hearing that I wrote a memoir, you remarked, "What could possibly be so important about your life that you'd write a memoir?" You couldn't have lit a hotter fire under me. Because that flame of shame burst into fuel that energized my fingers to fight the illusion of not-mattering.

Mrs. P. and Mrs. F.: You are two high school teachers whose dedication to my personal development far exceeded the confines of your classrooms. Both of you live in Israel, and you knew I was writing this book. You also knew the discomfort I had with the project, because I told you that. And you both deeply and lovingly held the hope, while bestowing your blessings, that it would all work out.

My friend/colleague in Israel: You asked me not to mention your name, so I won't. For in honoring your request, I honor you. But you still get the credit for doing two unforgettable things. First, for reading the manuscript with your educated eye editing the philosophical pieces in this work, ensuring their accuracy and appropriateness. Greater than that, you managed to convey in our meeting several years ago your appreciation of my thinking process and my ability to communicate with it. You probably won't know what I am talking about, because it was you just being your generous self. It found its mark in a searching, receptive soul ready to move forward when the right opportunity presented itself.

Rabbi Michoel Friedman (Atlanta, GA): Our professional paths crossed when my words and conceptual vision were dressed with your masterful graphic designs in service of shared clients. When you learned of my book project, you'd leave occasional voicemail messages which stayed on my phone for several years because they'd continue to prod me along the path of progress. You quite understand the unspoken, deep-seated struggles we humans wage in trying to move forward. Had your meaningful sentiments been any more heartfelt, I'd have imagined that I wrote them as a means for strengthening myself. The people you serve in your multiple professional roles are beyond simply blessed.

Ivan Sacks: You are that person who connects with others because you cannot help but understand what they need, and cannot rest until you satisfy them. As tourists visiting Dallas for the first time, we received a welcome unlike any ever before: You discreetly paid for our lunch as if we were your guests—except that we weren't. You had never met us before and we weren't having lunch with you. But that didn't stop you from extending that random kindness, which we discovered only when we tried to pay. Yes, there is such a concept as Ivan's free lunch, made even more satisfying by our ensuing priceless friendship. You are the man whose every email ends with "attitude is everything." You know what you are talking about, and you paint awesome rocks. The Dare to Matter rock you painted has now become known as the rock star from Dallas.

Allan Glazer: We met at a business expo, after which you became a reliable professional upon whom I called, particularly with some of the early marketing work for this book. In our conversations, I came to understand that you always had my highest interests in mind, and at heart. Your impeccable good will distinguishes you from many of your colleagues. So does your Zambian accent.

Mark Neely: For your expert instruction with recording my audiobook. As my actor friend, you are a class act when it comes to helping others maximize their voices. Your recent work with voicing the pandemic public service radio commercials were so well-done.

Sylvia: As my cherished cousin, you had a ready understanding of how your mother would appear in my story, and why. I do pray that what evolved has your blessings. I continue to admire your street smarts, your brand of mothering, and your financial integrity. Not to mention your Backgammon skills.

Brenna and Nate: For loyally showing up in this book, over and over again. Just the way you have appeared in my life—to catch me in the fall, to cheer with me in the rise, and for everything in between. Relying on your mountains of inner wisdom has moved me to scale my own. It is entirely possible, if I want to be honest here, that most everything I know originated with you. I do not forget turning to you when writing this book, begging to know two things: Should I stop writing it and did I make it all up? The book is here because your answers, and your personal example, were sufficiently clear and compelling. Your essence has overtaken the darkness in my path a million times—if not a million and one.

My Parents: For learning a new language…mine. Believe me, I know what a hard task that is. I speak that language, and I still struggle to understand it myself. You read much of the book, and were selflessly supportive of it, though you could have had quite a few reasons to object. Children do and say the darndest things…and exceptional parents such as you try hard to model the best in patience and forbearance. You have always done the best you could with what you have…what more could be asked of the two people that I am beyond fortunate to call my parents?

My Children: For not reading the book, you have my appreciation. You'd listen to some lines, and that was quite enough for most of you. (Except for Zeeva who listened to the audiobook and offered me valuable commentary.) All of you endured my amorphous ambitions for many years, sharing me with one community project and then another, allowing me my life outside of the mothering role that I am grateful to have. It may not always be a pleasure for you to be my children, but it is always a privilege for me to be your mother.

Our first three daughters— Aviva, Basya, and Zeeva, and your loyal spouses whom we are thrilled to call our children: Watching all of you parent is like watching you skate across the proverbial rink with joy and grace, making it look deceptively easy and enjoyable. I don't know if you let your children eat crayons, but you sure let them draw circles around you, with all the pleasure and purpose that they evoke in you … even after you've had quite enough of their mess. And dear **Grandchildren**, I know you don't expect me to push you more than twice on the swings during our limited park outings or to serve you freshly-baked cookies from my oven, but thanks for letting our singing and dancing be almost as delicious.

Someone has to be the youngest, and in our family, that is you, **Ayala**. And then someone is her only brother, and that is you, **Daniel**. You both let me know that you deserve shoutouts for being in the house while this book was being written, so here they are. You'd both tell me that you believed in what I was doing, though it best not interfere with making your nightly suppers (that you didn't like anyway). Daniel, you offered to help when I was being "paged," i.e., needing to show up at the page, which meant driving Ayala to the mall for something she didn't really need, and often cutting short our enjoyable nightly conversations. You both have taught me everything I know about parenting, and that is quite another story. In the four years of working on this book, I just cannot fathom how much you have grown. You have learned how to share the four-cushioned couch without kicking off each other. And even more significant, how to share your Laffy Taffy candies. Just last year, you, Daniel, even found an awesome (and brave) young lady who agreed to marry you. Julie is not only a lot taller than me, but thankfully can cook a lot better. Ayala, I have seen your type only once before . . . but you are already much further along the journey than I was at twice your age. You go, great girl!

Readers: You are the individuals who did the work of reading mine. I do hope the experience was pleasurable, even if demanding at times. Dare it all down as if you matter, because you do.

Zack: You allowed yourself to become known in this story, because you put yourself at my service— so that I could do the same for others. I guess now is a good time to tell you that I never believed you when you'd say that I would write a book, even books. I thought that you were just being you, overstating the possibility when it came to uplifting me. I think you will understand that I don't know what to say now. And even if I did, I wouldn't know how to say it. Because this is one of those rare times when my pen has become mute, overwhelmed by its limitation to express a proper gratitude for making my life into your love. Please continue holding the mirror; it is more constructive in your hands than mine.

Dear G-d, my pen is not quiet here. Rather, it is shaking with awe—for I have seen You in every step of this process. You have a magnificent agenda for Your world and for us, Your guests. Please let us step into it, the large world of mattering you bequeathed to humanity. What that request really means is: Enthuse us to bring honor to Your name. For in doing that, we build our capacity to receive the unending goodness, and the greatness, You desire to lavish upon Your creations.

ABOUT THE AUTHOR

S HIFRA is fascinated with the inner spaces humans inhabit.
As the producer and host of a weekly radio program on social and educational issues that aired live in the Mid-Atlantic region, Shifra was known for eliciting hard, honest responses from her interviewees when posing the questions that others were too hesitant to ask.

Underlying these conversations was one pressing question Shifra always wanted to answer: What makes our lives matter? Daring to step right into the heart of life's complexities, her search for answers to this question is refreshingly approachable and impactful.

Shifra currently serves as the vice-president of project development for a web-based writing and communications company that assists corporate and non-profit enterprises with shaping their verbal and written communications. Among diverse professional credits, she has crafted messages for an online greeting card company and has written and recorded radio commercials, corporate phone scripts, and organizational videos.

She has been invited to present on topics of spiritual, personal, and creative growth and development in a variety of academic and corporate settings, ranging from university students to women entrepreneurs.

Her lengthy list of community activism includes past service for the Association for Women in Communications, Washington D.C., and current service on the board of a non-profit organization dedicated to helping singles meet and marry.

Shifra resides in Maryland, where she occasionally puts her pen down so that she can roam around in pursuit of her next writing desk.

Please visit www.ShifraMalka.com.
Email: shifra@shiframalka.com

@ShifraMalka   @DaretoMatter   @DaretoMatter